BUILDING *Sweet Dream*

An Ultralight Solo Canoe
for Single or Double Paddles

BY

MARC F. PETTINGILL

Tiller

St. Michaels, Maryland

ISBN 1-888671-03-3

Text and drawings by Marc F. Pettingill   •   Cover photography by Marc F. Pettingill
       Front cover: Nancy Lekberg and Bob Frick in two *Sweet Dreams.*
       Back cover: Liz Pettingill (top), Bob Frick (center) and Nancy Lekberg (bottom)
              demonstrate *Sweet Dream* with single and double paddles.

Black and white photography by Bob Ander, Ander Commercial Photography,
              1317 Redgate Avenue, Norfolk, VA 23507 (unless otherwise credited)

Contributing artists:
       Terrance D. Young, *Adirondack Swirling.* Youngs Studio & Gallery,
              RR1, Box 189, Jay, NY 12941
       Garrett Conover, *While Readying the Fleet.* North Woods Ways,
              RR2 Box 159A, Guilford, ME 04443

Layout and design by Words & Pictures, Inc., 27 South River Road South, Edgewater, MD 21037.

Printed in the USA by Victor Graphics, 1211 Bernard Drive, Baltimore, MD 21223.

P.O. Box 447
St Michaels, MD 21663
Voice: 410-745-3750 • Fax: 410-745-9743

To my wife, Ann,
and my children,
Liz and Dan.

Acknowledgments

Most of what I know about small boat and ultralight canoe building I've gotten from personal experience and the many books on the subject that I've read. A notable exception is what I learned first hand in classes given by Ted Moores, Tom Hill, and Greg Rossel at The WoodenBoat School in Brooklin, Maine. Also, the time I spent while at the school with Henry "Mac" MacCarthy and Harry Bryan was an invaluable experience. Each one of these canoe-boat builders has contributed to my approach to canoe building. I need to recognize them for what they've given me and countless other students. I thank:

> Ted Moores, the consummate canoe builder; for his commitment to passing the lessons of the past on to others.

> Tom Hill; for championing innovative construction methods.

> Greg Rössel; for teaching us that if the tool doesn't work, modify it, or get one that does. If the right tool doesn't exist, make it yourself.

> "Mac" McCarthy; for his encouragement to another potential competitor, and his time's-a-wastin', what-have-we-got-to-lose, why-not-give-it-a-try approach to problem solving.

> Harry Bryan; for reaffirming that thinking small and dreaming big are not incompatible ideas.

I owe Phil Green a special debt that I cannot ever repay for his selfless help in bringing *Sweet Dream* from flickering idea to reality. To Phil I offer my most heartfelt appreciation.

Chesapeake, Virginia
September, 1995

Table of Contents

The Road Not Taken 8

Introduction: 9

    Paddling Through Time 14

Part I: Building the Hull 15

    List of Materials 17

        Cautionary Words on Saving Weight 18

    Recommended Tools and Equipment 18

        Epoxy Sources of Supply 18

        Okume Plywood Sources of Supply 19

    Picking A Hull Length 19

    Hull Layout Plans 21

    Building Sequence 25

        Mill the Parts for the Hull 26

        Cut out the Hull Shape 26

        Drill Holes for Electrical Ties 27

        Bevel the Stem Cuts 28

        Close Up the Stems and Chines 30

        Setting the Rocker and Bottom Arc 31

        Insert the Amidships Frame 32

        Temporarily Install the Outer Rails 32

        Align the Hull 34

        Cut the Side Halves to Length 34

        Join the Side Halves 35

        Install the Bottom Pad 36

        Fillet and Tape the Inner Chines and Stems 38

        Cutting the Sheer 41

        Install the Breasthooks 42

        Fillet and Tape the Breasthooks 44

        Trim the Breasthook Sides 46

        Shape the External Chines 46

        Tape the External Chines 46

        Shape the External Stems 48

        Tape the External Stems 50

        Permanently Install the Outer Rails 51

        Install the Inner Rails 54

        Trim the Hull at the Rails 55

        Trim and Radius the Rails 55

        Install the Thwarts 56

        Taper the Fiberglass Tape Edges at Stems and Chines 60

        Install the Seat 61

        Single Paddle Seat 61

        Double Paddle Backrest 62

    Celebrate Your Accomplishment 66

Part II: Finishing the Hull 67

    Detailing the Hull 68

    Sanding and Sandpaper 69

    Painting and Varnishing 73

    Special Bottom Coatings 90

    Determining and Marking a Waterline 91

    Annual Maintenance 93

While Readying the Fleet 94

Part III: Optional Accessories 94
Curved Structural Members 95
Curved One-Piece Backrest 101
Tuffet and Tuffet II 102
Asymmetrical Hulls 107

Part IV: Additional Building Information 109
Safety in the Shop 109
Epoxy 109
The Work Surface 112
Sturdy Sawhorses 114
Milling the Parts for the Hull 116
Batten 116
Outer Rails 116
Inner Rails 116
Thwarts 117
Single Paddling Seat Beams 117
Double Paddle Backrest Stretcher 117
Joining Plywood Sheets 118
Butt Joint 118
Fiberglass Tape Butt Joint 118
Scarph Joint 118
Scarph Joint 119
Joining the Scarphed Sheets 125
How Many Clamps? 127
The Stem Bevels 128
Builder-Made Tools and Fixtures 129
Aluminum Straight Edge 129
Router Guide 129
Dragon's Teeth 129
Filleting Tools 130
Rail Tapering Fixture 132
Bottom Pad for the 14-foot *Sweet Dream* 134
Making Filleted and Taped Joints 135
Regular *vs.* Bias Cut Fiberglass Tapes 136
Determining the Sheer 137
Breasthook Options 140
Tapering the Edges of Fiberglass Tape 142
Seating Options 144

Part V: Supplements 147
Paddle Styles, Shapes and Lengths 147
Double Bladed Paddles 148
Single Bladed Paddles 148
Hull Numbers and The *Sweet Dream* Register 150
Safety on the Water 151
Canoeing Safety Tips 152
FLOAT PLAN 153
Further Canoeing Adventures 154
Paddle Your Own Canoe 155
What's In A Name? 156
Post Script 160
Bibliography 162
Biography 163

Index 164

List of Figures 🦢

1. Adirondack Swirling 15
2. Views of the Hull 16
3. Hull Length Decision Guide 20
4. Okume Panel Layout Diagram 21
5. Hull Layout Plan, *Sweet Dream* 12 22
6. Hull Layout Plan, *Sweet Dream* 13 23
7. Hull Layout Plan, *Sweet Dream* 14 24
8. Amidships Frame Dimensions 32
9. Lap Joint 33
10. Radiusing the Chine Joints 47
11. Completed Thwart End Markings 58
12. Thick *vs.* Thin Masking Tape 78
13. Removing the Masking Tape 79
14. Curved Backrest Pad Press 101
15. Curved Backrest Pad Dimensions 102
16. Asymmetric Hull 107
17. Work Surface Cutting Diagram 112
18. Work Surface Exploded View 113
19. Sturdy Sawhorses 115
20. Outer Rail Cross Section 116
21. Inner Rail Options 117
22. Butt Joint 118
23. Fiberglass Tape Butt Joint 118
24. Scarph Joint 118
25. Setting Up to Scarph 121
26. Scarph in Progress 122
27. Scarphing Fixture 126
28. Centering the Pressure Bar 126
29. The Stem Bevel 128
30. Router Guide 130
31. Dragon's Teeth 131
32. Plastic Filleting Tools 131
33. Rail Tapering Fixture 132
34. 14-Foot *Sweet Dream* Bottom Pad Parts Arrangement 134
35. 14-Foot *Sweet Dream* Bottom Pad Scarphing Set-Up 134
36. Regular *vs.* Bias Cut Tape 136
37. Optical Illusion 138
38. Traditional Breasthook 140
39. Laminated Plywood Breasthook 140
40. Double Paddle Backrest Parts 142
41. Double Paddle Backrest 145
40. Backrest Stretcher Support Block Shapes 146
42. Single Paddle Seat 146
43. *Sweet Dream* Hull Number Plate 150
44. Paddle Your Own Canoe© 150

The Road Not Taken

Two roads diverged in a yellow wood,
And sorry I could not travel both
And be one traveler, long I stood
And looked down one as far as I could
To where it bent in the undergrowth;

Then took the other, as just as fair,
And having perhaps the better claim,
Because it was grassy and wanted wear;
Though as for that the passing there
Had worn them really about the same,

And both that morning equally lay
In leaves no step had trodden black.
Oh, I kept the first for another day!
Yet knowing how way leads on to way,
I doubted if I should ever come back.

I shall be telling this with a sigh
Somewhere ages and ages hence:
Two roads diverged in a wood, and I —
I took the one less traveled by,
And that has made all the difference.

Robert Frost 1916

BUILDING *Sweet Dream*

I am not entirely comfortable with the sentiment in Robert Frost's poem, "The Road Not Taken." You may remember the poem; you probably read it in high school or as a college freshman. It's the one that uses a fork in the road as a metaphor for choices made during a lifetime. It is too easy to fall into the convention, both literary and real world, that a road not taken is an opportunity lost forever.

I have a mental picture of Frost reading the poem aloud to a small group somewhere in New England. A child standing by the stove catches Frost's eye, and he stops reading with an enquiring look. The child says, "Mister Frost, I don't see what the problem is. If you go through French's pasture, the one with the spring house by the gate, you'll find t'other road just over the rise, on past the bull pine."

I accept that you can't go back in time to the fork that divided two roads of life. But if you want to be on the other road, don't look back with regret or trudge along in a rut that leads forever in the wrong direction; make your own path. Opportunity could lie not on either road, but in the pasture. There's also a meandering stream beyond the rise in the pasture, and who knows to what and where it might lead.

For many people building a boat lies on one of their other roads. It's something they've always wanted to do, but haven't. Every so often they see that other road through the trees and they think, "I wish that . . ." and, "If only I had . . ." I've written *Building Sweet Dream* to help convert those wishes and dreams into something substantial and meaningful, to encourage striking out to rediscover the "road less traveled by."

Many people think that building a boat as small as a solo canoe is an act of insanity or little consequence. They are dead wrong. There are few if any other activities that can generate even half the excitement, deep satisfaction, and on-going fun that building your own boat does. When you factor into the equation access to little-traveled waters, and the innumerable hours of paddling close to nature, the rewards are doubled and redoubled. Nothing else that I know of even comes close.

There is no better boat than a solo canoe. Properly designed it can be built without a lot of expensive tools or any wood working experience. It will be a continuing source of pleasure, satisfaction, and pride. The solo canoe is small and light; small enough to be built and then stored out of the way, overhead in a garage. It is light enough to put on and take off a roof rack, and be launched and recovered by one person. With a double paddle, no special paddle strokes must be mastered. The solo canoe is the perfect vehicle to travel great distances or poke around in quiet places after dinner. The canoe's roots dig deeply into prehistory and canoeing has a lively history in modern times that is a source for many pleasant hours of reading and discovery.

Through countless centuries, ancient builders and users refined the canoe to its simplest and most elegant forms. As a result, the canoe is one of the few aboriginal forms that survives into the modern world with few significant changes. While the canoe's shape is old beyond time, the materials and techniques used to build one needn't be. In *Sweet Dream*, I have joined old forms with contemporary materials and building techniques to create a light and responsive solo canoe for single and double paddling.

Sweet Dream

⚜ is easily and quickly built using basic hand and electric tools.

⚜ is buildable by one person. (An assistant is helpful at times, but is not necessary for any part of the work.)

⚜ gets maximum use of the materials purchased (85% of the two sheets of plywood goes into the hull and an optional set of paddle blades).

⚜ quickly develops the essential boat-shape.

⚜ is shapely, strong, and durable. Strength, durability, and safety are not compromised to ultralightness.

⚜ is visually appealing, and

⚜ gives excellent flat water paddling performance to both beginning and experienced canoeists.

Conceptually the "folded plywood" construction method follows in the wakes of the canoe designers and builders of the wooden canoe's heyday in the mid to late 1800s. At that time, soon to be famous canoe builders introduced new construction methods at the cutting edge of their technology. It was during that period that the strip built, wood and canvas, lapstrake, and even the paper canoe, all precursors to forms familiar today, were developed. Due to those pioneering efforts, today's wooden canoe builders and users are not limited to "traditional canoes" of only birch bark or dugout logs.

The folded plywood method uses 4mm okume (*oh-koo'-may*) marine plywood for its inherent strength and workability. The folded plywood creates controlled tension that imparts three dimensional curves to the ends

One person can easily lift Sweet Dream onto and off a roof rack.
Photo by Marc Pettingill

of the hull. *Sweet Dream*'s distinctive lines join smoothly contoured shapes at its ends with an arched bottom and hard chines amidships. Modified stitch and glue construction produces an incredibly strong monocoque all-wood hull with the clean, uncluttered interior usually found only on strip built or cold moulded wood canoes.

Sweet Dream can be built in one of three sizes, 12, 13, or 14 feet long, to accommodate overall weights of 125 to 300 pounds.

With the exception of the rails and thwarts, all hull parts are gotten out of a single 4x16 foot plywood panel made by joining two 4x8 foot standard plywood sheets. Once the distinctive hull shape is cut out, in just a few hours the hull takes its final form. Of course, it takes some additional time to fit breasthooks, rails, etc., and complete the detailing and finishing that are the hallmarks of a finely crafted wood canoe. Still, there probably is no faster way to build an all-wood canoe.

Although I designed *Sweet Dream* in response to needs I encountered while teaching canoe building in adult education classes and youth summer camps, my interest in small boats and canoes goes back to childhood summers spent on Bear Pond in Hartford, Maine.

I am not a formally trained naval architect. I'm not even a proper naval engineer. I just happen to have an abiding interest, an obsession even, with small boats and especially with wooden canoes. I was fortunate to attend a small federally funded college with a strong sea going tradition in New England. Much to my

detriment, I never figured out "The Calculus." In the time honored academic tradition that prevailed, you could not engineer in the manner naval unless beforehand you could calculate in the manner of Newton and Leibnitz.

Not being burdened with overpowering intellectual abilities, I concentrated my none too prodigious talents on modern European and American literature. As it turned out, I was more suited to the liberal arts than the literal ones. During my four year residency I was well grounded; many times in fact. I graduated in 1970 with an officer's commission and a BS in Engineering. Go figure. I am confident that nothing naval engineering or architectural wise in this manual can be laid at the door of my *alma mater*. I done it all by my lonesome.

In government service I was fortunate to have a career involving ship building and repair in which I specialized in wooden boats. In 1975, during my first tangle with budgetary cut backs, I asked myself what I'd rather do instead of my then current job. The answer was build canoes and small boats. I felt that my professional training was a good general background, but I needed specific small boat knowledge. I started my own course of post graduate study. During the following 18 years I read extensively, built models, gained proficiency in using hand and small power tools, built up a reference library, and otherwise extended my knowledge and abilities.

I left federal service in 1993, and went immediately to The WoodenBoat School in Brooklin, Maine. There I took classes from

When you travel by river, you discover something about roads. When you drive, the road defines the landscape, which becomes only the soiled and slovenly corridor through which you move, a measurement of the time you have passed and the time that lies ahead of you. But rivers both define and express a landscape, and they do it slowly, organically, and profoundly, the way a history defines a culture. From the water, roads seem adventitious and inconsequential; the occasional bridge no more disturbs the river than the vapor trail of a passing jet disturbs the vastness of the sky.

Franklin Burroughs, The River Home

Liz Pettingill, the author's daughter, demonstrates paddling techniques. Photo by Marc Pettingill

active canoe and small boat builders whose work I knew from my reading and whose ideas I liked. Little did I realize then that in mid-life it is dangerous to choose a second career the name of which is commonly preceded by the words "poor," and "young;" as in poor young artist . . . or boat builder.

In my second career, I have been able to spend some part of almost every day paddling, designing, building, writing about, or teaching others about canoes and small boats. I have designed two ultralight canoes, taught canoe building in adult classes and youth summer camps, put on public demonstrations at waterfront festivals, addressed a national meeting of math and science summer camp directors, published articles, and three canoes have won blue ribbons. Sometimes after a week of 16 hour work days I've wished that I had a real job to go to so I could get some rest. Actually, there are

Whitewater, flatwater, or local streams. The solo canoe will go anywhere a tandem canoe will go — a bit more slowly perhaps, but with a grace, style and elegance that is unmatched by any other watercraft. Solo canoes. They set you free to follow your own star in your own way.

Cliff Jacobson,
The Basic Essentials of Solo Canoeing

very few jobs that could seduce me from my long held dream to build small boats and canoes.

There are scant few people today who can afford a custom boat, even if it is a just a solo canoe. Many of those who can't afford a custom canoe would still like to own one. One way for a not quite young, and trying to be not abjectly poor boat builder to help both himself and them is to teach them how to build their canoes themselves. I've written this manual to share *Sweet Dream* with more people than I could possibly meet or teach in person.

Even though I know exactly what will happen in each step of the building sequence, every time I build a *Sweet Dream* I am amazed. It seems more like conjuring a wood canoe out of thin air than building one from scratch. I think that you, too, should experience that sense of wonder and satisfaction. You should also experience the excitement of paddling a canoe that you built yourself.

The rewards of building your own canoe continue after the hull is built:

⮢ Canoe building is doubly rewarding when it is shared with others. It is an excellent activity to share with children, grandchildren, spouse, friend or even like minded strangers in a class.

⮢ Building the canoe is only the first stage of a journey of discovery that can last a lifetime.

⮢ The canoe offers endless possibilities of places to go, and opportunities to learn.

⮢ The canoe offers unique opportunities to interact with the environment and people that are unavailable to the shore bound crowd.

I have separated the material in this manual into five parts. Part I covers the steps in the *Sweet Dream* building sequence. Part II deals with finishing the hull, which is to say painting and varnishing. Part III discusses optional accessories for advanced builders and needn't concern first time builders at all. Part IV contains the additional information to the building sequence. Part V presents some supplemental material to suggest additional reading or canoeing related activities.

I wrote the building sequence while building a *Sweet Dream*. I alternated building and writing. It took longer to write about most of the activities than it did to do them. When I reread the completed building sequence I realized that many of the techniques I call for seem to come, like the canoe, out of thin air. Remembering my early building experiences and thinking like a first time builder, I often had to ask, "Why is he doing this?" or "Where did this come from?" I knew that these questions deserved answers; the information would increase both the confidence and competence of first-time builders. I put the answers in **Part IV: Additional Building Information.**

Digging up reference works is fun and rewarding if you are in the business of building boats. If all you want to do is build just one good boat, having to go elsewhere for what you need may just be the end of the adventure. Part IV is meant to serve as a reference library. It contains the background and technical information that first-time builders need to use the tools, materials, and procedures. The information in this section is applicable to building numerous other contemporary plywood designs by Bolger, Devlin, Benford, Green, and others.

I've taken the reference material out of the building sequence so that when it comes time to build, the steps follow one another without interruption. My hope is that you will have read the building sequence and the additional information more than once before you start to build. Should a quick refresher be in order, the applicable section and its page number is given at the beginning of a building activity.

Don't let the number of individual building steps put you off. Building *Sweet Dream* is simple. It's like the man who ate an automobile. Every day he filed off some metal and ate it with his meals. He ate only a little bit of metal

Marc Pettingill demonstrates his techniques at the Mid-Atlantic SmallCraft Festival, St. Michaels, MD, in October 1995.
*Photo compliments of **Messing About In Boats**.*

at a time and after a while the car was gone. He even lived to tell the tale to his grandchildren. I've taken a similar approach. I've broken the building sequence into many small steps. Each is easily mastered.

Throughout this book I emphasize getting a particular task done at the lowest technological level that gives the desired result. Wherever possible special tools and fixtures are built from readily available materials as opposed to buying some single purpose equipment. One of the joys of boat building is overcoming problems with your wits and hands rather than your wallet.

I do not claim any exclusivity for myself or Phil Green in the design of "folded plywood" boats. (Some people call the technique "tortured plywood." We don't because nothing remotely like torture occurs in building *Sweet Dream*.) There are a number of other designer/

builders and a large company that sells boat plans that offer similar construction methods. It is no wonder; building in this fashion is exciting and immediately rewarding.

The factors of time and money are of prime interest to all potential builders. Figure $200 to $250 in materials excluding paint. Paint, varnish, brushes, etc., can go from $20 for a bare bones exterior latex finish to $200 for two-color marine one part polyurethane with varnished trim and a special bottom coating.

Tools are another matter. You probably already own some of the ones listed. Although *Sweet Dream* can be built with only hand tools, access to a table saw is very helpful. You really should have a 5" or 6" dual-action sander. Sanding the taped seams by hand would take an unimaginably long time. Rather than buying one, consider renting a 5"or 6" dual action sander. All the sanding can be completed in a weekend, although it would be tiring work.

How long it takes to build *Sweet Dream* depends on what you mean by "build." If you are moderately familiar with the tools and materials, the hull can be assembled in 30 hours excluding sanding the taped seams. If this is your first exposure to boat building and its tools, 45 hours is more realistic. Sanding the taped seams takes another 10 to 20 hours depending on how invisible you want the interior seams to be. Painting and varnishing requires 20 to 30 hours spread out over two to three weeks if you follow my recommendations on drying times between coats of paint and varnish.

For me, building and using small canoes is a source of unending fascination. In addition to the building activities and the people I meet, an important part of the fascination is the special places that I can go in a small canoe. Many of those places seem to have a living presence that evokes thoughts and ideas that are otherwise drowned out by the clammer of modern life.

One such place near me is Lake Drummond in the Great Dismal Swamp. To get to the lake requires a four-mile paddle against the current in a narrow, perfectly straight, tree and vine lined channel. The trip can be very boring, but the lake with its ancient moss-hung cypress is worth the effort. Recently while paddling to the lake in a semi-daze I found myself thinking along these lines:

Paddling Through Time

Paddling a canoe is to travel through time. A trip on a quiet stream can become a metaphor of life.

As the canoe moves over the surface, the water silently parts and then rejoins as the canoe moves on. The record of the passing is briefly written in wavelets, ripples, and swirls.

Just as the hull slips through the water, on a different plane the canoe parts the flow of time. The canoe is a slit in the ethereal stuff of time, it is the fragile space created by consciousness that humans call "Now."

Ahead, the future flows towards us and just beyond our touch becomes the present. The spinning whorls made by our paddles take the shape of miniature galaxies; momentary reflections of the *nearly* infinite. Our lifetime lasts only somewhat longer.

The questions: Why am I here?" What is the right way to live?" and "Where am I going?" linger in the shadows for mindful travelers to ponder.

Behind, the streams of time accept our passage, close with a whisper, and become the past. The chaotic vestiges of our passage flicker as memories, and then . . . stillness.

Compassion and selflessness are our true legacies to the world; they are the waters of our children's future.

The permanent legacy of our life- journey will be realized on a timeless plane where mind and matter exist as one in the abiding calmness.

Enough , it's time to build *Sweet Dream*.

6/150 ADIRONDACK SWIRLING   Terrance D. Young/92

Adirondack Swirling
Terrance D. Young, 1992
Used by permision of the artist.
First published in *Wooden Canoe*,
Vol. 19, No. 2, April 1996

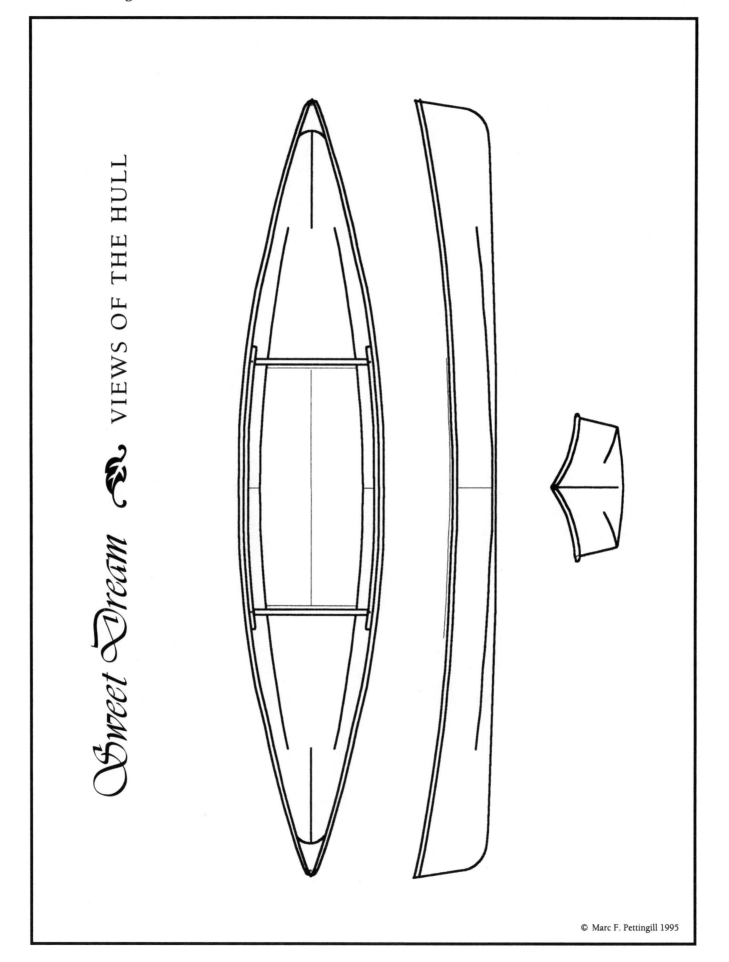

Sweet Dream 🐿 VIEWS OF THE HULL

Part 1: Building the Hull

List of Materials and Supplies

Before you buy any materials, read through the Building Sequence and Additional Building Information at least once.

Materials for the Hull

(Does not include supplies for painting and varnishing.)

2 sheets, 125cm x 250cm, 4mm Okume Marine Plywood.

4/quarter or 3/4"x 6"x 14' White Ash, Mahogany, Spruce, fir, white oak, etc. (7 bd. ft.). Planed to 3/4" and used for inner and outer rails, thwarts, and possibly the backrest stretcher. If 14' long stock is not available, two 8' boards can be joined with a 10:1 scarph before the rails are cut.

2 qt. West System® 105 Epoxy Resin

2 pt. West System® 206 Slow Hardener

1 pr. West System® 301-A Calibrated Mini Pumps

2 ea. 8 oz. pkgs West System® 405 Filleting Blend

1 ea. West System® 809 Notched Spreader (Optional.)

1 ea. 6" Plastic Squeegee (Used to make three filleting tools.)

200 ea. 3.6" Nylon Electrical Ties

24 ft. 1" Masking Tape.

40 ft. 2" Fiberglass Tape

20 ft. 3" Fiberglass Tape

1 ea. 50", 2 x 4 (Used as backing bar for Scarph Clamping Fixture)

1 ea. 50", 1 x 2 (Used as pressure plate for Scarph Clamping Fixture)

8 ea. 1/4" x 20 x 2" Silicon Bronze Carriage Bolts w/nuts and washers

12 ea. 3/8" Acid Brushes

16 ea. 1-1/2" or 2" Chip Brushes

5 ea. 40 or 60 grit, 5" or 6" Sanding Discs (Adhesive or hook and loop backed to suit sander.)

5 ea. 80 or 100 grit, 5" or 6" Sanding Discs (Adhesive or hook and loop backed to suit sander.)

100 ea. 1" Drywall Screws (Used for temporarily fastening outer rail.)

1 lb. 2" Deck Screws (Used for clamping pressure in Scarph Clamping Fixture.)

36" x 20" piece of 1/2" or 5/8" Plywood or Chipboard (Used to make the amidships frame, backing plates for side joints, and pressure plates for breasthook laminating

52" x 36" piece of 8 oz. Fiberglass Cloth (Optional. Used to make bias cut tape for exterior stems.)

Rubber, latex, or plastic gloves (1 pair if multiple use, 15 pairs if disposable.)

4 ea. OSHA approved nuisance dust masks

Epoxy mixing pots and stirring sticks

1 ea. 3/4" Straight Copper Pipe Coupling (Used to make backrest stretcher bearings.)

1 ea. 48" x 7/8" Hardwood Dowel (Used to make the backrest stretcher.)

2 ea. # 8 or #10 x 1-1/2" Machine Screws with wing nuts and 2 washers for each

1 ea. 4' x 8' sheet of 3/8" Plywood (Optional. Used to build work surface.)

4 ea. 8', 1 x 6 (Optional. Used to build sawhorses)

1 ea. 6', 2 x 4 (Optional. Used to build sawhorses)

Cautionary Words On Saving Weight

Sweet Dream is designed to be as light as practicable given the constraints of safety, and the strength of the materials used in its construction. At approximately 27 pounds, *Sweet Dream* is a light canoe. Every piece in *Sweet Dream's* hull is essential; none can be left out. It would be foolish, even imprudent or negligent, to substantially change the specified dimensions of any of the parts.

If lightness is a primary consideration, you may wish to omit the second layer of tape on the exterior chines and stems. These are primarily for abrasion and impact resistance. Consider the finish you will put on the hull. You can save two or three pounds by going very lightly on the paint and varnish.

The only acceptable material for the hull is 4mm marine grade okume plywood. 3mm okume is not acceptable, neither is luaun plywood even if it is marine grade. Okume is relatively expensive, but the time you spend building and finishing your *Sweet Dream* will represent the vast majority of the value of your canoe. You owe it to yourself and other users of your canoe to use only first grade materials throughout.

Recommended Tools and Equipment

Horizontal work surface at least 30" x 8'.
    Length must not be less than 8'.
Saber Saw w/sharp hollow ground blade
Japanese Dozuki Saw (Can substitute for the
    saber saw.)
Electric Drill or Torque Driver
1/16", 1/8", and 3/8" Drill Bits
1/4" and 7/8" Forstner Bits (For boring holes
    in thwarts and rails, and in backrest
    stretcher support blocks.)
5" or 6" Dual-Action Disc Sander
Low Angle Block or Block Plane
Hack Saw
Miscellaneous Sanding Blocks
50" x 2" x 1/8" Aluminium Straight Edge
Putty Knife

Utility Knife
Hammer
5 ea. 1" Brads
16' Tape Measure
8' Straight Edge (Can be made of 1/4" ply.)
14' Batten
14 ea. Screw Clamps, 2" or larger
10 ea. Spring Clamps, 2" or larger
1-5/8" Deck Screws
4 ea. 50 lb. bags of Sand, Limestone, etc.
3\4" Scrap Stock
Awl
Bevel Gauge
Carpenter's Level
Carpenter's Square
1 ea. OSHA approved organic vapor mask
    with cartridges
Safety Glasses or Goggles
3/4" Chisel
Optional:
Router with 3/16"round nose bit
Table Saw
X-Acto 7770 Circular Cutter (For cutting
    bias cut tape for stems)
Spoke Shave (For eight siding thwarts.)
Band Saw
3/4" #7 Gouge
Palm Sander

Epoxy Sources of Supply

If you can't find a source of epoxy near you, call these corporate offices to find their nearest retailer.

Fiberglass Coatings Inc.
P.O. Box 60457
St Petersburg, FL 33784
813-327-8117

Matrix Adhesives Systems (MAS)
1-800-398-7556
Smith & Co.
5100 Channel Avenue
Richmond, CA 94804
1-800-234-0330

System Three Resins, Inc.
P.O. Box 70436
Seattle, WA 98107
1-800-333-5514

West System Epoxy
Gougeon Brothers, Inc.
P.O. Box 908
Bay City, MI 48707
517-684-7286

4mm Okume Plywood Sources of Supply

Aircraft Spruce and Specialty Co.
201 W. Truslow Avenue
P.O. Box 424
Fullerton, CA 92632
714-870-7551

Boulter Plywood Corp.
24 Broadway
Somerville, MA 02145
617-666-1340

Edensaw Woods, Ltd.
211 Seton Road
Port Townsend, WA 98368
1-800-745-3336

Flounder Bay Boat Lumber
1019 3rd Street
Anacortes, WA 98221
1-800-228-4691

Harbor Sales Company, Inc.
1400 Russell Street
Baltimore, MD 21230
1-800-345-1712

Hudson Marine Plywoods
P.O. Box 1184
Elkhart, IN 46515
219-262-1174

Maine Coast Lumber
35 Birch Hill Road
York, ME 03909
1-800-899-1664

> *It is my opinion that the double paddle canoe gives the most fun for the money of any type of boat a person can possess.*
>
> L. Francis Herreshoff, *Sensible Cruising Designs*
> *International Marine, 1973, 1991*

M.L. Condon Company, Inc.
262 Ferris Avenue
White Pains, NY 10603
914-946-4111

Quality Woods Limited
Box 205
Lake Hiawatha, NJ
201-584-7554

Yukon Lumber Co.
520 W. 22nd Street
Norfolk, VA 23517
1-800-325-9663

Picking a Hull Length

Your first decision in building *Sweet Dream* involves selecting one of the three hull lengths. If you and your gear weigh less than than 100 pounds, or more than 300 pounds, I don't recommend that you build *Sweet Dream*. If you and your gear weigh over 275 pounds, I can recommend only the 14' version of *Sweet Dream*. Phil Green has quite a number of canoe designs from 7' 8" (!) up to 15' 6". I recommend that you send him $5 and ask for his catalog of plans. Write to: Phil Green Designs, 2 Keep Cottages, Berry Pomeroy, Totnes, Devon TQ9-6LH England.

Sweet Dream, like all boats and canoes, is not perfect; her design is a compromise of many technical factors. Likewise, you'll have to accept some compromises in your expectations of what she will, and even can do. The longer the hull the easier it is to paddle, but it is less maneuverable. The longer the hull the more freeboard you'll have, but you may find the hull has marginal directional stability in high winds.

The decision guide below is based on my belief that the most important factors for safety are adequate freeboard and stability. There are three simple rules for using the guide:

1. Begin at the left; find the weight that applies to you. If the total weight of you and your gear is between the figures given, choose the next higher weight level.

2. Be honest about the weight of canoeist and gear. It is better to estimate high rather than low.

3. Enter the matrix by moving to the right. At the question marks, if one of the factors at the top and bottom of the guide is significant to your canoeing, move towards that factor one level. If both factors are equally significant, stay on the same level and continue to the right. At the upper or lower-most levels, if a choice is not available, continue to the right without changing levels.

Exit the guide at the right with my *recommendation* for a *Sweet Dream* hull length. In the end, only you can choose which hull best suits your needs.

Sweet Dream's hull is built using two sheets of 4mm thick, 125cm by 250cm, (49-1/4 inches by 98-1/2 inches) okume marine plywood. The diagram on page 21 shows one-half of the roughly 4 foot by 16 foot panel after the two sheets are joined at one end, and the hull has been laid out. The only other wood needed to build *Sweet Dream's* hull is a 14'x4"x 3/4" piece of ash, mahogany, spruce, etc. for the rails and thwarts. The diagram shows the general arrangement of the various parts cut from the panel.

❧ **Hull.** The hull is laid out using one of the Hull Layout Plans that follow. The other parts shown on the diagram are made from the panel cut-offs after the hull has been cut out.

❧ **Breasthook.** Two pieces are laminated to make each of two 8mm thick breasthook blanks.

❧ **Bottom Pad Half.** The two pieces are joined along their long sides to make the bottom pad. The 14' hull requires four smaller pieces to make up its bottom pad.

❧ **Paddle Blade.** The material can be used to make a single or double bladed paddle.

❧ **Double Paddle Backrest.** The two pieces are laminated to make an 8mm thick blank. Either flat or curved backrest pads are cut from the blank.

	Single Paddle ↑	Semi-Open Waters	Speed	Beginning Paddler	
300 #					14'
275 #	?	?	?	?	14'
250 #	?	?	?	?	13'
225 #	?	?	?	?	13'
200 #	?	?	?	?	13'
175 #	?	?	?	?	13'
150 #	?	?	?	?	12'
	Double Paddle ↓	Swamps & Backwaters	Easy Turning	Expert Paddler	

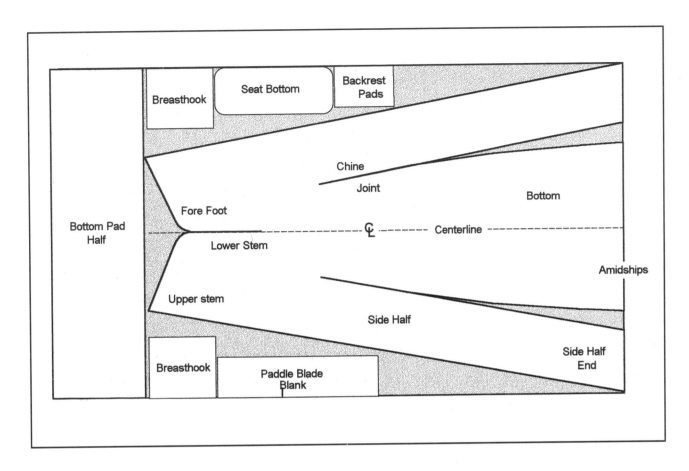

Single Paddle Seat. Two pieces are laminated to make an 8mm thick seat.

During building, some additional small pieces are cut from the scrap; parts for a simple feeler gage, pieces to make up the backrest stretcher support blocks, small pressure pads used with drywall screws to temporarily clamp the outer rail to the hull.

Dimensioned plans for the 12', 13', and 14' *Sweet Dream* hulls appear on the next three pages.

Charlie Ellin in Sweet Dream *with a double paddle.*

Photo by Marc Pettingill

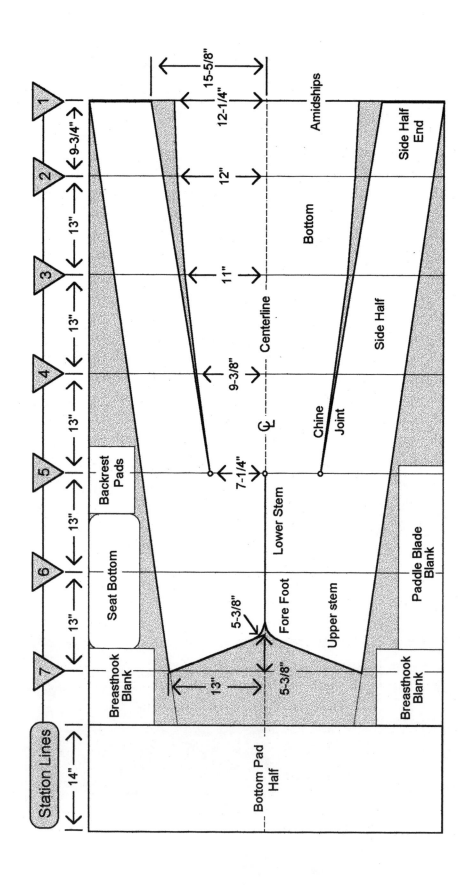

Sweet Dream 12 ❧ 11' 10" LOA

Hull Layout Plan

© Marc F. Pettingill 1995

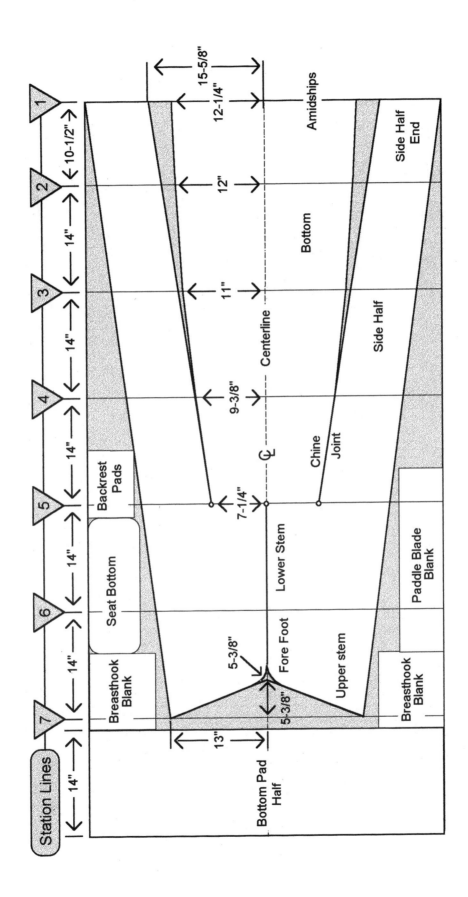

HULL LAYOUT PLAN

© Marc F. Pettingill 1995

Sweet Dream 14 ✎ 13' 10" LOA

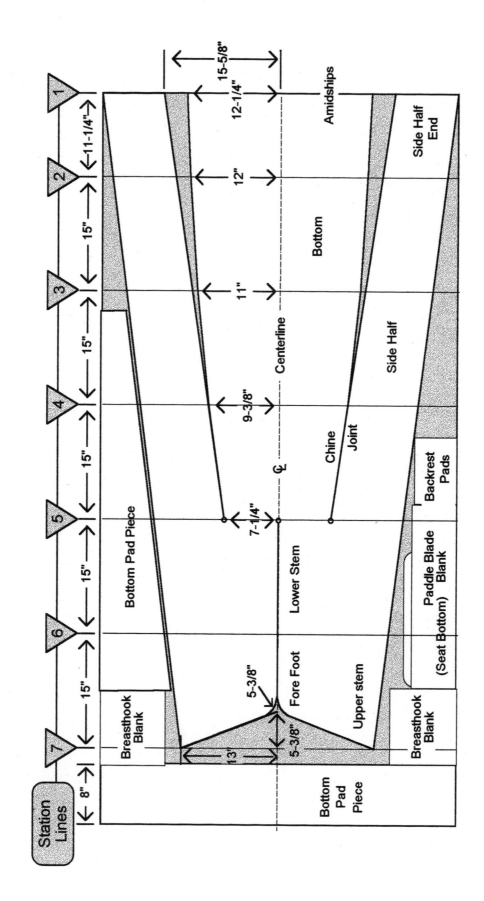

HULL LAYOUT PLAN

© Marc F. Pettingill 1995

Comments on the Building Sequence

It is not necessary to have prior boat building or carpentry experience to build *Sweet
Dream.* The Building Sequence goes into considerable detail because the folded plywood
building method has few precedents in other
canoe and small boat building styles. Whether
you are a neophyte or an old hand, it is essential that you become familiar with the building
sequence and the additional information in Part
IV before you begin building. While some of
the details may be obvious to experienced
builders, even they will find some of the
techniques unusual.

Throughout the building sequence when
the word "center" is used with reference to the
hull, it means the centerline of the hull running from stem to stem. When the word "amidships" is used, it means the middle of the hull;
a line across the hull that is equidistant from
each end.

Before you buy any materials or start building your *Sweet Dream*, read the building
sequence and additional information
through more than once and become
familiar with the whole building
process. The building sequence is broken
down into discrete activities, and further into
individual steps. The steps are numbered for
easy reference during the building process.
When a particular step is supported by background or technical material, that material
appears in a cited section.

I can well understand your coming to look
on your handiwork with affection. If you do,
you'll join a long-standing club whose many
members include Pygmalion, Professor Higgins,
and myself. However, in building a canoe it is
wise to avoid affectation. The canoe's timeless
grace and beauty do not need dressing up and

gadgetry. In fact, there is little that can be done
in the way of ornamentation that will not make
the hull look gimmicky or over-worked. Rather
than think ahead about special moldings for the
rails or an "authentic Indian" paint scheme, it is
better to invest your energy in living in the
moment as you build. By this I mean giving
your full attention to the task at hand. What
you do may not be perfect — it doesn't have to
be. Your final work will be better than your
first. The key is to get to the higher level of
skill as quickly as possible. This comes only
from concentrating on what you're doing.

The difference between production and
finely crafted canoes is the same difference as
between clothes bought off the rack and those
bought from a tailor. The difference is the fit. It
has as much to do with what is not there as
with what is: no excess, no bulges, no gaps;
rather, impeccable cut, smooth lines, and
restrained details. On the canoe concentrate
your effort on the cut and fit of the parts. Getting a good fit takes time to learn and to do. As
an amateur builder, time is one resource that
you have in abundance. You don't *have* to rush,
so don't; it's that simple.

The solo canoe enjoyed great favor and
widespread use in the later 1800s. Unfortunately, the governing body of the canoe association was made up of blue-bloods to whom
money was no object. They pushed the sport of
competitive canoe sailing to the detriment of
paddling. By 1896, the solo canoe was nearly a
pure racing sailboat and the paddle was but
clutter on deck. In the paddle races, the "Canadian canoe," what we know as the tandem
canoe, was dominant. The solo canoe faded into
history, and the tandem canoe was adopted by
the middle class as the first recreation vehicle.

Every city park that had even a puddle of water had a canoe livery. At every available chance young beaus and their belles went a-paddling. It was hardly canoeing, but it did provide a few hours of privacy in the teeming, overcrowded, newly industrialized cities.

The canoe's role as darling of the public's eye was short lived. Its sudden popularity in the cities, based mostly on its social uses, was overwhelmed by the introduction in turn of the chain driven bicycle with safety brakes, the automobile driven by a gasoline engine with an electric starter, and boats with outboard motors. As last ditch efforts, the canoe manufacturers tried just about everything to recapture their market share. In the 1920s you could get a canoe with sumptuous accommodations including oriental rugs, matched retractable stowage for a wind-up Victrola and 78 rpm records, and a dry bar with crystal glasses for serving non-alcoholic elixirs and tonics. How the canoe was got to and from the water, and how it was moved once there can only be guessed.

Don't get sucked onto the gadget and gee-gaw merry-go-round. It's never ending and, along the way, the canoe becomes less a source of re-creation and more a millstone. Today we're fortunate. If you want the modern equivalent of a Victrola, you can buy a metal-flake fiberglass runabout with a surround-sound stereo, all the comforts of home, and the requisite 200hp two-cycle motor. While satisfying your need for aural stimulation, you can generate pollution at ten times the rate of an automobile and by way of conspicuous consumption contribute to the GNP. Some call this progress, but I think not.

Sweet Dream Building Sequence ∽

Before you put saw to wood, there is some important basic information that you need to know. Please reread Safety In the Shop, Epoxy, and Work Surface, pages 109-114.

Mill the Parts for the Hull

Before working on the hull, it's best to mill the rails, thwarts, and other pieces so that they are immediately available when needed later. A table saw is the best tool to use. See Milling the Parts for the Hull, page 116.

Cut out the Hull Shape

Step 1. Join the two 4mm okume sheets into a 4'x16' panel. (See Joining Plywood Sheets, page 118.)

Step 2. Use your selected Hull Layout Plan to layout the hull on the side of the 4' x 16' panel with the smoothest joint.

Lay out the hull right on the floor. This is as close as we get to lofting in building Sweet Dream. *See Step 7.*

Step 3. Draw the hull centerline between the centers of the ends of the panel. Station Line 1 is at the exact middle of the panel. Measure and draw the six additional Station Lines on both sides of Station Line 1.

Step 4. Transfer the measurements given on the Hull Layout Plan to each station line on both sides of the hull centerline.

Step 5. Draw the lines from the marks on Station Lines 7 to the ends of the side halves with an 8' straight edge.

Step 6. Draw the lines from the ends of the chines at Station Lines 5 to the ends of the side halves on Station Lines 1 with a straight edge.

Step 7. Draw smooth lines connecting the marks for the chine edges of the bottom using a 14' batten.

Step 8. Draw the stems as straight lines between the marks on the centerline and the marks on Station Lines 7.

Step 9. Draw the curves at the fore foot with a handy round object about 11" across; plates do fine. The diameter can be up to 12" as your dinnerware requires.

Use the japanese saw to cut the lower stem joint. See Step 11.

Step 10. Cut out the hull. With the saber saw or japanese saw, cut as close to the hull lines as possible without cutting into or crossing them. While accuracy is important, it is more important not to cut across the lines into the hull. Practice cutting next to the line by first cutting off the

bottom pad halves on the ends of the panel. These two rectangular pieces will be joined later to make the bottom pad.

Step 11. When cutting the stems, use the saber saw to cut from Station Line 7, along the upper stem and around the curve at the forefoot. Stop where the two stem lines converge at the centerline. Cut the rest of the lower stem joint to Station Line 5 with the japanese saw. This cut should be as narrow as possible. A saber saw will do if you don't have a japanese saw.

Cut the straight line of the chine joint with the saber saw. Start by drilling a 1/4" hole near the scarph. See Step 12.

Step 12. When cutting out the area between the bottom and the side halves, make the first cut along the straight line that is the chine edge of the side. Next, make the curved cut along the edge of the bottom. Last, make the cut on Station Line 1 that separates the two side halves.

Step 13. Use a low angle block plane, file, and/or sanding block to trim the saw cuts to their lines.

Drill Holes for Electrical Ties

Step 14. Turn the scarphed panel over and draw the centerline between the two lower stem cuts.

The curve on the bottom cuts smoothly using the japanese saw. Cut the first six inches or so with the saber saw to get started. See Step 13.

Step 15. Mark set back lines at the edges of the stem and chine cuts for holes for the electrical ties. The ties will be used to temporarily hold the stem and chine joints until they are permanently joined with epoxy fillets and tape.

Step 16. On the upper stem and forefoot, the set back lines are drawn 1/4" from the edge of the hull.

Step 17. Drill 1/8" holes for the electrical ties. The drilled holes should be drilled inboard of, and just touching the set back line.

On the stems, drill holes for the electrical ties on both sides of the joint. See Step 18.

Step 18. Along the lower stem, the drilling pattern starts 1/2" from the end of the cut. The second through eighth holes are 1" apart. The ninth and successive holes are 2" apart. Leave 1" free of holes at the top of the upper stem at the sheer. Carefully measure and drill holes on both edges of the upper and lower stem, and the forefoot. The holes must be directly across from each other so that the stem sides close up without twisting.

Step 19. Draw setback lines 3/16" from the side and bottom chine edges. Along the chine edges, drill holes at this time only along the curved edge of the bottom. The drilling pattern starts 1/2" from the end of the cuts. The second hole is 1" from the first. The second through sixth holes are 1" apart. The seventh through eleventh holes are 2" apart. The rest of holes to amidships are 4" apart.

On the chines, drill holes for the electrical ties only on the bottom, the curved side of the joint. See Step 19.

Bevel the Inner Edges of the Stem Cuts

Step 20. See Stem Bevels, page 128, for an explanation of this important step.

Step 21. Using a low angle block plane, chisel, spokeshave and/or sanding block, cut a 1/16"x 1/8" bevel from the top of the upper stems to about six inches past the curve of the forefoot. The 1/16" dimension

While it is easiest to cut the bevels with a chisel, be careful! See Step 21.

Close Up the Stems

Step 23. Place two of the 50 pound weighted sacks next to each other lengthwise amidships.

Step 24. Use two pieces of heavy string or stranded copper wire about 24" long as ties at each end. Lead one tie through the uppermost holes on each side on the upper stem. Lead the other tie through the third holes on both sides. Take tension on one tie and knot it loosely. Next, take a little greater tension on the second tie. Close up the stem by alternately tightening the two ties. This way, should one tie break or slip, the stem will not open flat. As the stem sides come together at the forefoot, insert nylon ties there. Close up both stems.

of the bevel is across the edge of the plywood. The 1/8" dimension is along the top surface of the panel.

Step 22. The bevel changes shape from below the curve at the forefoot to the end of the stem cut. On the top surface of the plywood the measurement widens to 1/8". On the edge of the plywood, the bevel extends to the bottom side of the sheet.

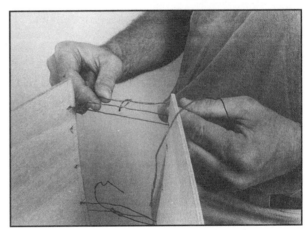

You may hear a slight cracking at the end of the lower stem at this point. Press on regardless! See Step 25.

Step 25. Insert and tighten nylon ties along the lower stem cut only AFTER the upper stem is completely closed up and ties inserted in each pair of holes and the stem sides aligned at the forefoot.

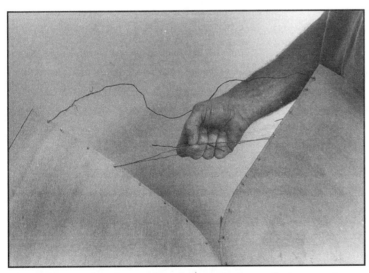

Close the stems by alternately tightening 2 pieces of wire or string. See Step 24.

---

efined by function, a boat is simply a contrivance that floats and is capable of carrying some kind of load over the water. Nowhere in its definition is implied or mentioned varnish, rabbets, keels, frames, hair-line joints, copper rivets, cedar, oak, or any of the other articles of faith and holy relics that many people and publications would have you believe are part and parcel of the mystery.

Skip Snaith,
Canoes and Kayaks for the Backyard Builder
International Marine, 1989

Step 26. It is easiest to tighten the nylon ties if they are all put in from the same side of the hull. Overtightening single ties will lead to broken ties and/or torn out holes in

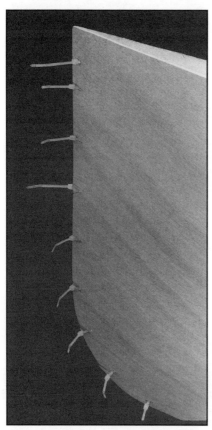

the hull. In the event of a tear out, redrill a pair of opposing holes about 1/4" to the side of the torn hole(s).

Step 27. Aligning the stem at the forefoot . As the forefoot closes up, check to ensure the edges of the two stem sides are in alignment both vertically and fore and aft. If neces-

Replace the wire or string used to close the stems with electrical ties. See Step 26.

sary, slip the blade of a thin putty knife between the stem sides to give a low friction surface on which to slide the sides into alignment. Do not proceed with closing up the upper stems until the forefoot is as close to perfectly aligned as you can get it.

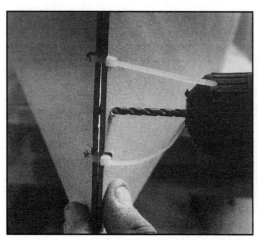

If an additional tie is needed to close the stem, drill through both sides at once. See Step 28.

Step 28. At a spot about 10" below the top of the stem, the stem sides often open up between the nylon ties. This point lies on the extension of the chine cut and it reflects the tension that has been created in the inner ply of the sides. As necessary drill holes in the two stem sides and install additional ties to get the stem to close up.

Step 29. Replace the string or wire with nylon ties. After closing the upper stem, close up the lower stem joint below the forefoot. Along the lower stem it is important to get the two sides pulled as close together as possible. If the lower stem joint is not pulled completely closed there will be an unsightly hump in the stem just outboard of the end of the joint. Push on the hull from below next to each tie and take some slack out of the tie. Do the same for the other ties, then repeat as necessary to get the lower stem sides to close up tightly.

Drill holes in the sides to match those in the bottom. See Step 30.

Close Up the Chines

Step 30. Starting where the bottom and side chine edges meet at Station Line 5, drill 1/8" holes in one of the side ends directly above the first three holes previously drilled in the bottom. Insert ties in the three holes in side and bottom and pull them moderately tight. Repeat for the other three chine ends. Continue closing up the chines by drilling three holes at each chine edge of the side half ends, inserting and moderately tightening ties, and continuing around the hull. Do not drill holes for the last three ties in each side half end.

Step 31. The side and bottom will come into contact at about Station Line 4. After you install a few more ties towards the center of the hull, the bottom should extend under the side and out to its outer edge. From this point to amidships, ensure that the side sits above the bottom.

Step 32. Fully tighten all the nylon ties in the chine joints. At this point the two side halves overlap amidships about 5/8" at the chine and 4"at the top of the sides.

Step 33. The hull now has its essential shape. From here on, the work consists of trimming and joining the side halve ends, locking the hull shape in with taped fillets, and adding the rails, breasthooks, and thwarts for strength.

Setting the Rocker and Bottom Arc

Step 34. Make up two, 3/4x 3/4x12" blocks from 3/4" thick scrap. Center the hull on the work surface. Place one of the blocks under each end of the canoe 4' from amidships (or at the ends of an 8' long work surface.) Make up two 18" long, 3/4x1" blocks from 3/4" thick scrap. Put one of the blocks with its 3/4" dimension against the work surface on each side of the hull, centered under the outer edge of the bottom amidships.

Step 35. Check under the hull. The two 50 pound sacks should be forcing the bottom in contact with the work surface for about 2' from amidships. The two blocks at the ends of the work surface set the amount of end to end curve or rocker in the canoe's

bottom. The two blocks at the chines amidships ensure that the bottom is arched throughout its length and not flat amidships.

Step 36. At this point the top edges of the side halves are straight lines meeting at an angle amidships. The top edges of the side halves only vaguely reflect the intended sweep of the sheer which will be cut later. Not to worry.

Step 37. Beginning at the fourth tie from amidships, let the side halves extend outside the bottom. With one hand, hold the two side halves on one side together and against the bottom so that their lower edges are at the height of the lower surface of the bottom. Ensure that the side halves overlap each other evenly at their lower edges.

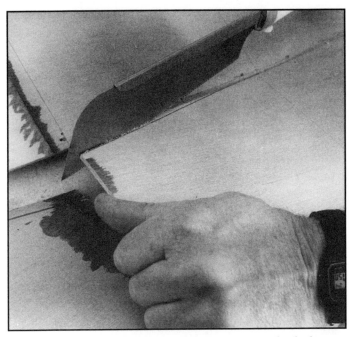

Trim the side halves. Removing this little piece creates a chine line amidships. See Step 38.

Step 38. Mark the upper surface of the bottom on the inner faces of the side halves. Remove the fourth tie from the chines amidships. Carefully bend the side halves outward. With the japanese saw, cut off the long thin triangular areas below the lines just drawn. Drill holes for the last three ties. Insert and moderately tighten the ties.

Step 39. Repeat on the other side of the hull. Tighten all the ties in the chine joints. Use the procedure for tightening the lower stem ties to get the ties at the ends of the chines as tight as possible. (*See Step 29.*)

Insert the Amidships Frame

Step 40. Mark and cut out the frame carefully. In addition to holding the sides at the correct width at the sheer, the frame is used as a hull alignment guide. Darkly mark the centerline on both faces of the frame.

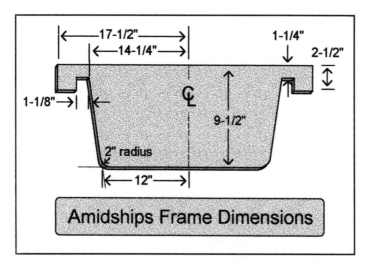

Amidships Frame Dimensions

Step 41. Move the two weighted sacks apart about 2". Put the frame into the hull amidships. Its wings rest against the upper edges of the hull sides. There should be about 3/8" clearance between the frame and the canoe's bottom.

Temporarily Install the Outer Rails

Step 42. See How Many Clamps?, page 127. Always clamp the rails to the hull as a pair. Clamp both the rails amidships first. Go to one end of the hull and clamp both rails to the sides at the stem. Go to the other end and clamp the rails there. Clamping this way reduces twisting, or racking forces on the forefeet which can loosen the ties there and cause misalignment of the hull.

Step 43. Slide the rails under the tabs on the ends of the amidships frame. Clamp the outer rails to the hull using spring clamps

in four places on each side. For each rail, use two clamps about 4" apart amidships where the side halves overlap, and one at each stem. The two clamps on each rail amidships keep the rails from flopping about while you go to an end of the hull to put on the clamps there.

Step 44. When removing the rails, later in the building sequence, unclamp the two rails at one end of the hull, then unclamp the rails at the other end of the hull, and finally unclamp amidships.

Step 45. When clamped to the hull, the rails will cross outboard of the stems. One rail passes below the other and it cannot follow the edge of the side to the stem. This is all right for now. DO NOT CUT THE RAILS TO LENGTH AT THIS TIME.

Step 46. Use a spring clamp to hold the two rails together where they cross. Using the excess rail beyond the stem, pull the rails together at the stem so that they force the the sides of the hull to touch at the top of the stem. Mark the rails where they cross the outer edge of the stem. Make a second

Marking the outer rails at the stems.
Even with the rails clamped to the sides, the
clamp holding both rails has a tendency to slip off.
See Step 47.

mark on each rail 1/8" outboard of the one just made. Repeat the marking at the other end of the rails.

Step 47. Remove the rails from the hull. Check that the distance between the inner marks on each rail is identical. If it is not, halve the difference between them, put new inner marks at this location on one end of each rail. Make a new outer mark 1/8" towards the end of the rails. Erase the first set of marks.

Step 48. Using the outboard mark on the rail ends, cut the rail ends so that they make a simple lap joint as shown in the drawing above.

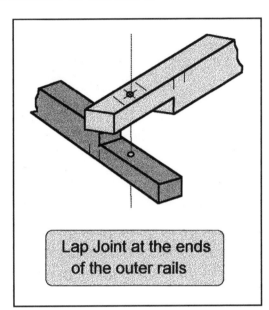

Lap Joint at the ends of the outer rails

is in the center of the crossed rails. Drill a 3/32" diameter hole through the rail at this mark. Recross the rails and with them held tightly against the hull sides, use the hole just drilled as a guide to drill through the lower rail.

Step 50. Fasten the rails together with a # 8 or #10x1-1/2" machine screw and wing nut with washers top and bottom. Tighten the bolt and nut through the rails.

Step 51. With this temporary arrangement at the rail ends, the clamps at the ends of the rails can be removed. Pinning the rail ends together relieves the considerable outward force that the rails otherwise exert when they are clamped to the sides at the stem. It will also prove useful later when marking the sheer. Amidships make a register mark across each rail and the edge of the side. Put the mark an inch or two to one side of the center of the over-lapped side half ends. This mark will be used to reposition the rails when they are removed just before being permanently attached to the hull later in the sequence.

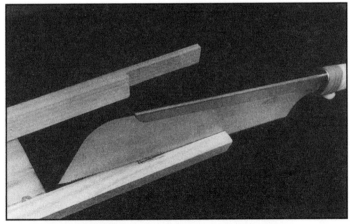

Cutting the lap joints in the end rails goes quickly with the japanese saw even though it is primarily for cross-cutting and not ripping. See Step 48.

Step 49. Remount the rails. Center the rails on the hull. Again, pull the rails together at the stem so that they force the the sides of the hull to touch at the top of the stem. Mark the point on the uppermost rail that

Carefully drill the holes in the rail ends. Once the drill has marked the lower rail, uncross the rails and drill through. See Step 49.

Align the Hull

Step 52. Check that the amidships frame centerline is aligned with the centerline on the inner bottom of the hull. If it isn't, give the frame a sharp knock on one end with the heel of your hand. The spring clamps will allow the rails and side halves to slide into alignment when the frame is given short, sharp knocks on its ends.

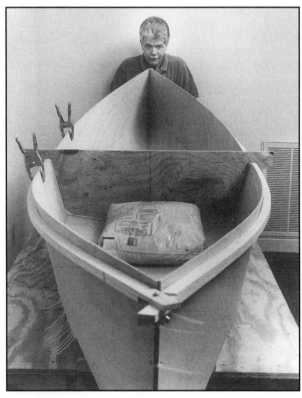

Not quite in alignment. A sharp knock on the right end of the centerframe will set things aright. See Step 53.

Step 53. Sight from stem to stem across the amidships frame. The top of the stems and the centerline on the amidships frame should be in a straight line. If they aren't, the problem is usually a twisted stem . Check the alignment at the forefoot.

Step 54. Retighten the ties on the stems as tight as you can get them. Replace any ties that break or do not hold tightly. If the end wont stay in alignment, or the points of the sides at the stems are not at the same level, it's probably because some pairs of holes are crooked and the ties are pulling at an angle across the upper stem. Take out any ties that cross the stem joint at an angle other than 90°. Add new holes 1/4" to one side of the crooked ones by drilling through both sides at once. Put ties in the new holes and pull them tight.

Cut the Side Halves to Length

Step 55. Next to aligning the hull at the forefeet, cutting the sides to length is one of the most important activities in the building sequence. To keep the hull in alignment, the clamping, unclamping, and rail removals that follow must be done on both rails at the same time.

Step 56. Replace the four spring clamps on the rails amidships one at a time with small screw clamps. Remember to use pressure pads under the jaws of the screw clamps.

Step 57. The four screw clamps are holding the side half ends together at the correct length and angle as determined by the combined effects of the four small blocks under the hull, the rails, and the amidships frame. There must be no slippage between the overlapping side half ends from the time the screw clamps are first tightened on the rails and the side ends are cut to length in Step 61.

Step 58. With two of your largest screw clamps, clamp the overlapping side halves together on one side of the hull as far below the rail as possible. Leave as much distance between the clamps as possible. Again and always, use pressure pads under the jaws of the screw clamps. Tighten the clamps securely. Repeat on the other side of the hull.

> *Practice makes perfect only when you start with the right idea in the first place, and no amount of repetition will make a poor approach any better.*
>
> Walter J. Simmons,
> *Building Lapstrake Canoes*

Step 59. Unbolt the rails at their ends, then unclamp them amidships. Slide the rails out from inside the clamps holding the overlapping side ends together amidships. Replace the two screw clamps and pressure pads on each side of the hull to hold the overlapping side half ends together at the upper edge of the hull.

Step 60. On the outside of the hull, adjacent to the the center of the joint in the bottom of the hull, draw a straight line midway between the sets of clamps from the top of the side halves to the chine. The line

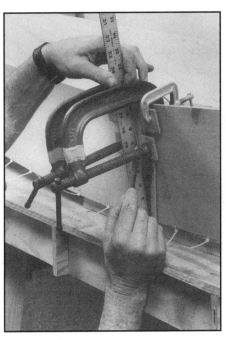

Set the clamps so that there is a clear strip between them to draw a line down the center of the overlapping side half ends. See Step 60.

Use the japanese saw to cut the side half ends to length. See Step 61.

should be approximately perpendicular to the work surface. The line must pass over both half side ends from rail to chine. Check carefully at the chine where the side half ends overlap by only 5/8" or so to ensure that it does.

Step 61. Cut down the line just drawn from the top of the sides rail to the chine. Use a saw with the thinnest possible blade; a japanese saw is the best tool for this job. The side halves are now cut to length and are ready to be joined.

Join the Side Halves

Step 62. The side half ends are joined with a fiberglass tape butt joint. From the remains of the plywood used to make the amidships frame, make two 9"x9" backing plates. These plates will be used to align and hold the side half ends together while an epoxy/fiberglass tape butt joint is started. The backing plates will be screwed to the inside of the side half ends and epoxy and fiberglass tape will be applied on the outside.

Step 63. On the outside of each side half, draw a line from rail to chine 2" from its end. On the line drill three 3/16" holes: the first 1" from the top of the side, the second 1" from the chine, and the third in the middle of the side.

Step 64. To keep from gluing the backing plate to the side ends, create a non-stick band at least three inches wide down the center of the backing plates. Plastic wrap, masking tape, or duct tape will do fine.

Step 65. To keep epoxy run-off from gluing the bottom to the sides or the block beneath the hull, put some pieces of film or tape between the side, bottom, and block. It should extend at least 3" on either side of the joint. Attach some of the film or tape to the work surface below the joint.

Step 66. Center the non-stick band on the backing plate over the end of one side half. The lower edge of the backing plate should be 1/4" or so above the chine edge of the side. Fasten the plate to the inside of the side end with three 1" drywall screws with 1" square pressure pads under their heads. Drive the screws through the holes just drilled in the sides and into the backing plate.

Step 67. Bring the two side half ends together so that their ends are in contact from top to chine. With a screw clamp, clamp the second side end to the backing plate. (If the clamp covers the upper hole in the side, it's OK.) With the side ends connected like this, the side looses some of its outward tilt. This is only a temporary condition.

Step 68. Check to see that the side ends are still in contact, and that their top and bottom edges are aligned. If so, drive drywall screws with pads through the lower two holes in the second side end and into the backing plate. Remove the clamp. Drive a screw and pad through the upper hole. Repeat the process on the other side of the hull.

Step 69. Cut two 12" pieces of 3" fiberglass tape. With a chip brush, apply epoxy to the hull side in a 3" wide strip centered on the

Cover the joint with 3" fiberglass tape and epoxy. Remember the masking tape on the backing pad. See Step 69.

crack between the side half ends (1 pump for both joints). Don't forget to wear protective gloves and safety glasses whenever you work with epoxy. Center the fiberglass tape over the joint and press it into the epoxy. Apply enough additional epoxy so that the tape is transparent. Don't try to fill the weave of the tape with epoxy; it will just drip off. Three or four additional applications of epoxy are needed to fill the weave.

Finish up the interior side joint with a layer of 2"-wide tape. The holes from the screws used to hold the side to the backing plate will be filled with thickened epoxy putty. See Step 72.

Step 70. Repeat on the other side of the hull. After an hour or so, when the epoxy is tacky, but before it has cured hard, trim the excess tape at sheer and chine.

Step 71. After at least four hours, when the epoxy has cured hard, remove the backing plates.

Step 72. On the interior of the hull the joint is made with one layer of 3" tape. The butt joint backing plates are not used. Apply epoxy and tape as on the exterior (1 pump for both joints).

Install the Bottom Pad

Step 73. Join the two rectangular pieces that were cut off the ends of the hull panel at the beginning of construction. Join the pieces along their long sides with either a scarph or a fiberglass tape butt joint.

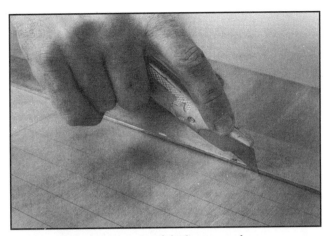

Score through the outer ply of the bottom pad with a utility knife. See Step 74.

Step 74. With a sharp utility knife, make cuts through ONLY THE OUTER PLY of one side of the bottom pad. Make the cuts at 1" intervals beginning 11/2" from the pad's centerline (and not the edge of the scarph joint if that's how the two pieces are joined). The cut side of the pad will go against the hull.

Step 75. On the uncut side of the pad, draw a centerline between the long sides. Transfer station lines from the Hull Layout Plan to the panel. The panel is long enough for only the first two station lines outwards from amidships. Subtract 1/4" from the bottom dimensions on the Hull Layout Plan and plot these shortened lengths on their associated station lines.

Step 76. With a batten, draw a fair curve connecting the marks just drawn and running off the ends of the panel. Cut out the bottom pad.

Step 77. To de-emphasize the bottom pad, its ends can be given a wide bevel; 1" to 1-1/2" will do fine. The bevel should be made on the uncut, or upper, side of the pad. Otherwise, the ends of the pad will be covered with a small fillet later.

Step 78. The fiberglass tape butt joint used to join the side halves added a layer of tape on the interior of the sides. These two layers together add about 1/32" to the thickness of the sides. This 1/32" must now be subtracted from the amidships frame's width. Thanks to the frame's taper, this is easily accomplished by raising the frame relative to the sides. Put the frame in position with 3/4" thick spacers between it and the upper edge of the sides.

Step 79. Reattach the outer rails to the hull using spring clamps amidships. Rebolt the rails at the stems. Check to see that the frame centerline is in line with the centerline on the hull. Check hull alignment from the stems across the center frame. Correct alignment as necessary.

Step 80. Trial fit the bottom pad. Remove the two 50lb. sacks from the hull. With its cut side facing down, slide the pad under the frame. Center the pad over the centerline on the hull and amidships. Replace the weighted sacks. There should be 3/16" or less between the pad and the sides of the hull. Trim the pad as necessary to clear the ties amidships.

Step 81. It is important that the pad be glued securely over its entire underside to the bottom. Mark the area of the bottom covered by the pad. Remove the amidships frame. Remove the sacks and the bottom pad from the hull. Sand the cut side of the pad and the area it will cover with 100 grit sandpaper.

There is one thing that I should warn you about before you decide to get serious about canoeing. You must consider the possibility of becoming totally and incurably hooked on it ... I find it hard to believe that not everybody is crazy about canoes. A canoe is the only thing I know that has no moving parts. There's nothing to break down and you don't have to feed a canoe ... I understand that people can become addicted to horses, but I'm sure it's nothing like canoe addiction. Canoe addiction can affect your whole life.

Bill Mason,
Path of the Paddle

Step 82. Spread a thin coating of unthickened epoxy on both the cut side of the bottom pad and the marked area of the bottom (8 pumps). Spread a thin layer of thickened epoxy on the scored side of the pad (10 pumps, 10 scoops). The West System© 809 Notched Spreader simplifies this job immensely. Place the pad in position, replace the amidships frame with its shims. Put two weighted sacks on the pad, one on either side of the amidships frame.

Quickly spread the thickened epoxy mixture on the bottom. The dark puddles are mixture that has been poured out of the mixing pot to slow heat buildup in the mix. See Step 82.

Mold the bottom pad to the hull with four weighted sacks. The centerframe is raised on 3/4" blocks at the rail. See Step 84.

Step 83. Align the centerline on the pad with that on the hull. Ensure that the centerline on the amidships frame is in line with that on the pad.

Step 84. Add two more weighted sacks stemward of the first two, one on either side of the amidships frame.

Step 85. Check to see that the bottom pad is in contact with the bottom everywhere around its perimeter. If it isn't, use additional smaller weights to make it so.

Step 86. If you chose not to bevel the ends of the pad earlier, use any thickened epoxy that squeezes out from between the pad and bottom to make a smooth fillet on the end of the pad. This fillet ensures

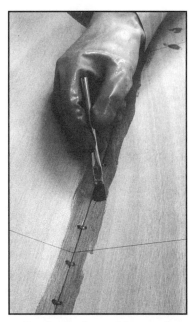

Preglue the inner chine out about 3/4" from the joint line. See Step 89.

that water cannot get under the pad, and it seals the grain on the end of the pad. The space between the outboard edges of the pad and the hull sides will be filled shortly by the chine fillet. Clean any epoxy squeeze-out from the joint between the bottom and sides.

Fillet and Tape the Inner Chines

Step 87. See Filleting Tools, page 130, and Making Fillet and Tape Joints, page 135.

Step 88. Before doing any filleting or taping, recheck the alignment of the hull. Check the tightness of all ties.

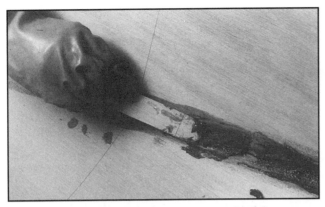

The fillet always looks a little messy as you load the thickened mixture into the joint. See Step 89.

Fix anything you don't like. Once the fillets are cured, the shape of the hull is locked in.

Step 89. Fillet half of an inner chine joint at a time. With an acid brush, spread unthickened epoxy along the joint and out about 1" onto the bottom and sides. (1 pump per chine) Mix a batch of thickened epoxy (3 pumps, 41/2 scoops). Use the medium size wood filleting tool to apply, then smooth the thickened mixture. The fillet should be deep enough to just cover the ties.

Step 90. At the ends of the joint, use the large plastic filleting tool to get a smooth transition to the hull. The fillet should blend into the hull about 2" past the end of the joint.

Here the joint to the right has been shaped and cleaned up with the wood filleting tool. To the left, the fillet is being blended into the hull with the large plastic tool. See Step 90.

Step 91. Repeat for the other end of the joint, and then do the other side of the hull.

Step 92. Wait an hour until the fillets have a rubbery texture and won't be distorted when fiberglass tape is applied. Cut a piece of 3" tape that extends 2" past the fillet. Using a 1-1/2" or 2" chip brush, pre-coat a 3" wide strip centered on the fillet (2 pumps each chine). Place the tape in the epoxy and press it into place. With the chip brush apply epoxy to the tape (3 pumps each chine). Use the brush to push the tape so that its edges are straight. Repeat for the other chine. After 20 minutes, cleanup any epoxy runs on the bottom with a rag or paper towel.

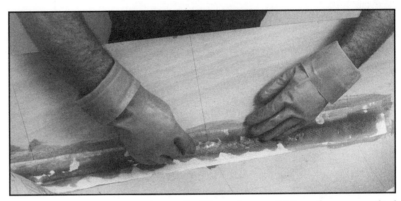

Press the 3" tape into unthickened epoxy applied to the rubbery hard chine fillet. See Step 92.

Step 93. Let the taped fillet cure overnight. Cut off the ties along the chines. Because the nylon pieces that are left in the holes are relatively soft, they needn't be removed from the hull.

Fillet and Tape the Inner Stems

Step 94. With an acid brush, precoat the stem sides with epoxy 2" out from the center of the joint (1 pump for both stems). Mix enough thickened epoxy to fillet the inner stems one at a time (6 pumps, 9 scoops for each stem). Use the small radius filleting tool at the upper stem to create a fillet that is approximately 3/4" deep.

Step 95. To get the thickened epoxy into the upper stem joint, put as much filler on the

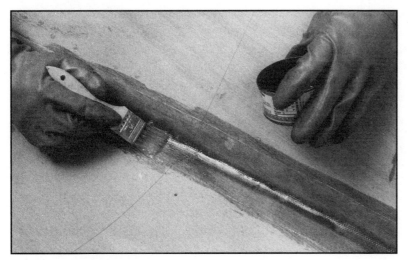

Coat the taped fillet with unthickened epoxy. See Step 92.

Get the thickened epoxy out of the mixing container and into the stem as quickly as possible to increase the time you'll have to form and smooth the fillet. See Step 95.

small filleting tool as it will hold. Reach into the stem and with a wiping motion, deposit the filler on the hull side near where the filler is needed. Now use the tool to move the filler into the joint.

Step 96. To maintain sufficient depth to cover the nylon ties, the fillet must widen as it extends past the forefoot and onto the

lower stem. Use the medium width wooden filleting tool at the lower forefoot. As soon as possible, switch to the plastic tools. The fillet should be about 1/2"-5/8" deep until well past the forefoot. At the end of the lower stem joint the fillet is about 2" wide. The fillet should blend smoothly into the bottom about 3" inboard of the stem cut.

Step 97. Work quickly; the filleting mix gets quite draggy as it cures. Try to get a smooth transition from tool to tool. If you over work the fillet the surface will get very rough. Do the best you can and stop filleting around.

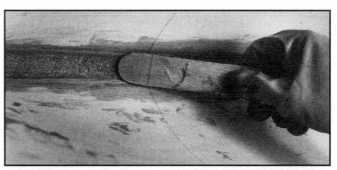

Form and smooth the fillet in the upper stem and forefoot with the small radius wood filleting tool. See Step 96.

Blend the chine fillet into the hull with the wide plastic filleting tool. See Step 97.

Step 98. Use the flat end of the large tool as a scraper to clean excess filler from the hull sides. Make sure that there are no lumps or ridges of excess thickened epoxy on the hull sides right next to the feather edge of the fillet.

Step 99. Wait an hour until the fillet has a rubbery texture. If the surface of the fillet is really rough with ridges and lumps higher than 1/16", you'll have to wait until it's cured and then sand it smooth before applying the tape. Sand when the fillet is firm but not hard. If you can get to this about four hours after the fillet was applied, it is fairly easy. If you wait for 24 hours, the fillet will be very hard and sanding is considerably more difficult.

Apply unthickened epoxy to the tape for the stem before putting the tape over the fillet. See Step 100.

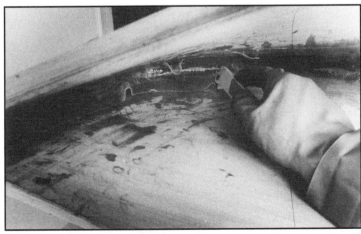

Where the tape curves around the forefoot, it will bulge outward from the fillet in several places. Cut a dart in one side of the bulge and overlap the tape. The dart is easily cut with the circular cutting tool. See Step 100.

Step 100. Apply one layer of 3" wide tape over the fillet. This tape is most easily applied if it is presaturated before it is put on the fillet. Cut darts in the tape as necessary to get it to lie flat against the hull sides around the forefoot. Two darts on either side is typical; stagger the darts on either side of the tape.

Step 101. Let the tape cure overnight. Cut the ties off the stem.

Cutting the Sheer

Step 102. See the information on Determining the Sheer, page 137.

Step 103. Check the lap joint at the ends of the rails. The upper surface of both rails must be even. Trim or shim the rail ends as necessary to make them so. Throughout the following steps, the rails remain bolted together at their ends and clamped to the hull amidships with their upper faces 1/32" below the top of the side. At the stems the rails will sometimes be clamped at the top of the hull or released and moved down, out of the way.

Adjust the rails so that they cross the adjustment lines at the same distance from the top of the hull side. See Step 104.

Step 104. Unclamp the rail ends at the stems and move them downward 4" or 5". Midway between where Station Lines 5 and 6 meet the top of the hull side, draw 2" long lines on the outside of the hull perpendicular to the top of the side. As a convenience, I will call these lines "adjustment lines."

Step 105. At the stems, reclamp the rails even with the top of the sides. Take measurements from top of the sides to the top of the rail at the adjustment lines. Adjust the rails so that the four measurements are the same. Mark the top of the rail on the adjustment lines. DO NOT MARK THE ENTIRE LENGTH OF THE RAIL.

Measure downward 3/8" from where the "natural" sheer line crosses the adjustment line. See Step 105.

Step 106. Unclamp the rail ends and move them out of the way. Make a mark on the adjustment lines 3/8" below the one just made. Clamp the rails to the hull at the lower mark on the adjustment line. Hold the rail in position with clamps at the adjustment lines in addition to those amidships and at the stems.

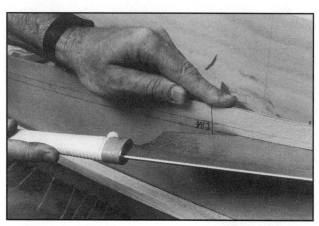

Cut the sheer with the japanese saw. Stay 1/32" or so above the line. See Step 108.

Step 107. Take measurement of the rails to the top of the sides at Station Lines 4 and 6. Adjust the rails to make the measurements the same at each set of station lines. Mark the upper surface of the rails from end to end onto the hull. Remove all the clamps and move the rails down the hull out of the way.

Step 108. With the japanese saw, cut the hull side 1/32" above the sheer line just drawn. Reclamp the rails in position amidships.

Install the Breasthooks

Step 109. Laminate two 10"x 7" breasthook blanks from four pieces of okume cut from the scrap left after the hull was cut out. See your Hull Layout Plan for the location of the pieces for the breasthook blanks. The grain on the upper side of the blank should run parallel to the 10" side.

The two breasthook planks can be laminated at the same time. Be sure to put plastic between the blanks themselves, and between the blanks and the pressure plates. See Step 109.

Step 110. See Breasthook Options, page 140, for options in installing the breasthooks and for the shape of their inboard ends.

Step 111. Draw a centerline on the long axis of the laminated breasthook blank. Place the blank on the sheer so that 1/4" of the blank extends past the leading edge of the stem.

Here the laminated breasthook blank is turned upside down to show the lines made by tracing the hull. See Step 114.

With spring clamps, clamp the bolted rail ends to the hull inboard of the breasthook blank so that the rails are about 3/4" below the sheer at the stem.

Step 112. Align the outboard end of the breasthook blank centerline with the center of the stem. Align the inboard end of the blank with the centerline on the amidships frame by sighting across the blank towards the frame.

Step 113. Hold the blank firmly in place and trace the outside and inside of the hull onto the underside of the blank. Using the breasthook blank as a guide, mark the thickness of the breasthook parallel to the sheer on the outside of the hull on each side.

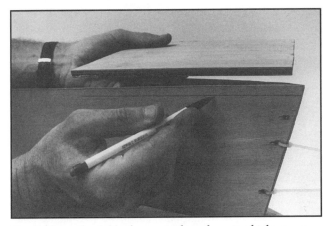

Use the breasthook blank as a guide to draw its thickness on the hull side. See Step 115.

Step 114. Draw your chosen inboard end shape on the underside of the blank. Cut the inboard end to its exact shape. Cut out the breasthook shape leaving 1/16" extra on the sides.

Step 115. Place the breasthook on the top of the hull in its correct position with the hull markings on its underside. Mark the inboard end of the breasthook onto both the top and side of the sheer. Extend the mark down the side at right angles to the sheer and ending at the breasthook thickness line.

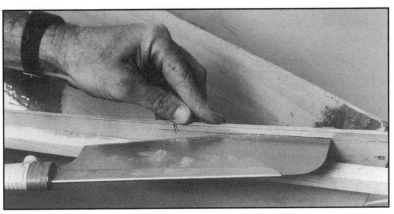

Cut out the breasthook notch. Under my thumb, the line for the breasthook's length is to the left, the vertical saw cut is to the right. Offsetting the initial cut provides a margin for error when the breasthook notch is trimmed with a chisel. See Step 116.

Step 116. With the japanese saw, cut 1/16" forward of the line just drawn from the sheer down to the breasthook thickness line. Be careful to cut parallel to the mark showing the angle of the breasthook's inboard end when viewed from above.

Step 117. With the japanese saw, cut just above the breasthook thickness line on one side of the hull from the stem to the saw cut previously made. Repeat the cut on the other side of the hull.

Step 118. Dress the saw cut to the breasthook thickness line with a sharp chisel. When the breasthook is placed in the cutout, its upper surface should be 1/32" or less below the sheer.

The breasthook notch has been flattened and trimmed to length. Note that the cut at the left end of the notch has moved closer to the line. It's a good thing some wood was left there to work with. See Step 118.

Step 119. After the breasthook is properly positioned relative to the sheer and resting squarely in the notch without rocking, cut the inboard end of the notch to its proper length.

Step 120. Repeat the above steps on the second breasthook.

Fillet and Tape the Breasthooks

Step 121. The following steps are done with the rails clamped to the hull amidships and just inboard of the breasthooks. The rail ends remain bolted together and in place about 3/4" below the sheer at the stem.

Step 122. Pre-glue the notches in the hull sides with unthickened epoxy (1 pump for both breasthooks). With an acid brush, apply epoxy to the edge of the hull in the notches and at the inboard ends of the notches. Apply epoxy to the entire underside of the breasthooks and on their entire inboard ends. (The latter will pre-seal the end grain of the breasthooks.) Reapply epoxy to the edges of the notches where the epoxy has been soaked up by the end grain center ply.

Step 123. Add filler to the remaining epoxy to make a peanut butter consistency

mixture. (1-1/2 scoops). Apply the mixture to the notch in the hull. The epoxy is easiest applied by using the upper edge of the notch to wipe the mixture off the side of the stick used to mix the filler into the epoxy.

Step 124. Place the breasthooks in place. Ensure that they are firmly in contact with the inboard end of the notch. Check the alignment of the breasthooks with the hull centerline at the stem and the centerline on the amidships frame. Place a heavy object such as a gallon jug filled with water on top of each breasthook.

Step 125. Carefully scrape the squeeze-out off the outside of the hull. On the inside of the hull, use the small filleting tool to create a fillet with any squeeze-out that may be there. Wait about three hours for the epoxy to cure to the rubbery stage.

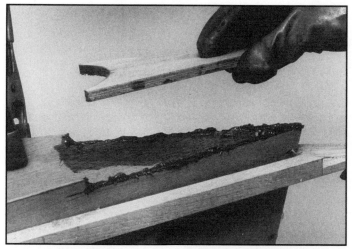

Preglue the notch, inner hull sides, and breasthook inboard end and entire underside. Apply thickened epoxy to the notch and carefully position the breasthook in the notch. See Step 123.

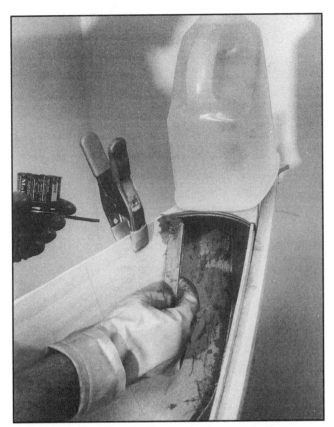

Pull the fillets right to the end of the breasthooks; it will smoothly taper to nothing. See Step 127.

Step 126. The following steps are most easily accomplished with the canoe turned up on its side. The bolted rail ends remain clamped 3/4" below the sheer. Remove the center frame and the two weighted sacks. Turn the hull on one side and put one of the weighted sacks in the hull amidships to hold it upright.

Step 127. With the medium filleting tool, fillet the breasthook to hull joints (3 pumps, 4-1/2 scoops for both breasthooks). Use the filleting tool to put the thickened mixture into the joint. Hold the medium tool flat against the hull and at right angles to the hull-breasthook joint, and shape the fillet. After the fillets are formed, clean any excess filleting mixture off the sides, breasthooks, and upper stems.

Step 128. Turn the hull on its other side and fillet the other breasthook.

Step 129. Wait an hour and tape the fillets. Cut four 8" long pieces of 3" tape. Remove the corners on one end of each piece of tape so

that there is a point approximating the angle of the breasthook at the stem. Removing the corners of the tape prevents excessive tape build up in the corner of the stem and the breasthook.

Step 130. Pre-impregnate the tape before putting it in place (1 pump each breasthook). With an acid brush, preglue the fillet and 1-1/2" out on the hull. Skewer the pointed end of the tape with a sharpened dowel or pencil. Put the tape in place on the fillet so the point is up in the corner of breasthook and stem. Apply a little more epoxy and seat the tape on the fillet. With sharp scissors or a razor blade, trim the end of the tape at the inboard end of the breasthook.

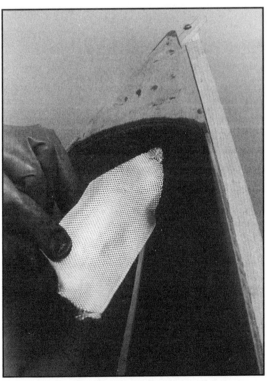

Use a thin stick or long sharpened pencil to position the presaturated tape on the fillet. (The tape here has no epoxy on it to give a strong contrast.) See Step 130.

Step 131. Turn the hull on its other side and tape the other breasthook fillets. Do not discard the acid brush when taping is finished. Wait 15 minutes and check the tapes. The tapes on the upper side of the hull sometimes pull away from their fillets. If that happens, push the tape back in place with the brush. Let the taped fillets cure overnight.

Trim the Breasthook Sides

Step 132. With a sharp low angle block plane, trim the edges of the breasthooks even with the hull sides. Let the lower edge of the sole of the plane ride on the hull and carefully trim the breasthook so that it has the same vertical taper as the sides. You are trying to match the slight fore and aft curve in the hull sides as well.

You can judge how much breasthook remains to be trimmed by feel rather than by eye. See Step 132.

Step 133. As you plane off the last 1/64" or so of the breasthook side, adjust the plane iron for a very shallow cut. The iron should be adjusted flat across the sole of the plane, or set with the slightest skew to cut more on the lower edge of the breasthook.

Step 134. Drill a 3/8" hole through the breasthook as close to the stem as possible. Use a 10"x1/4" piece of hull scrap to measure the distance under the breasthook from its inner edge to the stem. Transfer this measurement to the upper face of the breasthook. The mark just made represents the outer edge of the 3/8" hole, and NOT ITS CENTERPOINT.

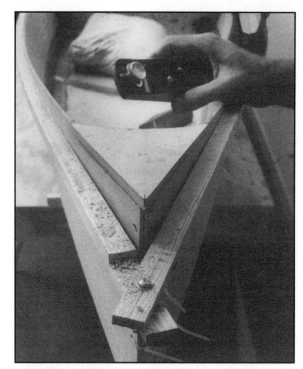

The left side of the breasthook has been trimmed flush with the side of the hull. It took about three minutes. See Step 133.

Shape the External Chines

Step 135. From this point on, work on the hull can be done on sawhorses. Put pads on the sawhorses or at the end of the work surface to keep from denting or marring the sheer when the hull is upside down. At this point the hull and breasthook joints are cured hard and the hull is approaching its final stiffness. The pinned rails should still be bolted together and clamped to the sheer amidships and inboard of the breasthooks.

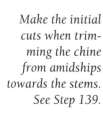

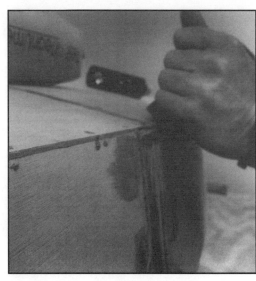

Make the initial cuts when trimming the chine from amidships towards the stems. See Step 139.

Step 136. Invert the hull. Put one of the weighted sacks on the middle of the bottom.

Step 137. The goal here is to cut a smooth 1/4-circle curve in the chine. The figure, "Radiusing the Chine Joints," page 47, shows the progression from sharp edged chine to radiused chine. Using a sharp plane, cut a bevel in a chine that bisects the angle between side and bottom. Work from amidships outward. You'll be taking a lot of material off amidships and successively less as you approach the ends of the chine. Cut the bevel until the third ply on the side just shows amidships. The face of the bevel will be about 1/2" wide amidships. The completed bevel is shown in the second drawing in the figure .

Step 138. After you cut the bevel on one side of the hull, cut the bevel on the opposite side. Match the second bevel to the first. Compare the bevels and match the width of the plys, appearance of plys with reference to the station lines, and any other bench marks that occur at each layout line.

The angle of the face of the initial cut is halfway between the bottom and the side. Proceeding towards the stems, the angle of the face rolls downwards slightly as the sides approach being vertical. Note that more wood has been taken off the bottom than the sides as bottom overlaps the side. See Step 140.

🐦

Step 139. Trim off the corners of the the bevel. The resulting cross section is shown in the third drawing in the figure above.

Step 140. Use the low angle block plane to blend the bevel into a smooth radius with the side and bottom. If the low angle block plane was used to cut the three flat bevels, stop and resharpen it. When checking for fairness of the radiused surface, run your hand perpendicularly across the chine feeling with fingers and palm. High spots usually occur in the end grain of the center ply and at the transition to the unplaned surface of the side and bottom.

Step 141. Amidships, plane off the 'glass tape on the side as necessary to prevent high spots or a tightened radius.

Step 142. At the end of the chines, plane from the ends inwards. You will be planing down into the second ply a little way past the end of the chine.

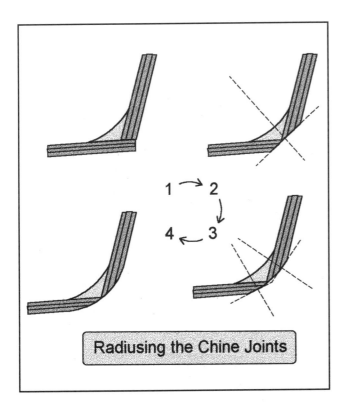

1 → 2

4 ← 3

Radiusing the Chine Joints

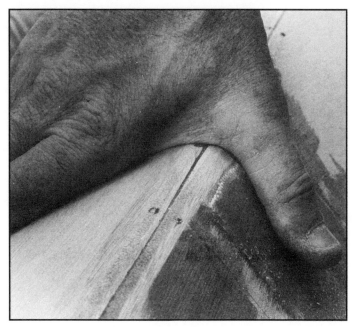

Round the chine so that it makes a smooth transition from side to bottom. Do the final smoothing with 100 grit sandpaper on a sanding block. See Step 140.

Step 143. As the radius approaches completion, plane from amidships towards the stems on the bottom, and from the stems inward on the sides. The completed chine is shown in the fourth drawing in the figure, Radiusing the Chine Joints, on page 47.

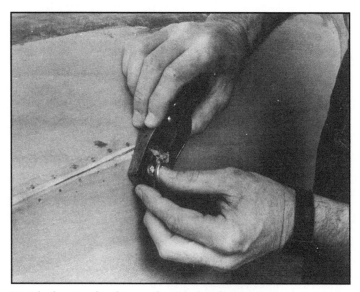

Finish shaping the chine ends with the plane iron set very shallow. Note that the trimmed area widens slightly as it nears the chine end. See Step 143.

Tape the External Chines

Step 144. Smooth the radiused chine with a hard sanding block and 100 grit sandpaper. Sand out 1 1/2" on the sides and bottom to prepare the sides and bottom for taping.

Step 145. Fill any voids in the chine joint with thickened epoxy. These should be relatively small and can be taped over before the filler is cured. It is not necessary to fill the tie holes.

Step 146. Tape one chine at a time. Cut a length of 3" tape that extends 3" past the ends of the chine joints. With a chip brush, preglue the chine joint (1 pump each chine). Roll the tape onto the joint and apply additional epoxy (3 pumps each chine). Use the brush to center the tape on the joint and straighten the edges of the tape. After 20 minutes, clean up any epoxy runs on the sides.

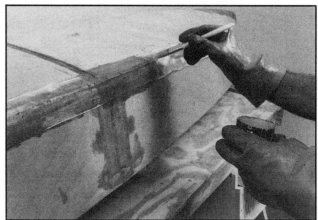

Applying tape to the outer chine is a straight-forward job. See Step 146.

Step 147. Wait an hour until the epoxy is tacky and apply a layer of 2" tape to each chine (3 pumps each chine).

Shape External Stems

Step 148. Turn the hull upright. Clamp the rails in position along the upper edge of the sides and breasthooks. Mark the lower

Apply the second layer of tape to the chines after the first layer is quite tacky. This way the first layer won't move around as you adjust the second layer for smooth, straight edges. See Step 147.

edge of the rails onto the hull. Unbolt the ends of the rails and remove them. Invert the hull and put a weighted sack on the middle of the bottom.

Step 149. Place a yard stick or the aluminum straight edge along the centerline and across the end of the lower stem joint. You'll see a hump in the joint just outboard of its ends. Typically the hump is about 1/8" tall. The tighter the ties were set before the lower stem was filleted, the smaller the hump.

The hump at the end of the lower stem is shown by the shadows under the straightedge. See Step 149.

Step 150. With a sharp block plane, carefully plane the hump down. At the highest point on the bump, you will plane completely through both the outer ply and the center ply, and into the third ply.

Step 151. Work slowly and carefully. Use a sharp plane and set the iron very shallow. Take off only the minimum amount necessary. Use the yardstick frequently to locate the high spot; it moves up and down the joint as it is planed. Stop planing when the third ply is first exposed. At this point there still may be a little daylight showing under the yard stick. No further wood should be removed from the bump. Remember that the full 4mm hull thickness is made up by the fillet and tape on the inside of the joint.

Step 152. Flatten the lower stem joint up to the forefoot by planing the 90° corners off the sides. The width of the cut plys should taper evenly from widest at the end of the joint to narrowest at the beginning of the forefoot curvature.

Trim off the hump with a sharp plane; the remnants of the electrical ties trim away without a problem. Keep the straight edge handy and use it often. See Step 150.

Step 153. Flatten the leading edge of the forefoot and upper stem. To prevent splitting off the upper ply of the breasthook, first make a few cuts upwards from the breasthook. Plane the rest of the forefoot and upper stem towards the breasthook. The cut face should be perpendicular to the centerline.

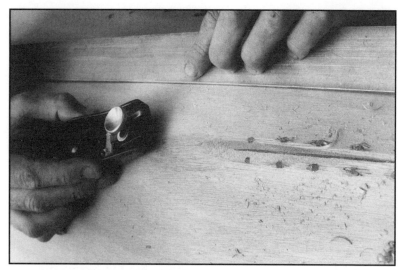

The trimmed area takes on an elongated tear-drop shape. Here the hump has been trimmed down to where the third ply is just showing. Whether or not the hump is completely removed, it's time to stop trimming. See Step 151

Step 154. The width of the final face of the cut on the leading edge of the stem depends on whether you will use regular or bias cut tape. For regular tape, plane until the face is 3/8" wide. For bias cut tape it can be as narrow as 3/16".

Step 155. After the forefoot and stem are flattened and perpendicular to the centerline, radius the stem and forefoot to a half round cross section. It is better to have the radius a little blunt than somewhat

pointed. The smaller the radius, the more difficult it will be to get the tape to wrap around the stem.

Step 156. Radius the edges of the stem between the forefoot and the end of the lower stem joint. Below the forefoot the cross section of the joint smoothly changes from halfround to something roughly elliptical.

Step 157. Where the bump was planed down at the end of the lower stem joint, there is now a flat spot. Plane or sand the edges of the spot to create a smooth transition from it to the surrounding hull. Take as little off as necessary and no more. Remember, the fillet on the inside of the hull extends outwards about 1 1/2" on either side of the centerline.

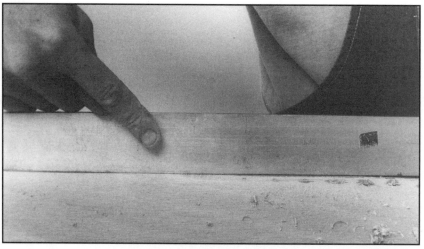

Compare this picture with the one on the bottom right of page 49, Step 149; very little of the hump remains. See Step 151.

Tape the External Stems

Step 158. This is where bias cut tape really shines, see Regular and Bias Cut Tapes, page 136. Do one stem at a time. If regular tape is used, two or three darts will be needed to get the tape to lie smoothly around the forefoot. Stagger the darts on the two sides of the forefoot.

Step 159. Cut a piece of 3" tape to run from 3" inboard of the stem joint to 2" past the

Keep the plane level across the hull when trimming the lower stem. I find it easiest to pull the plane towards me and sight along the stem. See Step 153.

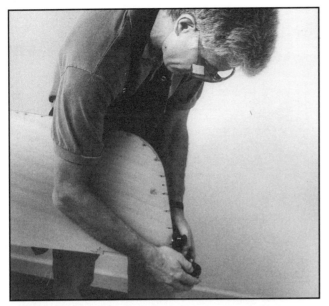

Begin to flatten the upper stem by planing upwards starting at the breasthook. See Step 154.

stem. Sand and preglue 1-1/2" on either side of the joint (2 pumps for pre-glue, pre-saturation, and filling the tape for each stem). Presaturate the tape before taking it to the hull. Place the tape into the epoxy and begin to coax it into position. Cut darts in the tape as necessary in regular tape. Shingle the darts at the forefoot so that the side of the dart closest to the sheer goes over the other side. Darts shouldn't be required in bias cut tape.

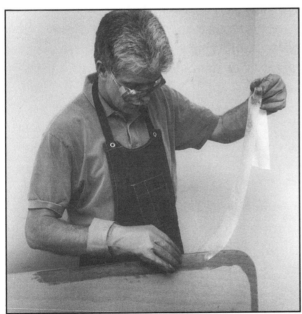

Applying presaturated tape to the outer stems is rather simple until you reach the forefoot. The photo on page 136 shows why bias cut tape is preferred on the outer stems. See Step 159.

Step 160. Wait an hour and add a layer of 2" tape using the same techniques (2 pumps). Stagger any darts between those in the first layer. Let the tape cure overnight.

Permanently Install the Outer Rails

Step 161. (Optional) Tapered rails visibly lighten the ends of the canoe. Tapering the rail ends is not an essential feature but the results are well worth the effort. See Rail Tapering Fixture , page 132.

Step 162. Permanently installing the outer rails requires many clamps. The rails will be attached to the hull using epoxy and no permanent fasteners. The rails and sides must fit flat against each other to get a good solid epoxy joint. The rails twist from the angle of the side amidships to nearly vertical at the stems. The rails must also take on the three dimensional curve of the sheer. While the rails are being glued on, the uncured epoxy acts as a lubricant as the rail tries to slip back into its natural shape. Spring clamps can't be trusted alone in this application.

Step 163. I don't have enough screw clamps for this job — it would take about 50 of them. I improvise by using 1" drywall screws and pressure pads to clamp the outer rails to the sides amidships. In this area the screw holes will be hidden by the inner rail. If you have less than 32 clamps, one every 3" the entire length of the rail, make up the difference with additional drywall screws and pressure pads.

Step 164. Center one of the inner rails on the hull just below the sheer. For built-up rails mark the center of each block on the sheer. For solid rails, put marks every 3". Drill 1/8" holes in the hull sides on the marks and 1/4" from the sheer. (Drill additional holes as necessary for any additional drywall screws and pads that you will be using.) Make up two, 1x1" pads from waste hull material for each drywall screw that you will use to clamp the rail. Drill a

1/8" hole in the center of each pad. Put two pads on each of 20, 1" drywall screws. The two pads shorten the length of the screws so that they do not penetrate through the full width of the 3/4" wide rails.

Step 165. With a sharp chisel and/or sanding block, remove the fiberglass tape under the outer rails where they cross the butt joints in the sides and on the stems. Be careful not to remove the tape where it wraps around the stem between the ends of the rails. Lightly sand the inside of the outer rails and above the line drawn earlier on the hull.

Step 166. Using scrap hull material and 3/4" stock, make up two sets of "dragon's teeth" for clamping the rails to the hull at the breasthooks. See additional information on Dragon's Teeth , page 130.

Step 167. Even though only one rail is glued on at a time, there are a lot of things to be done in a short time. This will be a severe test of your deodorant. An assistant will be most helpful. It's best to do a trial fitting with your assistant or by yourself before you've got to contend with wet epoxy too. You have to move quickly; the epoxy is curing while you work. Use slow cure hardener. If you are building in hot weather, do this in the coolest part of the day.

> $\mathcal{A}$ ny man who wants to can produce a good boat. It takes some study, some practice, and, of course, experience. The experience starts coming the minute you begin, and not one jot before. I sometimes hear the wail, "I have no experience." Start. Start anything, and experience comes. Some say building a boat is one of man's nobler efforts. Maybe so; it's a lot of fun, anyway. As one of my builder friends says, "It's only a boat; go ahead and build it." If the first effort is a bit lumpy, so what? There will be another much less lumpy later on.
>
> R. D. Culler, *Skiffs and Schooners,*
> *International Marine, 1978, 1990*

Step 168. As a general rule, always apply clamps to the rails from amidships towards the ends. The exception is spring clamps used to hold the rail ends at the inboard end of the breasthooks as screw-pads and screw clamps are applied from amidships outwards.

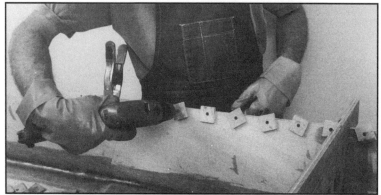

1" drywall screws and pads on 3" centers are a good alternative to screw clamps for attaching the outer rail. Amidships the holes will be covered by the inner rail. See Step 170.

Step 169. Remember to clamp the rails to the hull as a pair, not one at a time. This applies even though one of the rails has epoxy on it and the other doesn't. Check to ensure that you have register marks on the hull edges and rails to tell where the middle of the rail is placed. To ensure that you know each step in the operation, do a dry run of Steps 170 to 174.

Step 170. The dance goes like this: using acid brushes, apply epoxy to one rail and hull side (2 pumps). Spread epoxy on the hull while your assistant does the rail. Put epoxy on the breasthook end grain first, then do the rest of the hull. Go back and do the breasthook edges again; they'll be dry. Clamp each rail to the hull with four spring clamps; two amidships, one just inboard of each breasthook. Have your helper put screw pads in the holes ahead of you. Keeping the rail 1/32" BELOW the sheer, use the torque driver to drive the drywall screw pads in pairs from amidships outwards alternating ends; two on one end, two on the other, etc.

Step 171. When you run out of screw pad holes, switch to screw clamps. Space them evenly between the screw pads and the breasthooks. Use pressure pads under the clamp jaws. Remember to check that the upper face of the rail is 1/32" below the sheer. At the breasthooks, remove the spring clamp, and clamp on a set of dragon's teeth with at least two screw clamps. Clamp a set of dragon's teeth to the far side rail as well.

Screw clamps and pressure pads won't leave holes in the hull. On the nearside rail the dragon's teeth were clamped to the rail before gluing started. The other half of the dragon's teeth is near at hand on the breasthook. See Step 171.

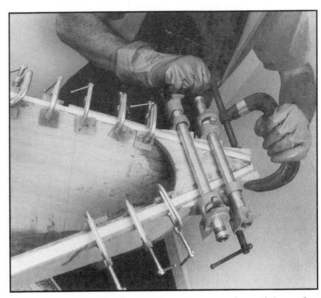

Check to make sure the upper face of the rail is slightly above the breasthook. This way the rail can be sanded flush with the top of the breasthook without breaking through the top ply of the breasthook. See Step 173.

The far side rail is being glued on. The last three clamps use the tail on the dragon's teeth as a pressure pad. Note how the pressure pad on the last clamp just catches the end of the breasthook. This minimizes the chance that the end of the breasthook to hull joint could be cracked before pressure is applied across the breasthook. See Step 172.

Step 172. As the rail comes into contact with the breasthook, the top of the rail should be 1/64" or less **ABOVE** the top of the breasthook. Use bar clamps on the two widest steps of the dragon's teeth, pressure pads aren't needed here. Distribute all your screw clamps and any left over spring clamps between the clamps already in place.

Step 173. Check the lower edge of the rail; it should be flat against the hull side. If its not, more screw clamps and/or screws and pads are needed. The holes left by screw pads can be filled and sanded so they won't show under paint so they are a good alternative.

Step 174. With a square ended piece of scrap, clean any epoxy squeeze-out from the rail/hull joint. With a paper towel clean any epoxy runs off the hull. Wait at least four hours for the epoxy to cure. It is best to wait overnight to get a good solid cure before removing the clamps.

Step 175. After the dry run, remove all the clamps and screw pads in reverse order from stems back to amidships. Replace the dragon's teeth with spring clamps just inboard of the breasthooks. Remember to leave a spring clamp at the rail ends just inboard of the breasthooks until last. Place the clamps on the work surface and in the hull near where they will be used. Take a break, discuss what happened with your helper, consider ways to make the operation go as smoothly as possible.

Step 176. Epoxy the rail to the hull for real. This is not a drill.

Step 177. Epoxy one rail, wait overnight for the epoxy to cure. DO NOT LEAVE THE DRYWALL SCREWS IN LONGER THAN 12 HOURS. When the screws were driven, they dragged a little epoxy with them into the hole they made in the rail. If you wait more than twelve hours, the screws can get glued in solid. When you try to remove them, their heads will shear off. If you're lucky, they will break below the surface. If not, try to grab the stub with Vice Grips® and screw them out. If that doesn't work, the screw shafts need to be ground down below the surface of the hull. If the shaft is going to be behind the inner rail, hollowing the back of the inner rail will work too.

Step 178. When the second rail comes off to be sanded and have glue applied is the only time that the rails are handled individually. Find your helper, if he/she is still talking to you, or get a new one, and glue on the second rail. After the second rail is installed, profusely thank your helper.

Clamp the inner rail to the hull so that it is even with the top of the outer rails. See Step 182.

Install the Inner Rails

Step 179. See Inner Rails, page 116, for a discussion of inner rail options. With a sharp chisel and/or sanding block, remove the fiberglass tape where the inner rails cross the butt joints in the sides. Center the rail on the hull and transfer the register mark on the hull to the inner rail. Mark the rail's outline on the hull.

Step 180. Sand the standoff blocks on the rails and inside the rail outline on the hull. There is no need to fill the holes left by the screw pads when the outer rail was attached if they will be covered by the blocks.

Coat the entire back of the inner rail to make a good waterproof seal. The tape on the hull will catch any squeeze-out from the rail/hull joints. Since both the standoff blocks on the rails and the holes for the screw pads in the hull are at 3" intervals, the blocks will hide the holes. See Step 181.

While a satisfactorily strong joint can be made with clamps on every other standoff block, it is best to use clamps on every block. The curled tape under the rail has caught a few pesky drips. See Step 184.

Optimally, a screw clamp should be applied over each block in the rail. Usually a screw clamp on every other block will do. Put spring clamps between the screw clamps.

Step 181. Apply epoxy to the entire back of the rail, up into each of the cut outs on a built-up rail, and to the entire rail outline on the hull (1 pump).

Step 182. Starting amidships, clamp the rail in place just below the sheer and **even with the top of the outer rail.** Don't forget pressure pads under the clamp jaws. Add spring clamps between the screw clamps.

Step 183. The rail gets successively more difficult to bend into place as the ends

Carefully trim the sheet down to the rails. Sometimes the grain in the inner and outer rails runs in opposite directions and it is impossible not to get tearout in one or the other. In this case, a sanding block with 100 grit paper will do the job nicely. See Step 185.

are clamped. A solid rail can be a real bear to get positioned. Clean all epoxy runs off the hull. Allow the epoxy to cure hard.

Step 184. Remove the clamps. Attach the second rail. If you have enough screw clamps, both inner rails can be installed at the same time.

Trim the Hull at the Rails

Step 185. Using a freshly sharpened low angle block plane, remove the 1/32" of plywood that extends above the rails. At the breasthooks, the rail should be just higher than the top of the breasthook. Use a sanding block to trim the rail level with the breasthooks.

Trim the Rail Ends

Step 186. With the japanese saw, trim the rail ends parallel to the leading edge of the stem, at the beginning of the stem's half round profile. With the low angle block plane and a sanding block, trim the rail end to a quarter-ellipse profile when viewed from above.

Radius the Rails

Step 187. Sharp or small radius corners on the outer rails are subject to dents and dings that can crack the finish and cause discoloration of the wood beneath. The larger the radius on the corners of the outer rails the better.

Step 188. Radiusing the rails is like radiusing the chines only on a smaller scale. First cut a bevel that splits the angle between the rail's top and outer face. Next plane off the new angles at the edges of the bevel. If you can see the resulting four new angles, plane them off. Finish up with a sanding block and 100 grit sandpaper. Repeat the process on the lower corner of the rails.

Step 189. On the inner rails, it is only necessary to break the sharp corners with a small radius.

A thwart blank is in position centered above standoff blocks. The feeler gauge is used to get the width of the hull just under the rails at the front edge of the thwart. Marking one end of the thwart with a piece of tape can simplify the procedure. See Step 195.

Install the Thwarts

Step 190. See Thwarts, page 117. The thwarts' fore and aft locations are not super critical. The thwarts should be positioned just outboard of the ends of the bottom pad. On a built-up rail, install the thwarts below standoff blocks. There should be 2" or 3" of rail outboard of the thwarts.

Step 191. Check the width of the hull to the outside of the plywood amidships. It should be 28-1/2". If it is within 1/4" either way, leave it like it is; it's fine. If the hull width is more than 1/4" off, make up a helper stick to push or pull it to the right width.

Step 192. The cuts on the ends of the thwarts are compound angles; the hull is angled both fore and aft, and from bottom to top. The underside of the rail is at an angle to the plane of the thwart. The top of the thwarts must be trimmed at the same angle as the rail so that they rest firmly up against the rail. These too are compound angles. Getting both these cuts at the correct compound angles and the thwarts cut to the correct length can be difficult. Trial and error usually leads to many botched attempts.

Step 193. Here is a method for marking the thwarts for the cuts that works first time for me. All that is needed is a sharp pencil, a 6" piece of 3/4" scrap, three simplifying assumptions and one serendipitous omission. I'll point out the latter as they come into play. Describing this sequence takes a lot of words but its not hard to do. Practice marking and cutting a proxy thwart made of a piece of scrap 3/4" stock before cutting the real thwarts to length.

Step 194. Trim two pieces of scrap hull material to 1/2" wide and 18" long to use as a feeler gauge to determine the exact width of the hull under the rails at the thwart location. Make a sharp point on one end of each piece of the scrap. The pieces must be tapered to a point in both depth and width.

Step 195. Place a thwart in position on the inner rails. Place a spring clamp on each rail immediately next to the thwart on its amidships, or inboard, side. Hold the two pointed pieces of the feeler gauge together at their middles with their points outward . Hold the two pieces in your non-writing hand and adjust their length so that they touch the hull just under the rails at the thwart's outboard edge. Hold the two pieces tightly and mark the inner edge of the rails onto the gauge pieces.

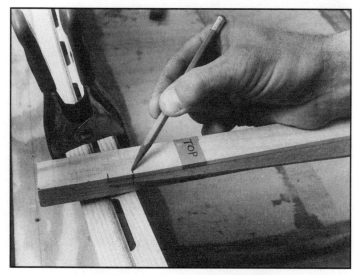

Transfer the rail thickness and hull width measurements from the gauge to the thwart blank. Note that the taped end of the thwart is on the near side of the hull. See Step 196.

Step 196. Hold the gauge so that it doesn't change length and transfer the two marks and the distance between the points at the ends of the gauge to the side of the thwart blank along its stemward facing upper corner. Roughly center the marks lengthwise on the thwart. After the four marks have been transferred, flip the thwart end for end so that the near side marks are now on the far side of the hull and all the marks face downwards.

Step 197. Keeping the thwart against the clamps, slide it until one of the marks on the far side is aligned with the rail's inner edge. With a pencil, mark the edge of the inner rail on the underside of the thwart. Repeat for the other marks on both ends of the thwart. (The first simplifying assumption is that the two sides of the hull have the same curvature.)

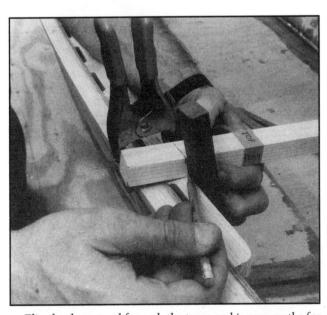

Flip the thwart end for end; the tapes end is now on the far side, with its bottom face upwards. Position the rail to transfer the angle of the inner rail to both marks. See Step 197.

Step 198. Flip the thwart end for end, back to its original orientation. The four lines just drawn should be facing upwards and replicate the curve of the rails. The outer marks represent the ends of the thwart, the inner marks represent the inner extent of the bevel to be cut on the top of the thwart.

Return the thwart to its original position and mark the top bevel line from the innermost of the two lines on the top face. See Step 199.

Step 199. Place the 6" long piece of 3/4" scrap stemward of the thwart and flat against the top of the rails. With the thwart against the clamps, slide the thwart across the hull to align the upper edge of the piece of scrap with the inner mark at the top edge of the thwart. Draw a line along the upper edge of the scrap onto the side of the thwart. This line marks the bevel on the thwart that will fit up against the bottom of the rail. (The second simplifying assumption is that the top face of the inner rails is parallel to the bottom face.)

$\mathcal{M}$any fallacies have arisen as to what consists good boat building practices and have lead to much unnecessary cost in construction. The truth is that "good boatbuilding" is no more than "good enough to do the job and last the required time," and has no particular relationship to rabbeting, notching, or boxing in the framework.

Howard I. Chappelle,
American Small Sailing Craft

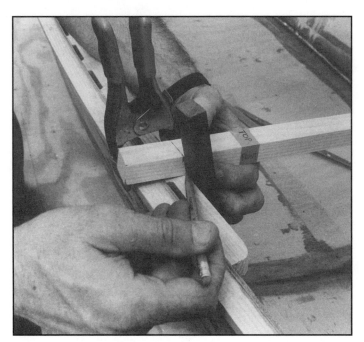

Mark the end of the thwart line from the outermost of the two marks on the end of the thwart. See Step 200.

Step 200. Position the piece of scrap flat against the inner face of the inner rail and touching the side of the thwart with the marks on it. Align the rail so that the edge of the scrap against the rail intersects the outer mark at the top edge of the thwart. Draw this line on the side of the thwart. This line marks the end of the thwart. (The third simplifying assumption is that the face of the inner rail is parallel to the inner surface of the hull.)

Step 201. The serendipitous omission is that to get an exact thwart length, the outer mark should be squared down the side of the thwart to the bevel line. The line parallel to the inner face of the rail is then drawn through the intersection of the squared down line and the bevel line. By not doing this and drawing the line that parallels the rail face line from the mark at the edge of the side, the thwart is shortened about 1/32" on each end. Shortening the thwarts slightly is good; the thwart ends should not be in contact with the hull when they are bolted to the rails.

Step 202. Repeat the markings with the scrap piece on the other end of the thwart. See the figure, "Completed Thwart End Markings. "

Step 203. If you are handy with the japanese saw, there are now enough marks on the thwart to make both the cuts to get the bevel and the thwart length. If you aren't, you may want to repeat the marking sequence on the rear face of the thwart. Connect the two sets of markings across the bottom of the thwart.

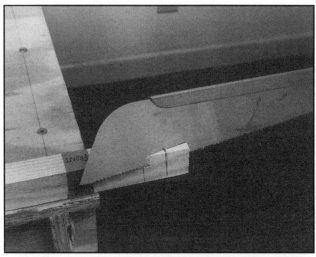

Trim the thwart about 3/4" long on either end, then cut the top bevels. See Step 205.

Step 204. Trim the thwart blank 1/2" longer than the outer line on the thwart's top.

Step 205. Next, cut the thwarts to length and the correct compound angles. With the japanese saw, cut on the bevel line; it's the one that makes a shallow angle with the top of the thwart. Save the small wedge

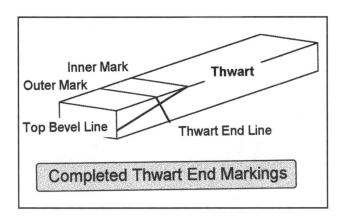

Inner Mark · Outer Mark · Thwart · Top Bevel Line · Thwart End Line

Completed Thwart End Markings

shaped piece that is cut off. It will be glued to the bottom of the thwart so that the nut on the bolt that secures the thwart to the rail will seat squarely.

Step 206. Redraw the thwart end line on the face of the top bevel. With the japanese saw, cut the thwart to length by cutting on the remaining lines on the top, sides, and bottom of the thwart.

Step 207. Repeat the cuts on the other end of the thwart.

Step 208. Check how the thwart fits at the desired position. It should be just a little loose.

Step 209. Repeat the marking and cutting on the second thwart. Remember to save the four wedges cut from the tops of each thwart. Save the feeler gauge pieces to use when cutting the single paddle seat beams or the backrest stretcher to length later.

Step 210. Clamp the thwarts in the selected location on the rails with 1/32" spacers between the ends of the thwarts and the hull. There will be very little wood at the end of the thwart outboard of the bolt hole. This is the weak point in the thwart to rail joint. If the hole drifts outward as

The thwart usually fits without further trimming. See Step 208.

it is drilled, there may not be enough room for the nut, never mind enough wood for strength.

Step 211. With a 1/4" Forstner or brad point bit, bore holes through the rails and thwarts. The hole should be perpendicular to the top of the rails which is at a slight outward angle.

Step 212. The Forstner bit has side wings and a brad point and is less likely to wander than a standard drill point. If a Forstner bit is unavailable, a brad point bit is acceptable although not quite as good. Even the brad point bit is much less likely to wander than a standard drill point.

Step 213. It is difficult to drill the bolt hole perpendicular to the surface of the rails freehand. A drill guide made out of a block of wood about 1-1/2" thick with a 1/4" hole bored through its center and perpendicular to the lower face of the block will help to drill square with the surface of the rails.

Step 214. Start the hole in the rail 1/32" deep without the drill guide. Insert the bit through the drill guide, register the end of the bit in the started hole, and clamp the guide to the inner rail with a screw clamp. By centering the shaft of the bit in the hole

Redraw the thwart end line on the top bevel and cut the thwart to length. See Step 207.

in the top of the guide as the hole is bored, there is a good to better chance that the hole will be perpendicular to the upper face of the rail and thwart.

Step 215. (Optional) With a spokeshave, eight-side the thwarts. Eight siding creates the illusion that the thwarts are thinner and narrower than they actually are. Mark a cut-to line on the top and bottom of the thwarts 1/4" from the edge. On the sides, the line is 3/16" from the edge. The eight siding should fade out no less than 3/4" from the ends of the thwart.

Eight-siding the thwarts requires a sharp chisel or, better yet, a spokeshave. The high-dollar bench dogs holding the thwart are drywall screws with pads set at an angle to pull up tight as the screws are tightened down. See Step 215.

The completed thwart ends with the wedges glued in place, trimmed and drilled, and the thwart eight-sided. See Step 216.

> *The simplest design is usually the best is a good rule by which to judge a design. It is easy to make things complicated and expensive, but it requires a great deal of thought, combined with experience, to keep a design simple, practical, and inexpensive. The eraser should be the most useful tool used by a designer, and he should never be afraid to use it!*
>
> Francis S. Kinney,
> *Skene's Elements of Yacht Design*

Step 216. Glue the four wedges to the bottom of the thwarts at their ends. The thin edge of the wedge points inwards and extends 3/4" onto the thwart. There is no need to use epoxy; Elmer's® Carpenter's Glue or Titebond® with a screw clamp works fine. When the glue is dry, trim the wedge ends to match the thwart ends. Drill 1/4" holes through the wedges.

Step 217. Attach the thwarts to the rails with 1/4"x20"x2" silicon bronze or stainless steel carriage bolts, nuts, and washers. It may be necessary to cut or file flats onto the washers so that they fit on the bolts without touching the hull sides.

Taper the Fiberglass Tape Edges at Stems and Chines

Step 218. See Tapering the Edges of Fiberglass Tape, page 142. The goal here is to create a smooth taper across the tape from full thickness about 3/4" into the tape to no thickness at the tape edge. When making the taper, be careful not to cut into the hull outboard of the tape.

Step 219. Be especially careful sanding at the ends of the external chines. The changing curves in the hull make it very easy to sand through the tape. Consider doing these areas with a palm sander or by hand. If the tape gets sanded through, apply a double layer patch of tape and epoxy. When it has cured, blend the patch with the surrounding area by hand.

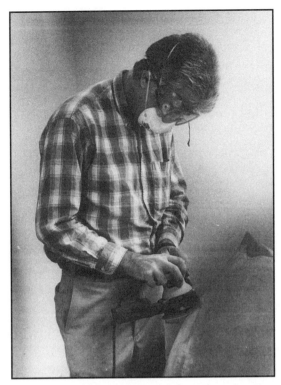

When sanding the taped joints, take extra precautions to keep the dust off you. Here I've used goggles in lieu of safety glasses, donned a nuisance dust mask, and covered my arms. The actual sanding was done out of doors as the dust is very fine; it drifts everywhere and gets into everything. See Step 219.

Step 220. To complete the joints after tapering them, recoat the unsanded portion at the center of the tape with epoxy to fill the weave. When the epoxy is cured, sand with 80 grit sandpaper. To fully hide the weave in the tape, a third, and even fourth coat of epoxy may be required. Apply the epoxy carefully and use masking tape to prevent build up at the edges of the glass tape and on the bare wood of the hull. The masking tape must be removed before the epoxy cures to rubbery hardness to prevent its becoming part of the hull.

Install the Seat

Step 221. See Seating Options, page 144 and Tuffet and Tuffet II, page 102.

Single Paddle Seat

Step 222. Begin building the single paddling seat by laminating two 8"x16" pieces of 4mm ply together (1 pump). See the Hull Layout Plan for the location of these pieces. Evenly spread epoxy on one side of both pieces. Clamp the pieces between two pieces of board or plywood with plastic wrap or wax paper between the pieces and the boards. Six or eight clamps should do. When cured, round the corners of the seat to 1/2" radius with the saber saw, or japanese saw and sanding block.

Step 223. The seat is hung on two 3/4"x1" seat beams that run from rail to rail. The front edge of the seat should be about 7" aft of amidships. The block on a built up rail that is just aft of 7" will be the location of the forward seat beam. The after seat beam is located where it will support the back of the seat. The beams can be located such that the seat overhangs the beams up to 1" at its forward and after edges. It is important that the forward beam be located at the center of a block on a built-up rail because it supports the majority of the paddler's weight.

Step 224. The single paddling seat is most comfortable when it is tilted forward with the front edge of the seat about 3/4" lower

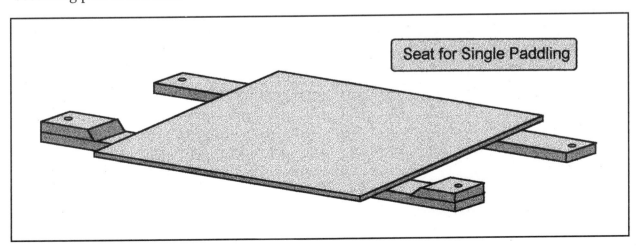

Seat for Single Paddling

than the back edge. This is easily done by placing a 3/4" spacer between the forward seat beam and the underside of the rail.

Step 225. Using the feeler gauge and the procedure that was used to find the exact length of the thwarts, find the exact length of the forward seat beam under the rails. Center and mark the length on the side of a 30" piece of 3/4"x1" thwart stock. Cut two pieces of the same material 1-1/2" long for the blocks to lower the forward beam. The end of the block that faces towards the centerline can be beveled or radiused to improve its appearance.

Step 226. Glue the blocks to the ends of the seat beam so that 1/4" of the block extends outboard of the beam length marks. Elmer's® Carpenter's Glue or Tite-bond® with screw clamps works fine.

Step 227. When the glue is dry, mark and cut the beams to length using the same procedure used for the thwarts, see page 56. Treat the forward beam as if it were 1-1/2" thick from end to end. Mark the exact beam length on the side at the top of the blocks. It will be helpful if the piece of scrap used to transfer the angles up from the rails is 1" to 1-1/4" tall. When finding the exact length of the after seat beam, treat it just like the thwarts. Cut the beams to length. Save and glue the wedges to the bottoms of the beam ends.

Step 228. Clamp the beams to the rails in their intended positions. Place the seat on the beams. The seat does not sit squarely on the beams due to the forward beam being 3/4" lower. Bevel the front upper edges of the beams so that the seat rests squarely against the beams.

Step 229. Clamp the beams in their intended locations and drill 1/4" holes for mounting bolts as was done for the thwarts. Glue the wedges onto the bottom of the beams. Redrill the bolt holes.

Step 230. Bolt the beams to the rails with 1/4"x20"x2-1/2" silicon bronze or stainless steel carriage bolts, nuts, and washers. Center the seat on the beams. Mark the beam locations on the bottom of the seat. Apply epoxy and clamp it in position (1 pump). Use scraps of wood across the top of the seat and on the bottom of the beam to prevent scarring by the clamps.

Double Paddle Backrest

Step 231. The standard double paddle backrest has eight components: two backrest pads; a pad carrier that connects the pads to a stretcher that rotates to adjust the pads to the angle of the paddler's back; two support blocks at the ends of the stretcher; and two copper bushings. See page 101 for an optional curved, one-piece backrest pad.

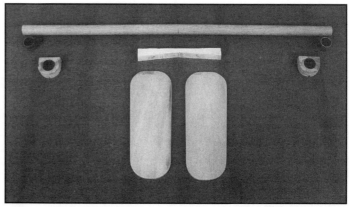

The parts of the standard backrest. There is a 90° V-notch cut in the far side of the pad carrier at center of photo. See Step 231.

Step 232. Begin construction by laminating two 8"x8" pieces of 4mm plywood together. When the epoxy is cured, transfer the shape of the pads to the blank, and cut them out. See Seating Options for the shape of the pads, page 144.

Step 233. The pad carrier is a piece of inner rail stock, 3/4"x3/4"x4". On one face of the carrier make two cuts with the japanese saw that meet at the center of the carrier at an occluded angle of 160°. Smooth the faces just cut with a sharp chisel.

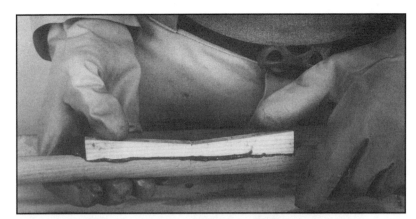

Fill in the V-notch in the carrier with thickened epoxy, center the stretcher in the groove and clamp in place. Carefully clean off the squeeze-out. See Step 235.

Step 234. The carrier needs to be securely attached to a 30" long piece of the 7/8" hardwood dowel that will be the stretcher. Rather than cut a half-round 7/8" diameter groove in the carrier with hand tools, it's easier to let thickened epoxy do most of the work. Cut a 90° groove from end to end in the face of the carrier opposite the 160° angled faces with the japanese saw. Try for an included angle of 90°. If you don't get it exactly, it's all right. Take the groove right to the edge of the carrier. You'll be surprised how easy it is to cut the groove with the japanese saw.

Step 235. Mark the center of the carrier on one of its uncut faces. Mark the lengthwise center of the stretcher dowel. Mix a batch of thickened epoxy and fill the groove in the carrier (1 pump, 1-1/2" scoops). Match up the center marks on the carrier and stretcher and clamp the dowel in the groove. Clean off the squeeze-out and let it cure.

Step 236. Epoxy the backrest pads to the carrier with 1" separating the pads, and the carrier 5" from the bottom of the pads.

Step 237. The stretcher is supported by blocks under the rails. As the sides of the hull are angled both fore and aft and vertically, the holes through the support blocks are at a compound angle. A non-traditional method to get the holes aligned across the hull will save a lot of hassle.

Step 238. The support blocks are made of pieces of 4mm okume predrilled with holes slightly oversize for the 3/4" copper coupling that is used as bushings on the end of the spreader.

Step 239. Cut twelve 3"x 4" pieces from the hull scrap. Put two of the pieces aside. Drill a 3/4" hole in the center of the other ten pieces. After the holes are drilled, cut a 1/8" slot from the hole to one of the long sides on two of the pieces. These slots will serve as drains for epoxy that squeezes into the holes as the pieces are laminated.

Step 240. Cover both sides of two of the pieces with duct tape or plastic. Slice through the tape and fold it so that it covers the edge of the hole. These pieces are used at the back of the laminate stacks that make up the support blocks to ensure that the coupling extends through and registers the four pieces that will make up each block. The tape covered pieces will not be a permanent part of the support blocks.

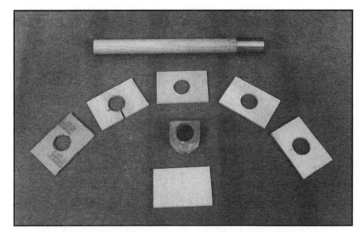

Here are the pieces for a backrest stretcher support block, arranged around a completed and shaped block. The extra width in the pieces forms a broad area on which to clamp during the laminating process. See Step 239.

Step 241. The support blocks are mounted with their centers 13-1/2" aft of the side joint amidships. Cover the side of the hull from chine to rail with duct tape or plastic wrap from 11" to 15" aft of the side joint.

This is to catch runs when the block is laminated in place on the hull. Be sure to cover the underside and inboard face of the inner rails as well.

Step 242. Cut the 48" hardwood dowel into two pieces; one 30" long to be the stretcher, and one 18" long. The short piece will be used with the copper coupling to align the pieces of the support blocks as they are laminated. The blocks are laminated in place so that the holes in the pieces of okume can be aligned at a compound angle to accept the stretcher running across the hull.

Step 243. Laminate one support block at a time. Each laminate stack consists of five pieces each having a 7/8" diameter hole in its center. The pieces, in order from the hull outward, are: the piece covered with tape; the piece with the slot pointed towards the chine; and the three other pieces with holes cut in them.

Step 244. Mix a batch of unthickened epoxy (1 pump). With an acid brush, spread epoxy on one side of the piece with the slot in it, and the topmost piece. Spread epoxy on both sides of the other two pieces. Build the stack with the copper coupling extending through the holes. Take the stack to the hull and center it, under the rail at 13-1/2" aft of the side joint.

Step 245. Clamp the stack loosely against the hull with a screw clamp or two or more spring clamps. Put the 18" piece of dowel in the coupling. Point the dowel at a spot on the opposite side of the hull that is 13-1/2" aft of the side joint and 1-1/2" below the rail. The clamps need to be just loose enough that the pieces in the laminate stack can slide against each other. When you are happy that the coupling and dowel have aligned the stack, clamp the stack tightly against the hull with four screw clamps. Place the clamps as close to the hole as possible. Remove the coupling and dowel from the stack.

Step 246. When the epoxy has cured, remove the stack, and take off the tape-plastic covered piece at the back of the stack.

Step 247. Laminate the block on the other side of the hull. Mark the blocks "Port" and "Stbd" as appropriate.

With the stack loosely clamped in position, use the dowel, and an extension as required, to align the pieces of the support blocks. The light colored tape is holding the plastic film which goes between the laminate stack and the hull, and wraps around the inner and outer rails as well. See Step 245.

Once the laminate stack is clamped tightly to the hull, remove the dowel and copper coupling and let the stack cure. See Step 245.

Step 248. When the stretcher is mounted in the blocks, it tends to contact the hull at the bottom of the holes in the support blocks. If it does, it can cause hairline cracks in the paint on the outside of the hull which in turn can cause premature failure of the coating. The undrilled piece of 3"x4" okume that was put aside earlier will be used to make a backing for the block that has a larger contact area with the end of the stretcher.

Step 249. Glue the backing pieces to the blocks. Carpenter's glue is adequate. On the back of the blocks draw a line 1/16" above the hole and parallel to the upper edge of the block. Cut off the excess above the line at 90° to the front and back faces of the blocks.

Step 250. With a 3/4" bit (a Forstner bit is preferred) drill down the hole and into the last piece only until the bit just breaks through at the back. This also cleans up the sides of the hole to accept the coupling again.

Here are a pair of completed stretcher support blocks. On the left the block is turned over showing how far the hole was drilled into the last okume laminate. See Step 250.

Step 251. Clamp both blocks and their backing pieces in position on the hull. Check the alignment of the two holes across the hull using the coupling and the 18" length of dowel. As necessary, use the dowel and a piece of 100 grit sandpaper as a file to remove wood inside the hole so that the bushing turns freely.

Step 252. Trim the block to a pleasing shape. Leave at least 3/8" at the bottom and sides

of the hole to support the backrest stretcher. (See the figure Backrest Stretcher Support Block Shapes, page 146 for alternate shapes.)

Step 253. Epoxy the blocks to the hull and rail with the holes centered 13-1/2" aft of the side joints. Clamp the blocks to the hull and up against the rail. Alternately, secure the blocks to the rails with carriage bolts.

Step 254. Even though there is now additional material at the back of the holes, it is best to put thin spacers made of resilient material at the back of the holes. With the feeler gauge used to fit the thwarts, determine the width of the hull at the lowest point of the holes in the support blocks. Transfer the hull width to the spreader. Cut the spreader to length subtracting the thickness of the two resilient spacers if used.

Step 255. Transfer this measurement to the stretcher. Ensure that there are equal lengths on both sides of the center of the stretcher.

Step 256. Make two cylindrical bearings for the stretcher by cutting the copper pipe coupling in half with a hack saw. Sand or file the burrs off the cut ends and rough up the insides of bearings.

Step 257. Unbolt the thwarts from the rails. Insert the resilient material in the two blocks.

Step 258. Mix up a batch of thickened epoxy (1 pump, 1-1/2 scoops). Before adding the thickener, dab some epoxy on the ends of the stretcher to help seal the end grain. Coat the inside of the bearings and the last 1/2" of the dowel with the thickened epoxy. Slip the bearings over the ends of the stretcher. Clean up the squeeze-out. Wrap both bearings and a little ways up the stretcher with very thin plastic wrap like food wrapping.

Step 259. Insert one end of the stretcher into its support block. Pull the sides of the hull apart and put the other end of the stretcher in its hole. Push the bearings outward on the stretcher as far as they will go. Rebolt the thwarts in place.

Step 260. When the epoxy is cured, unbolt the thwarts, and remove the stretcher and the plastic wrap. Reinsert the stretcher in the blocks and check that it rotates freely. As necessary, remove wood from the holes with the dowel and sandpaper.

Step 261. Insert the stretcher in its support blocks. Reinstall the thwarts.

Celebrate Your Accomplishment

Congratulations, *Sweet Dream's* hull is complete. Its time to for you to take a break and *CELEBRATE*.

All too often, we wait for someone else or the calendar to initiate recognition of important events in our lives. The heck with that; it's time to blow your own horn. For a few minutes, take the time to recognize your own achievement. This is a special day; play loud music, dance around the hull, laugh, clap, sing. Do it! The celebration is of and for you, and you alone. **YOU DESERVE IT.** Like life, you will get out of your celebration in proportion to what you put in. Invite your inner child to see and wonder at what you've done. Don't be surprised if you cry. This is your victory and there was no loser.

Soon you'll paddle your own canoe.

Part 2:
Finishing the Hull

When I started writing this manual, my plan was to write only about building *Sweet Dream's* hull. I intended to mention paint and varnishing only in passing. As I noted earlier, I wrote the building sequence while building a *Sweet Dream.* When I completed the bare hull, I knew that there was still a lot more effort involved before the canoe would be usable. I knew that most builders would have little experience in painting and varnishing. I knew also that a well built hull deserves a good paint and varnish job. I went back to my keyboard and wrote this part. While the building sequence is written rather tightly, declarative and directive sentences for the most part, the rest of the book will be looser, more conversational in tone.

I am a canoe designer and builder by choice. I am a canoe painter out of necessity. I get a better than average finish on my canoes, but I have to work hard to get it. I have worked out a system that gets paint and varnish on with a minimum of fuss, and a high degree of repeatable success. As I stood looking at the completed hull, I slowly realized that of all I've learned in building canoes that I am proud of, learning to paint well was the biggest hurdle. After I built my second boat, I was still not happy with my painting and varnishing. I knew that they did not reflect the care, craftsmanship, and quality that I had put into the hulls.

I bit the bullet and took a class on painting and varnishing from George Fatula at The WoodenBoat School. It was time and money well spent. What follows is my interpretation and adaptation of what George teaches. Don't think for a minute that my presentation is half as good as George's. He has applied enough paint to float a battleship and forgotten more about painting than I'll ever know. At best, my presentation should be considered a synopsis of how to apply paint and varnish.

Absent from my presentation is one important detail; technique. By technique I mean having the tools in your hand and trying to emulate the movements and pressure demonstrated by

Modern canoeing came into its own as the nation became more urbanized. I believe the reason personal and recreational uses of the canoe increased was because the canoe remained very much the same as it was. Few of man's early inventions have absorbed and survived technological progress so brilliantly; few primitive concepts have come through so clearly. The clean line and simple functional forms of the Indian birchbark have not been improved, nor has the cost greatly increased—it is still comparatively inexpensive. The silent action drawing it forward remains the same—the hand-driven paddle with no fixed fulcrum, and no fuel and no crew required. Furthermore it continues to be light and transportable. Indefinitely ancient, eternally youthful, a tangible reminder of freedom and unclouded rivers, the canoe lasts into our time from days when man lived closer to nature and it retains the aura.

Walter Magnes Teller,
On the River

The reflection of the sawhorse on the right side of the hull gives an indication of the smoothness of the paint that can be achieved with the foam roller and brush technique. The interior paint was deglossed with a flattening agent added to the paint before it was applied. Part 2 explains the foam roller and brush technique in detail.

the teacher. I will explain what materials to use, and the roller and brush process I use to apply them. Unfortunately, I cannot give you the hands-on experience with immediate feedback that you get in a well taught class.

Finishing is an entirely different activity than building. Up to this point the hull structure has been paramount. From this point on, it is best to think of your beloved canoe as just an object to support the finish. In applying paint and varnish, everything that matters is in the few thousands of an inch at and just below the surface of the hull.

Detailing the Hull

"Detailing" is doing all the little things that for reasons of time, and therefore money, are infrequently done on a production hull. Detailing is doing the little things now that later you'll wish that you had if now you don't. Detailing is the hallmark of professional custom and high quality amateur work. There are a hundred little things that can be done. These include:

ᦔ Making sure all edges are radiused.

ᦔ Filling small voids at the edges of the taped joints with surfacing compound if the joint is supposed to be invisible.

ᦔ Filling any nicks or dings in the hull.

ᦔ Cleaning epoxy out of the joint between the rails and the hull so tape will adhere evenly and produce a sharp dividing line between the paint on the hull and the varnish on the rail.

ᦔ Giving the end grain at the ends of the rails, thwarts, inner edge of the breast-hooks, and the drain hole in the breast-hook, at least three pre-coats of varnish so that they finish evenly with the rest of the wood.

ᦔ Topping off and sanding flush the epoxy plugs in holes in the sides amidships and in the bottom pad.

ᦔ Touching up the taped joints with epoxy if the weave still shows through.

ᦔ Sanding the hull and back side of the inner rails in the rail cutouts. Sanding the underside of the rails.

ᦔ Cutting the carriage bolts securing the thwarts and seat beams or backrest stretcher support blocks so that they have only two threads showing beyond the washer and nut.

There's more but I won't go on. I'm sure that you get the idea. How much detailing you do is your decision. These little things can be omitted without any ill effects on how the canoe performs. On the other hand, the cumulative effect of these many little things is a canoe that has a noticeable but indefinable crispness. People take notice, but they can't quite put their finger on why the canoe looks so good.

If you really get into detailing, here's a trick for when you're varnishing. It is difficult to get varnish onto the surfaces of the rail cutouts with a regular brush, no matter how small, without making a mess. Cut 2"x1/4" strips from a 1/8" thick foam roller. The japanese saw will easily cut the cardboard tube. This tool will coat the surfaces of the cutouts between the rails and the hull without making a mess. The coats of varnish it applies are very thin, so it's best to double the number of coats applied elsewhere on the trim.

When the hull is built and detailing is completed, your *Sweet Dream* is about half finished.

Sanding and Sandpaper

Sanding is the major component of preparing the hull for paint. You sand before any paint is applied, and you sand between coats. The final coat of paint or varnish can look only as good as the surface preparation that precedes it. Understanding sanding and sandpaper is an essential part of a good paint job.

In the Industrial Revolution, the salvation of mankind was to be the pay check. With it, a laborer (sometimes called a "wage slave") could buy from other paycheck earners the things that in an earlier time the worker would have produced him or herself. Factories employed thousands of unskilled laborers to finish products made in dreary factories in dirty, over-crowded cities by the new machines. In furniture factories, the job of preparing the pieces for the final

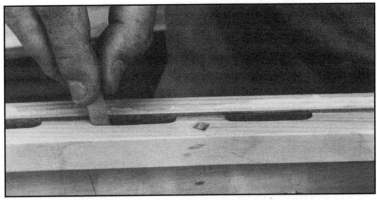

The slots in built up rails can be varnished without making a mess with a 1/4"x2" piece of foam roller. After the first few coats it is helpful to run masking tape on the hull just below the rail to prevent build up of varnish below the slots that would have to be sanded off the hull when it is readied for primer.

finish fell to laborers with no prior experience with the prevalent tool, the furniture scraper.

The furniture scraper is a thin flat piece of tempered steel, maybe 5" x 3". Its edges are sharpened with a file and used to scrape surfaces smooth. An even better approach is to turn the edges of the scraper with a burnisher which produces a sharper edge that also lasts longer. On most woods the edge lasts up to an hour before resharpening is required. Unfortunately, using the scraper requires some skill. Getting a razor sharp, perfectly straight edge with the file and burnisher needs even more skill.

The answer to getting a large output with consistently prepared surfaces with unskilled labor lay in finding an alternative finishing tool to replace the furniture scraper. Sharkskin was also used for finishing wood, but it was relatively hard to get. "Sandpaper" was invented to fill the gap. At first sandpaper was just what the name implies, sand or ground glass cemented to paper. (I am omitting from this discussion "french polishing," and other processes that use powdered abrasives. These are for the most part highly specialized, time-intensive techniques used in the final stages of finishing processes on the highest grades of custom work.)

Since the 1800s, and more particularly in the last 50 years, sandpaper has evolved into a sophisticated and versatile tool. Its manufacturers would prefer that it be called an abrasive sheet. I will mostly use the term sandpaper or just paper, as that's what most people call it in everyday use.

There are three basic parts to sandpaper:

☙ the backing, usually paper or cloth,

☙ glue, adhesive, or binder, and,

☙ the abrasive material.

To these basic parts can be added optional features such as:

☙ a coating on the abrasive material to discourage clogging, and,

☙ a means to temporarily but securely attach the sandpaper to a hand held block or a power tool.

For the most part, the sandpaper typically used in wooden boat building has a paper backing. Sanding belts and water resistant sandpaper are exceptions; they have cloth backings. Special purpose abrasives can be had with plastic or metal backings.

Glue holds the abrasive material on the backing. On large grit paper, the glue is very thick to hold the large abrasive particles. On small grit papers it is imperceptibly thin. It must not be so brittle as to break away with minor bending of the backing. It must not melt when subjected to the heat from the friction of vigorous hand sanding or machine sanding.

The abrasive does the actual removal of material. You can still buy sandpaper with sand as the abrasive; it is very low quality and should be avoided. Other common abrasives are garnet, flint, silicon carbide, and aluminum oxide.

Grits, the size of the bits of abrasive, go from 16, great lumps bigger than a goose bump, to over 1200, more for polishing than sanding. Grits between 40 and 320 interest us as builders of boats that will actually be used.

A coating is often applied to sandpaper to discourage clogging of the abrasive by particles that have been removed from the surface. This coating, a sort of release agent, is typically a stearate. Its color can be white, gold, green, or maroon. When a coating is present, it uniformly covers the backing and abrasive.

Sandpaper has become a much more versatile tool since the addition of means to attach it directly to a sanding block or power tool. These include hook and loop fasteners, and a tacky non-drying adhesive.

There are many combinations of the above features. Rather than discuss each possible combination, I will discuss what works for me.

Except for special purposes, I use nothing but adhesive backed, stearate coated, silicon carbide sandpaper. This combination gives me the highest consistency finish and the longest lasting and most versatile abrasive at relatively low cost.

☙ With the adhesive backing, the sandpaper can be attached to any smooth surface to make a custom sanding tool in whatever shape you need. It sticks to unfinished wood, plastic, rubber, and even felt. (More on felt in a moment.) I can't remember the last time I used a wood file. I put a piece of sandpaper on a piece of wood of whatever shape I need; flat, round, curved, whatever. Adhesive backed paper is more expensive than regular paper but every square inch is usable; none is wasted.

☙ Silicon carbide abrasive stays sharper longer. In use, the silicon carbide abrasive fractures and exposes new cutting

The canoe is the American boat of the past and of the future. It suits the American mind: it is light, swift, safe, graceful, easily moved; and the occupant looks in the direction he is going, instead of behind, as in the stupid old tubs that have held the world up to this time.

John Boyle O'Reilly,
Athletics and Manly Sport

surfaces. Again, it's more expensive than sand, flint, or garnet but you use less of it. The adhesive typically used with silicon carbide is stronger and less brittle so few abrasive grains break away from the backing and scar the surface. The adhesive is also less heat sensitive and doesn't break down under hard use. (Notice that I said hard use and not heavy pressure; more on that too in a moment.)

ᴈ The stearate coating further extends the useful life of the paper by discouraging clogging which can cause hot spots on the paper, breakaway of the abrasive from the backing, and marring of the finished surface.

ᴈ Last but not least, it is available at my local discount hardware store.

The special uses that might be an exception are papers bought to fit a power sander which you already own. If the sander is an older model, it probably has built-in spring clamps to hold plain backed paper. For a few dollars you can buy a stick-on plastic surface that converts the sander for adhesive backed paper. It's a simple conversion that is well worth the cost. As an even lower cost modification, high quality duct tape applied to the sanding pad will also create a satisfactory surface for adhesive backed paper.

Sandpapers with the hook and loop attachment system are more expensive than adhesive backed paper. Their attraction is supposed to be that papers of different grits can be switched back and forth and reused on a single sanding block or power tool. Hook and loop sandpaper on a dual-action electric sander works fine on relatively flat surfaces, where a relatively large portion of the sandpaper is in contact with the work. It works fine on the inner and outer chines. The hook and loop system does not work well when only a small portion of the sandpaper is in contact with the work such as at the outer forefoot, inner stem, and the ends of the inner chines. The loops on the back of the paper tear out before the abrasive is worn out and the paper is useless. All in all, the adhesive backed paper system is clearly better for this application.

Getting the right sandpaper is not a guarantee that it will do the job; it must be used

Make your own sanding blocks to fit your needs. The hard rubber store-bought block at the upper right is too heavy and unwieldy for sanding on curved surfaces. Clockwise from upper right are: three foam rubber pads of different densities made from found materials, two Scotchbrite pads of differing roughness; two felt-backed pads made of 4mm okume with handles; cylindrical blocks made of dowels, one with pipe insulation padding; and two large felt-backed wooden blocks. The modular size for most of the blocks is 2-14/"x4-1/2" or one half of a palm sander-sized sheet of sticky backed sandpaper.

traveled along twin, parallel paths. On one, a red, seventeen-and-one-half-foot canoe was my vessel. In it Marypat and I paddled nearly two thousand miles of Canadian waterways. For 416 days, we strove towards a goal, lived in and grew to cherish pristine country, accepted the environmental hardships that inevitably came our way, and adapted our lives to harmonize with our surroundings.

The second trail led into the wilderness of my mind and heart. It is a journey much more difficult to quantify or adequately describe, and has yet to reach its end. Profound but invisible landmarks stand along that pathway–lessons in friendship and love, benchmarks in physical and mental discipline, a deepening awareness of vulnerability, appreciation for the value of silence, a reassessment of priorities. The circumstances of the physical expedition served as a means to embark on the personal odyssey. Each voyage enriched the other.

Alan S. Kesselheim,
Water and Sky, Reflections of a Northern Year

properly. The abrasive removes material by being moved quickly, under light to moderate pressure across the surface being sanded. Heavy pressure screws things up.

Heavy pressure when either hand sanding or using a power sander rapidly builds heat on the sandpaper. In turn the abrasive breaks down or breaks off, the stearate coating wears off or fails, and sanded material is fused to the paper, marring the finished surface. When hand sanding, light to moderate pressure is called for. With a power sander, let the machine and gravity do the work; don't force it. Break-down of the abrasive can come in seconds if heavy pressure is applied.

To forestall clogging when sanding flat surfaces, frequently blow or dust off the accumulated material that has been removed from the surface. Usually a power sander causes enough commotion and agitated air flow that it blows the removed material around. Needless to say, a sander with a vacuum attachment is a great help.

Sandpaper should always be used with a sanding block. For starters, the block gives you something to hold on to. It also provides a consistent surface so you don't sand waves into the surface. For shaping edges and surfaces, the block should have a hard surface. For finish sanding, a little more sophistication is in order.

In my experience, the useful life of sandpaper is greatly extended if a thin layer of resilient material is permanently glued to sanding blocks before the paper is attached. This material need be no more than 1/16" thick and have some give to it. Rubber or neoprene sheet, and felt work fine.

I am partial to felt; I got mine from an old fedora. The adhesive on the sandpaper is sticky enough to adhere to the felt securely but not tenaciously like it does to rubber. When it is time to renew the paper, it comes off easily, bringing a few bits of the felt with it. After a few years or so, the felt is worn away and must be renewed.

In addition to wooden blocks, it is helpful to have some blocks made of foam rubber of varying density. These blocks can be purchased from a good paint store or automotive paint supplier. The standard blocks are conveniently one half the size of a sheet of sandpaper for an electric palm sander. The blocks come in different densities. The very light density blocks are used with very small grits like 220, 320 and beyond.

I've said a lot about sanding and you'd think I think sanding is fun. Wrong, I hate it. It's dusty, tedious work. I want to be quit of it as soon as possible; I want to do it quickly and correctly the first time so that I can move on. All the above are tricks I've learned that help me get the multiple sandings during the painting process behind me.

I don't buy power tools unless they are clearly superior to doing a job by hand. I am a little embarrassed to admit that I have four electric sanders; 1/2 sheet, palm sander (1/4 sheet), 6" dual action rotary, and detail sander. Within its range of use, each one sands better and faster than I can by hand. The one time that I do not use an electric sander is when sanding between coats of paint. The paint film thicknesses that I apply are very thin; a moment's inattention or slight misapplication of pressure with an electric sander, and I've gone right through to the undercoat. I'd rather sand by hand than reapply the paint, or try to blend in a patch.

Again, use at least a nuisance dust mask and safety goggles/glasses when using an electric sander.

Painting and Varnishing

Any finish that discourages the intended use of your canoe is a waste of your time, effort, and money. Arguably a hull interior or an entire hull finished bright is a thing of beauty. It is also a great burden on the builder and user. Any scratches or abrasions in the okume caused during building will show darkly under the clear finish. (Due to the thinness of okume's surface plys, sanding out all but the lightest scratches is not an option.) Likewise, epoxy spilled on the okume during construction will show as discolored splotches.

Over the life of the hull, the clear coating will have to be reapplied frequently. Sunlight burns varnish away. UV block in the varnish only slows the loss. In heavy use or in tropical climates, one or two coats of varnish may need to be reapplied every year, or even twice a year. Who needs the bother?

To my eye too much varnished wood does not improve the look of a canoe. Use varnish on the hull and trim as sparingly as your ego will allow. If you just can't stop yourself, use varnish to highlight a simulated sheer strake and/or on the interior sides, but not the bottom.

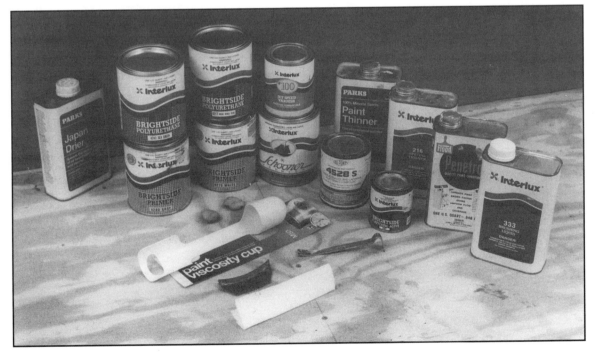

Here are the paint supplies that I typically use to finish a hull. Starting from the lower right there is: Brushing Liquid, a slow vaporating thinner; Penetrol©, a paint conditioner (the third can is a very rapid evaporating thinner that I no longer use); generic paint thinner for clean up and thinning. In front of these are two small cans of flattening agent, one from Interlux, and one by Dupont that has been discontinued recently. Next are two cans of oil/alkyd based varnish; the one on top is a quick drying formula that can be used for the first three coats, while below is a yellow-tinted varnish with UV filter. Next are two cans of primer; white for use under light-colored topcoats, grey for use under dark colors. On top of the primers are cans of one-part urethane paint , for interior and exterior. To the far left is japan dryer, which could be used with oil/alkyd paint and varnish, but not with urethane paint. In center front, top to bottom: smooth rocks to use as agitators; plastic paint viscosity cup; tool to open cans without distorting the edge of the top; a quart can-sized gutter guard cut from a store-bought gallon-sized guard; a folded paper towel gutter guard that is discussed in the text.

Better yet, restrict brightwork to trim and high-lights; rails, thwarts, breasthooks, and seat parts. Four coats of marine grade varnish with UV block is the minimum acceptable. Six coats are better, eight coats are recommended.

If you are going to use your canoe heavily, paint the entire boat, inside and out, trim and all. Otherwise, for typical use consider painting both the interior and exterior of your canoe, and varnish the trim. Quality paint will last three to five years before recoating is necessary.

A smooth, shiny, wet-look, high gloss paint job on the hull exterior can be stunning. However, getting the required smoothness of the wood and undercoat/primer is repetitious and extremely labor intensive. A semi-gloss finish will mask many small irregularities.

While most marine paints come only in gloss finishes, most paint manufacturers also sell a deglosser or flattening agent separately. Gloss and even semi-gloss finishes on the hull interior can cause excessive glare, distraction, and eye strain. Higher proportions of deglosser to paint will produce a flat surface that is superior in looks and abrasion resistance to one achieved by sanding.

Just about any exterior grade paint can perform adequately. The different types of paint have their pros and cons. Here are some that come quickly to mind.

༈ *Exterior latex.* Inexpensive, relatively low toxicity, easy clean up with water. Fully adequate protection for a canoe that sees only short periods in the water. Semi-gloss finish, relatively low in abrasion resistance, frequent touching up may be required. Latex paint skins over quickly but it requires three weeks or more to dry fully. Allow at least a week between coats if you sand, however lightly, between coats. Floetrol®, a latex paint conditioner made by Flood®, makes latex flow on smoothly. Cannot be thinned for viscosity or film thickness control.

༈ *Exterior alkyd enamel.* Only slightly more expensive than latex, vastly improved abrasion resistance, especially in "porch and deck" formulations. Both gloss and semi-gloss finishes are available. Clean up requires petroleum based thinner and presents some health threat due to release of volatile organic compounds, VOCs. Can be thinned for viscosity and film thickness control and modified to suit conditions with plasticizers, dryers, etc. Colors in porch and deck enamels are usually limited to white, tan, shades of gray, black, brick red, and dark green.

༈ *Marine grade alkyd enamel.* Arguably better hardness and abrasive resistance than the best grades of exterior enamel. Users of marine paints are a very small segment of the entire paint using population. Reliable sources report that paint manufacturers say that their porch and deck paints and their marine paint often have the same formulation. The higher prices for their marine paint result from advertising costs, special colors, and small lot handling and transportation costs. Predatory pricing by marine oriented retailers is not unheard of either. Clean up requires thinner and presents some health threat due to release of volatile organic compounds, VOCs. Can be thinned for viscosity or film thickness control. Can be modified to suit conditions with plasticizers, dryers, etc.

༈ *One part marine polyurethane.* Harder, smoother, and shinier than enamels; more expensive too. Somewhat limited range of colors. Clean up requires thinner and presents some health threat due release of volatile organic compounds, VOCs. Can be thinned for viscosity and film thickness control. Can be modified to suit conditions with plasticizers. A really good coating, perhaps the best that can be justified on a recreational hull.

🕱 *Two part polyurethane.* Very good shine, hardness, and smoothness. Full-gonzo racers love it. Achieving these results requires slavish devotion to preparing the hull. The above benefits also come at a high cost, not only in dollars, but also in a high health risk. In the form of liquid or vapor, the stuff is highly toxic to all living things. The thinners it requires are especially wicked stuff. Follow the application instructions to the letter including those for disposal of waste and soiled rags. If you simply must have this coating, do the right thing and have it professionally applied. (I currently have no direct experience with this stuff, and I don't ever expect to.)

🕱 *Automotive acrylic enamel.* A few builders that I know are using this coating and rave about it. The results they get appear to be equal to the one part polyurethanes. It is available in a wide, almost infinite, range of colors. I suspect that its toxicity is similar to one part polyurethane. (Although I have no direct experience with this stuff at this time, it looks to warrant some investigation in the future.)

🕱 *Oil/alkyd based varnish.* An old stand-by that has gotten better with time. Can be obtained in water-clear and yellow tint. I feel that the water-clear looks much like plastic. The yellow-tinted lends depth and warmth to the finish. Always get a brand that has an ultraviolet (UV) inhibitor. Accepts the full range of additives.

🕱 *Water-based varnish.* I have used this only once and my reactions were mixed. On the plus side, the stuff really does dry in just a few hours. It dries very much harder than oil/alkyd varnish, as well. I used water-clear and, if anything, it seemed to have a faint bluish tint. The wood looked dead. By this I mean the wood itself did not seem to glow as it does under oil/alkyd varnish. Both these problems can be overcome, but

I must admit that I still don't use water-based varnish. New color formulations are now available that have a yellow tint. To get the oil/alkyd glow, put on two or three thinned coats of oil/alkyd varnish, and follow with coats of water-based varnish.

🕱 *Two-part epoxy based paint and varnish.* Because I am happy with the one-part urethane paint and oil/alkyd varnish that I am familiar with, I haven't used either of these.

Any of the above paints and varnishes is formulated to provide a thin (except for latex paint), tough, water resistant film that is more or less impervious to the ill effects of abrasions, UV degradation, chemicals, pollution, etc. Paint intended for top coating will not substitute for: undercoater, primer, gap or hole filler, surfacing compound, etc. Asking paint to perform any of these functions invites premature coating failure requiring at least frequent touching up, and at worst a complete refinish from the wood out.

When it comes to the choice of paint, you pay your money and take your chances. As with epoxy, I use a single brand of paint. I use Interlux® paints and varnishes exclusively. I know what they can do and how to handle them to get a consistently "near yacht" finish. I can concentrate on reducing the human element in their application rather than wondering and fretting about all the technical details of thinning, mixing, etc.

T ime spent in a wooden canoe of fine lines and able handling qualities is intoxicating. Restoring vintage canoes or building such craft from scratch can be consuming. It will ruin a man or a woman for any other work. This is not to dismiss all canoe builders as rapscallions, curmudgeons, or reprobates. But in the majority of cases there are the symptoms of an addiction, or at least a suspension of common sense where canoes are concerned.

Jerry Stelmok and Rollin Thurlow,
The Wood and Canvas Canoe

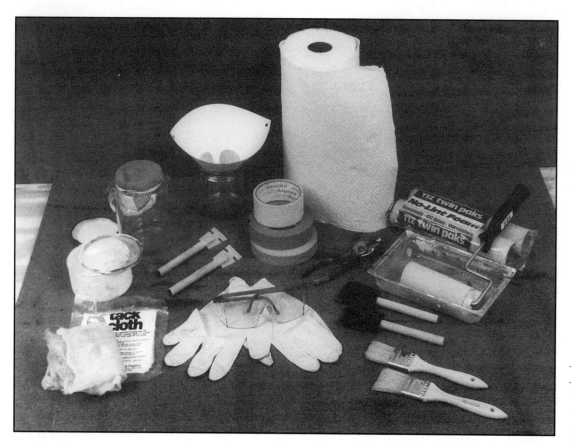

The equipment used in the foam roller and brush technique going from lower left and clockwise: tack cloths, one in wrapper, one unfolded and ready for use; a large tuna fish can with coffee can plastic cover as a top; glass jar with screw-on air-tight top with a piece of panty hose paint filter; glass jar and store-bought filter; paper towels'; Tiz brand foam rollers; small paint tray and cut down roller on 4" roller frame' foam brushes; chip brushes; plastic gloves and safety glasses; paint stirrers made from used foam brushes with the foam covering removed; masking tape of various types; and pliers to remove a used roller cover from the roller frame.

Interlux® makes a marine grade alkyd enamel, and one and two part polyurethane paints. I have used both the enamel and their Brightsides® one part polyurethane. For most applications I prefer the Brightsides® for its consistently smooth hard finish, abrasion resistance, and durability. I use the enamel when price is an overriding factor, as in most teaching situations.

I have not seen the need to go to the two part polyurethane and don't know anything about the thinners, proportions, etc. required. The application with roller and brush will work I'm sure, but I can't give advice on mixing and thinning.

Getting a smooth hard top coat is as much a matter of adequate preparation as it is applying the paint. Adequate preparation means a lot of sanding interrupted by applying the various coatings and their drying time. It is senseless to use sandpaper of grits greater than 120 on bare wood that is to be painted. Ditto for undercoater. Sand between color coats of paint or varnish with 220 or 320 grit paper.

To get good results, paint top coats should be applied over at least two coats of undercoat or primer. Both of these will fill pores in the wood; neither will fill scratches, gouges, holes, etc. For these a filler or surfacing compound is called for. Undercoat is intended for use below the waterline and is not really necessary on a canoe that is dry stored. It is harder than primer and more difficult to sand. However, when properly sanded to a thickness between opaqueness and translucence, either primer or undercoater provides superior smoothness for succeeding color coats.

After sanding, vacuum the hull and wipe it with thinner. Just before applying paint, use a tack cloth to remove the last bit of dust from the surfaces. The tack cloth is impregnated with a sticky substance that remains tacky after repeated usage. Wear gloves when using a tack cloth. Pull the cloth apart so that it is a single layer. Refold it loosely so that it's a square about 5" on each side.

Wipe the cloth lightly over the sanded surface, keeping the cloth in motion whenever it is in contact with the surface. Try not to touch the surface with your other hand; it has sticky residue on it from the cloth. If this residue is transferred to the surface, it can result in a telltale five-fingered pattern of recurring localized paint failure.

Wipe, do not rub with the cloth. Rubbing can put a thin coat of the sticky stuff on the surface which can cause paint or varnish not to adhere. Turn and refold the cloth frequently so that there is a fresh, sticky side to pick up the dust.

If you store the cloth in an airtight container you can get three or four uses out of it. After using the cloth, clean your gloves with a little paint thinner on a rag to remove the sticky residue.

Varnish builds overall film thickness slower than does paint. The first few coats of varnish are more sanding sealers than finish coatings. The job of the first few coats is to penetrate deeply into the underlying wood and make a hard smooth surface for the following coats to adhere to. A typical thinning schedule for coats of varnish is:

❧ First coat, 1 part varnish, 3 parts thinner.

❧ Second coat, 2 parts varnish, 2 parts thinner.

❧ Third coat, 3 parts varnish, 1 part thinner.

❧ Fourth and all subsequent coats, add only 10 -20% thinner as needed.

Do not expect to see gloss until the third coat. Use abrasives one grit higher than for paint. For a really smooth finish on the breasthooks, wet sand with 320 or 400 grit before the last coat. Be careful when wet sanding; the grit cuts much faster than when dry sanding. It is very easy to sand right down to bare wood.

If you are going to varnish the rails and breasthooks, apply at least four coats of varnish to them before applying paint to the hull. This seals the grain on the varnished parts and any spills or drips can be easily wiped off when they're wet or sanded off when dry. Masking tape is not necessary for these coats of varnish.

Apply the varnish 1/4" or so onto the hull. This seals the joint between varnish and paint. I apply the last two coats of varnish after all the paint is on. It means there's a little more taping to do than if all the varnish coats were put on earlier. But because the paint is on, the hull doesn't have to be handled between the coats of varnish and it's less likely you'll get dings in the varnished rails.

As paint and varnish dries, it loses volume in the form of volatile components gassing off. This is to say that paint and varnish shrink as they dry. They shrink in thickness and parallel to the surface they are on. A sharp corner at the edge of the surface can cut right through the paint or varnish as it dries and shrinks.

Always sand a slight radius on the edges of anything to be painted or varnished. The radius doesn't have to be very big; something on the order of 1/32" is big enough. Use 180 or 220 grit sandpaper to make the radius if you want it

To follow the drops sliding from a lifted oar,

Head up, while the rower breathes, and the small boat drifts quietly shoreward;

To know that light falls and fills, often without our knowing.

Theodore Roethke,
The Shape of the Fire

to be small. When sanding between coats, be especially careful not to cut through the coating on the radiused edge. Sand the edges only every other coat, and use 220 grit with the lightest possible pressure.

Paint and varnish are not formulated to cover in a single coat, even when applied over undercoater or primer. Multiple thin coats are always the way to go. Thin coats are easiest applied with a 1/8" thick yellow foam roller immediately followed by tipping with a foam brush to knock down the bubbles. (An explanation of the "foam roller and brush" technique follows shortly.)

With the exception of two part polyurethanes and true epoxy based coatings, paint and varnish dry from the outer surface inward. As a result one thick coat of paint will dry to true sanding hardness more slowly than two thin ones. Most paint is too thick as it comes from the can; it must be thinned between 10 and 20% before use. Despite what it says on the can, only thin coats of paint and varnish will dry sufficiently for sanding and recoating in 24 hours. It is best to wait three or four days before applying the last coat of paint or varnish.

Paint and varnish are dry enough to recoat when sanding produces tiny, light little particles that blow away in the slightest air movement. If the sanding residue is large and course, or rolls up into balls or little ropes, or immediately clogs the paper, the coating is not dry enough to be sanded. Wait another 12 hours and try again.

The drying of alkyd enamels and varnishes can be accelerated with japan dryer. I use the stuff very little so can only say, follow the directions on the can. I have heard tell of paint drying in only four hours with a great whacking dose of the stuff. What the dried surface looked like though was never mentioned.

There are many types of masking tape. By far the least expensive is the run of the mill, tan-colored kind. It can do an adequate job if not asked to do too much. It comes in two thicknesses; acceptable, and too thin. The pack-

aging never says how thick the stuff is, but the thicker stuff is about twice the price. The thinner stuff is better at going around tight corners, but that's about all. It tears as it comes off the roll and when it is being removed from the hull: it's a real headache and not worth the few pennies saved. Never use or leave the tan tape in direct sun; it hardens the adhesive on the tape and makes it difficult to get off the roll or the finished surface.

If you use tape to mask off parts of the hull during painting, remove the tape as soon as possible after paint or varnish is applied. Forget claims of the tape being able to stay on for three, four, or seven days. This is the time the tape remains usable *before* paint is applied. Remove the tape as soon as the paint or varnish has skinned over and it won't run. This can be after as little as 10 minutes. It is never longer than30 minutes.

Remember that when paint or varnish dries it shrinks. At the edges of an unrestrained paint film, the shrinkage pulls the edge into a smooth radius. If masking tape is left on too long, and the paint dries fully, one of two bad results is likely. In the least bad case, the edge of the paint will be rough and uneven. Flakes of paint can be pulled away from the hull when the tape is removed after the paint is fully dried. In the worse case, earlier coats of paint will be pulled off too.

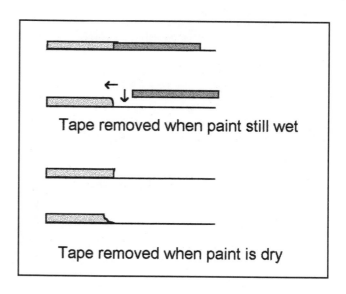

Tape removed when paint still wet

Tape removed when paint is dry

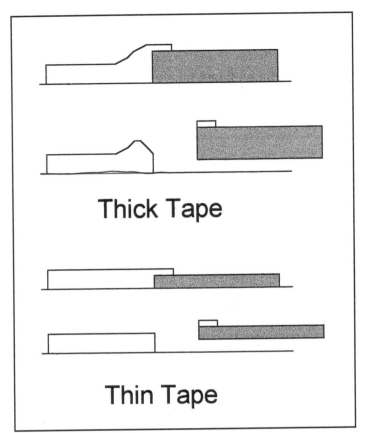

In my experience, the quality of the paint edge is a function of both the thickness of the tape and when the tape is removed. When thick tape is removed, it leaves a mound of paint at the edge of the paint which has trouble leveling. Thin tape on the other hand leaves no mound and the paint edge is sharp. The best thin tape is a light green plastic. It costs about twice as much as the better tan paper tape. It is worth every penny if you want a clean, crisp line every time.

Using a deglosser or flattening agent to produce a satin or flat finish calls for some planning. The deglosser is a thick mixture of "neutral color solids" in a fast evaporating vehicle. It is strange stuff; at first it thins the paint mixture, then its vehicle evaporates faster than anything else in the paint, and the paint thickens. When using deglosser, you often have to add thinners to paint after   the initial mix.

The neutral color solids in the deglosser also make the paint film somewhat translucent. It covers very poorly. The best way I've found to use deglosser is to put on two or three coats of straight paint, and then follow with a top coat of paint with deglosser in it. The first coats of straight paint provide color and opaqueness. The last coat is really just a wash to get the deglossed surface. You have to try different proportions of deglosser to get the degree of flatness you want. To get a true flat finish, don't be surprised if you need a 2:1 proportion of paint to deglosser, and 1:1 varnish to deglosser.

It is time to talk about the process of applying paint with a foam roller and foam brush. The goal here is to apply a thin coat of paint that has a consistent film thickness and no visible sign of the separate applications of paint that cover the hull. When properly done the hull looks like it was spray painted.

Required equipment:

7" or 9" Tiz® foam rollers
4" Roller frame
1-1/2" or 2" Poly-Brush® paint brush
5" x 8" Roller tray
12 Paper towels; 8 full size, 4 torn in half
 lengthwise to make 8 half-size towels.
6-8 oz. container with tight fitting lid
Du Pont™ M50 #2 plastic viscosity cup
 (Optional)
Paint
Additives:
 Brushing Liquid
 Penetrol®
 Japan dryer (except for urethane or epoxy
  paints and varnishes)
 Generic paint thinner or mineral spirits
Strainer (Optional)

Before discussing the process of mixing and applying the paint, I'll briefly discuss each of the components of the system listed above.

Tiz® foam rollers come in packages of two. They are made of a yellow 1/8" thick foam cover glued to an inner cardboard tube. Cut the rollers in half with the japanese saw. Do not use the foam rollers with black foam, they breakdown with some thinners.

Full size rollers are too big for painting a small boat or canoe. When working on curved surfaces, they tend to drip at their ends. The full sized roller tray that must also be used facilitates the rapid evaporation of solvents and additives from the paint mixture. The thickened paint is impossible to blend together at the "wet edge" of each application of paint. These conditions make it very difficult to get a satisfactory painted surface. I find that using a smaller roller overcomes these difficulties.

Poly-Brush® brushes have wood handles and very small open cells in the foam. Other brands of foam brushes with plastic handles have larger open cells which release thin viscosity paint too fast. They are also prone to leaving simulated bristle strokes in the paint. Although the plastic handled brushes are less expensive, they cannot be substituted for Poly-Brush® brushes.

The 4" roller frame accommodates the cut down rollers.

> *Let your boat of life be light, packed with only what you need — a homely home and simple pleasures, one or two friends, worth the name, someone to love and someone to love you, a cat, a dog, and a pipe or two, enough to eat and enough to wear, and a little more than enough to drink; for thirst is a dangerous thing.*
>
> Jerome Klapka Jerome,
> *Three Men in a Boat*

Although the foam roller and brush each have a rather narrow performance envelope, together they can replicate a finish applied with a spray gun. The roller is an excellent tool for transporting paint from the roller tray to the surface to be painted and for applying the paint in a thin coating with consistent film thickness. The drawback to the roller is that it leaves small bubbles in the paint. They can't be helped; it is the nature of the beast. The Poly-Brush® brush is the perfect tool for flattening the bubbles left by the roller.

Since the roller does so well applying paint to large surfaces, I use a Poly-Brush® brush solo only for applying varnish on the rails,

breasthooks, thwarts, and backrest assembly. The secret to getting a smooth, consistent film is in not overloading the brush. If there is too much varnish in the brush, it tends to make a sort of puddle where it first touches the surface. This can lead to runs and drips. I find that just touching the last 1/32" or at most 1/16" of the chisel point into the varnish very briefly draws up enough varnish for controlled, even flow. A properly loaded brush doesn't have to be wiped on the container lip before use.

Apply the varnish by flowing it on with deliberate strokes. As it comes off the brush the varnish should make a smooth, continuous coating. If it's streaky, there is too little varnish in the brush. Hold the brush lightly between thumb and first two fingers. After a while, you may get to the point where you can judge the amount of varnish left in the brush by the increase in drag. You can't develop this "feel" by clutching the brush in a fist.

If you move the brush at the correct speed, there will be few, if any, bubbles in the varnish. If you go too fast, there will be hundreds of them. Once the varnish is on, mess with it as little as possible. One or two light, slow strokes to kill some of the bubbles is OK, but after that you risk overworking the varnish and it will show your brush strokes. Don't let a few bubbles trouble you, they usually will burst on their own.

The small roller tray plays an important role in maintaining consistent paint viscosity. 5"x8" roller trays are not commercially available. I use the plastic tray from a package of refrigerated pasta. Some pasta containers are better than others: Contadina's™ tray is thicker and less prone to bending or warping than the Di Georgino™ tray. For quick clean up the tray can be lined with aluminum foil.

The paper towels are used for clean up; wiping up spills and drips when mixing and applying the paint, cleaning the roller frame, tray, and foam brush. It is wise to have one of the towels presaturated with thinner for quick removal of spills on the surface to be painted, the floor, your shoes, etc.

The container with tight fitting lid is used to hold the paint as it is mixed before it is transferred to the roller tray. Once the paint is mixed to the desired viscosity, maintaining that viscosity is one of the keys to a consistent film thickness and a smooth finish. Whenever the paint is exposed to ambient air, it loses thinners and conditioners and becomes more viscous. The loss of thinners leads to increasing film thickness, inability to blend applications of paint at the wet edge, and reduced ability of the paint to pull into a flat surface as it dries. The covered container can be a small glass jar with a screw cap, a plastic container with a press-on lid such as from Philadelphia® brand cream cheese, or a large tuna fish can and the plastic lid from a one pound can of coffee for a cover.

The #2 viscosity cup is not absolutely essential, but it's a great help in getting consistent viscosity. If the viscosity of the paint mixture is constant, you can concentrate on the technique of applying the paint. Viscosity cups are available in plastic and metal. The Du Pont™ M50 plastic ones cost about $3, the metal ones are about $50; mine is plastic.

You don't need a lot of paint to paint *Sweet Dream*. You need only 200cc of paint to do one coat on either the inside or outside of *Sweet Dream*. As there are 946ccs in a quart of paint, you can easily get four coats from a can, five if you're careful. Since the individual coats are quite thin when applied with foam roller and brush, three coats are required for coverage as opposed to the two coats generally recommended for brush application. Very dark colors, especially reds, greens, and blues, always require a third, and sometimes even a fourth coat. It is advisable to use a grey primer under dark colors.

Applying paint to a boat is not the same as painting your house. Let's face it, when you're at the top of an 18-foot ladder the most desirable feature in a paint is coverage in one coat. Getting back to terra firma is far more important than smoothness and gloss. House paints, especially latex, do well at covering in one coat. Unfortunately most amateur boat builders want the paint they apply to their boats to both cover in one coat *and* have superior smoothness and gloss. In my experience, you can't have it both ways. When painting a boat coverage becomes a secondary consideration, getting the desired smoothness and gloss is the primary concern and that requires modification of the paint with additives.

As it comes from the can, paint is a raw material, similar to a sheet of plywood or unplaned lumber. Additives bring the paint to a point where it will perform in the desired manner. Additives come in two general categories: those that are used primarily for controlling viscosity; and all the rest such as plasticizers, driers, flattening agents, etc. When mixing paint the "all the rest" additives are added first, then the viscosity controlling modifiers are used to get the desired viscosity.

Penetrol® made by Flood is a paint and varnish conditioner that helps the paint flow on and pull into a smooth flat coating as it dries. Flood recommends it be used at a 1:8 proportion to the paint. I always use it in alkyd enamels and one part polyurethane paints and varnish.

Japan dryer accelerates drying of alkyd enamel and varnishes. DO NOT USE JAPAN DRYER WITH POLYURETHANE PAINT. Its recommended proportion is 1:64 (2 oz. per gallon). Since you'll be mixing four to six ounces of paint at a time only a few drops are needed.

If you use a flattening agent or deglosser, add the deglosser to the paint and let the mix sit uncovered for 15 minutes to allow the very fast evaporating thinners to gas off. Then add thinners to get the desired viscosity.

Before adding viscosity controlling additives, check your paint mix with the viscosity cup. At the desired viscosity, the cup should empty in 18 to 20 seconds.

Viscosity controlling additives, generally called thinners, come in fast and slow evaporating formulations. I use one part fast evaporating thinner to three parts slow evaporating thinner to bring the paint mix to the desired viscosity. I use Interlux® 333 Brushing Liquid, which has a high percentage of kerosene, as a slow evaporating thinner. I feel that a higher percentage of slow thinners help the paint pull flat as it dries. I use generic paint thinners and mineral spirits as fast evaporating thinners.

The paint strainer is a paper cone with plastic screening at its tip. A piece of panty hose is a good, low-cost alternative for filtering paint and varnish. It is best to strain paint and varnish whenever you suspect that there may be lumps or foreign objects in it.

Before I discuss applying paint with the foam roller and brush, I'll touch on three more topics that can affect the quality of the finish. These are storing and handling unused paint, getting rid of as much dust as possible from the shop, and bugs.

Once a can of paint is opened, the paint remaining in the can is exposed to the ambient air that is contained in the can above the paint. Even when the lid is air tight, and it always isn't, some of the paint in the container can cure. The more air in the can, the more the paint can cure and form a hard surface. This hard surface is visible evidence of wasted paint and money. In his book, *Instant Boats*, "Dynamite" Payson discusses cutting a circle of waxed paper to fit inside the can and float on top of the paint to form an airproof cover. It's a good idea that works. I feel that there is some danger of some of the wax being dissolved by the solvents in the paint and so I use aluminum foil. It will float on top of the paint if the can is handled carefully. Either covering is a bit messy to remove from the can.

As a separate measure, keeping the gutter around the lip of the can clean will help maintain the air tightness of the can. Paint usually gets in the gutter when pouring paint off into another container. Some people punch holes in the gutter to allow paint to drain back into the can. In my experience punching the holes also distorts the gutter. More likely than not the can is never really air tight thereafter. I find it better to keep paint out of the gutter to begin with. I fold one of the half-size paper towels into eights and force one lengthwise edge of the towel into the gutter. I pour over the towel which also forms a spout so that the drips don't run down the can. Done carefully no paint gets in the gutter.

Thoroughly mixing a can of paint can be a chore, especially if it has been sitting on the shelf for a while and the pigments have fallen out of suspension. Whenever possible, get your supplier to mix the paint on a machine when you buy it. Often you'll have to mix by hand. The hidden problem is that the can of paint is opened to the air and loosing thinners and other additives the whole time that you stir and lift the pigments back into suspension.

I minimize this problem by putting an agitator in the can. When you shake a can of spray paint you can hear something rattling around in there; that's the agitator. It's in there because you can't open the can to mix the paint. I put an agitator in every can of paint I open. I use a smooth, clean rock about the size of a quarter, or a 3/8" or so bolt. With the agitator you can shake most of the pigments back in suspension and have the can open a very short time to do some final stirring just before pouring off the paint you need.

The sea being smooth, How many shallow bauble boats dare sail Upon her patient breast.

William Shakespeare,
Troilus and Cressida, Act I, sc. iii, l. 34

If you absolutely must have a dust free finish, then you also must have a dust free space to paint in. Good luck, and welcome to the real world. Remember that what we're finishing here is just a canoe; not a grand piano, a lacquered jewelry box, or a Fabergé egg. If you're like me you can't even get a canoe out of the shop the first time without putting a ding in it. A little air borne dust in the paint or varnish won't hurt. Neither will a lot of dust, but it sure doesn't make you feel good.

Like me, you'll probably have to paint in the same space that you build in, so there's dust everywhere. A permanently installed dust collection system would be a godsend. Not having one, while inconvenient, is not fatal. Here are some steps that will help minimize dust getting into your wet paint and varnish.

First, minimize the amount of dust you add to the work space. Whenever possible, use a razor sharp edge tool rather than sandpaper to trim and fit parts. Do as much sanding as possible outside the space. Do a reasonable job of cleaning the space. The vacuum cleaner is a good tool but it has a dark side. The exhaust from the cleaner is not dust free. Further, if the exhaust leaves your machine down near floor level, it can lift a lot of fine dust up into the air; just what you don't want. Use an exhaust hose to direct the exhaust air outside the space.

Now you have to deal with the dust suspended in the air. A simple way to pull the dust down is to fill the air with a fine mist from a hand mister. The secret here is to mist heavily the night before you paint. Cover the boat and get as much mist into the air as you dare. Next morning, come back and heavily mist the floor to keep the fallen dust stuck to the floor. Wipe the cover with a damp cloth and remove it with as little commotion as possible. Wipe the surface to be painted or varnished with a tack rag and apply the finish as quickly as possible.

There is a fine balance between not gassing yourself with paint fumes and filling the air with a dust cloud lifted by air currents from open windows and doors. It is best to work with an air mask and air from outside. Realistically, a half face mask with organic vapor filter canisters will protect you from the volatile thinners that are gassing out of the paint.

There is one more source of dust that must be addressed. Both the foam roller and brush are dust magnets. I don't know why; maybe it has to do with a weak electrostatic charge. Maybe the dust is in them when they leave the factory. I don't know. I do know that even if I keep both my rollers and brushes in airtight containers they are loaded with dust when I use them. So I have to clean them before I use them. I both vacuum and tack rag the foam rollers after they have been cut in half, and the foam brushes before I use them. (OK, I admit it, on an anal-retentiveness scale of 1 to 10, I'm an 11.)

After all the above, absent a NASA approved dust free environment, there will still be dust motes in your paint. Such is life. If the dust is very small and evenly spread across the hull, and is heavier on horizontal surfaces, it's ambient dust in the air. If the dust is heaviest near the open window or door, that's where it's coming from, either directly or as a result of being lifted by air currents. If the dust is largish pieces which occur most where you started to paint, it is coming from your equipment.

This brings us to bugs. If you get only three or four bugs in each coat of paint you're doing fine. All bugs are genetically programmed to throw themselves into wet paint. Painting at night is to invite a natural non-skid surface. The wet-paint-is-to-die-for gene, the Devarona-Louganis gene, was useless to bugs for 100 million years. Only in the last two centuries have bugs been able to become fully self-actualized. The genetic programming is inversely proportional to the size of the bug: for little bugs it is irresistible; big bugs will sometimes tarry until the paint has skinned over. Even bugs that can't fly will climb the walls and trek across the

I apply paint on the interior hull by moving from my left to my right and rolling from rail to rail. The rails and upper edge of the okume at the sheer have had five coast of varnish applied earlier to seal the grain. The interior hull to rail edge is not tapered off; any paint that gets on the edge can be wiped off with a little thinner on a paper towel after the whole interior has been painted.

around the hull. During the painting process you will be working to make it look like the paint is a single sheet of paint, as if it went on all at once. To get this effect you must plan where to leave edges of freshly applied paint that can't be immediately painted over. It is best to leave these dry edges on natural occurring breaks in the hull such as the chine. It is also best to plan an application sequence that has paint going on at the limit of your reach first, and then subsequent applications in closer to your body. This way you aren't reaching across wet paint and possibly dripping paint onto an already painted area.

My painting sequence (I am right-handed) for the exterior of the hull is to start at one stem and paint on both sides of the hull until I reach the chines. I then paint a section of bottom and the near side. I then go around the hull and paint the portion of that side that could not be be reached from the other side. I then paint a section of bottom and near side. I go to the other side, where I started, and repeat until I reach the end of the chines. I finish up painting rail to rail as I pass the chine ends and approach the other stem.

On the interior of the hull, I go from one end to the other, moving from my left to right and staying on the same side of the hull. I change sides of the hull only to get up under the breasthook on the far end. The roller won't reach into the interior angle of the stems and up into the corner formed by the hull sides and breasthooks. Remember that the foam brush does only a marginal job of transporting and applying paint, so it doesn't do very well in these areas either. I use a bristle brush to do the interior stems and the hull sides back to the inner edge of the breasthook. Because I don't want to put up with the bother of cleaning a good quality brush, I use one of the cheap

ceiling to get into position for a triple back flip with a full twist in the pike position into your paint. (Degree of difficulty 3.8)

Unless it's a large bug that's stuck in paint that you applied just moments before, it's best to leave it until the paint is dry and then sand it out, hopefully without cutting through the paint. Try to remember that you and your wet paint are playing a pivotal role in a grand cosmic scheme. Should you remember to ask, it will be explained to you in the afterlife.

Before applying paint, you have to form a clear mental picture of how you will proceed disposable chip brushes. Before I use the brush I pull on the bristles to remove as many of the loose ones as possible. Inevitably a few bristles end up in the paint but these can be lifted out with the corner of the brush.

Using the Foam Roller and Brush

At long last, it's time to discuss putting on paint or varnish with the foam roller and brush. The situation is this: you have just gone to the bathroom and taken the phone off the hook; the paint or varnish is mixed and waiting in a covered container; the hull has been sanded, vacuumed, wiped with thinner; any required masking tape has been applied, and you've wiped the area to be painted or varnished with a tack cloth; the space is relatively dust free and air motion is at a minimum;

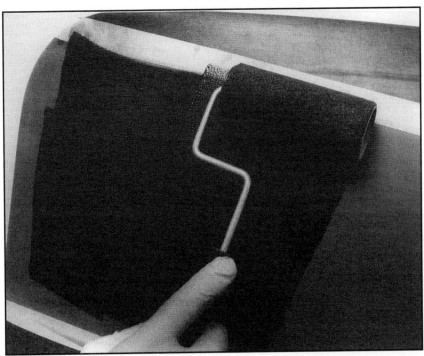

This is the beginning of the first color coat going over two coats of primer. Both the waterline for the graphite-filled special bottom coating and rails are taped off. The first vertical stripe of paint was very thin so I relocated the roller. From the size of the bubbles in the paint, I see I overloaded the roller.

you have your plastic gloves and safety glasses on and the roller, tray, and brush are nearby.

One more thing, always have a backup roller cover and foam brush cleaned and ready for use. That way when you drop one of the ones in use, you can get a replacement and keep painting with little interruption. It is good to have a second foil covered paint tray made up too, for the moment you drop everything in slack-jawed wonder as you look back and see how good it looks. Don't laugh! I've done it twice; once during the photo session for this book!

It will take about 30 minutes to do either the inside or outside of the hull. For those 30 minutes you are the slave of the roller, brush and "wet edge." Remember that the first coat of paint is not only the hardest to apply, it also shows inconsistencies in the film thickness as blotches. Not to worry, any blotchiness will disappear as successive coats are applied and you get experienced in the technique.

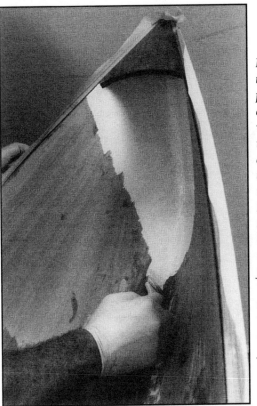

I use a chip brush to apply both primer and paint at the stems where the foam roller can't reach and a foam brush tends to create runs and drips. I paint the underside of the breasthooks even when the tops are finished bright. The 2" masking tape on the rails is actually taping off the rail to hull joint on the hull exterior.

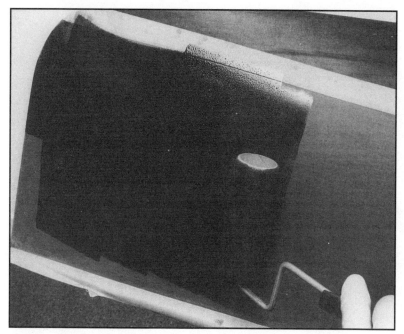

Use the roller horizontally to evenly distribute the paint. Because this roller is heavily loaded, I will widen the strip to the right to spread out the paint. The bubbles just above the roller are about the right size and distribution for proper film thickness. Above and to the left of the roller the bubbles are too large; if the paint is not redistributed, it will run after being tipped with the brush.

it. Turn the roller 90°and go over the paint with horizontal strokes.

If the paint shows even the slightest tendency to run, you are applying it too thickly. Widen the paint stripe on the hull to distribute excess paint over a large area. Next time, put less paint on the roller. Take heart, it's all a matter of experience which only comes from doing. Two or three more coats are needed and your technique will improve greatly with each application. Try to leave a relatively thick line of paint on the edge of the stripe in the direction you are proceeding around the hull. This edge is the infamous "wet edge," and on it hangs the whole question of whether the paint will look like one smooth coat or a patchwork affair. Hang the roller on the edge of the roller tray with the little hook-like things on the handle.

Pick up the foam brush. Dip the last 1/8" of the tip of the brush into the paint in the tray. Holding the brush lightly between the thumb and first two fingers, quickly and lightly wipe the painted surface

Pour about a tablespoon of paint into a small container and paint under the breasthook and out 6" or so on the hull sides. Even up the paint film with a few tipping strokes with the foam brush. Set the bristle brush aside to do the other breasthook later.

Pour about two or three tablespoons of paint from the covered mixing container into the tray. Replace the lid on the container. Take the tray in your non-dominant hand and swirl the paint so that it covers the bottom of the tray. Tilt the tray so that excess paint gathers at one edge. Load the roller by rolling it across the bottom of the tray. As you lift the roller let it spin a little so that paint gets pretty much all over the foam. Complete coverage of the roller is desirable but not necessary. Keep the roller tray in your non-dominant hand.

Apply paint to the hull in overlapping vertical strokes in a stripe about 9" wide. Use moderate to heavy pressure on the roller. The paint should have an even distribution of pin-head or smaller bubbles in

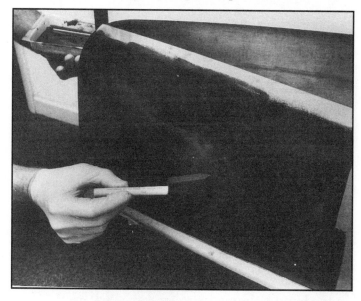

I am tipping in 6" wide vertical bands and moving from left to right. Hold the brush very lightly with your first three fingers. Remember that the brush must be moving when it first contacts the paint on the hull and as it is lifted from the paint before the end of the stroke.

The paint to the left has been tipped and looks pretty good, but don't stop to admire your handiwork. After carefully but quickly reloading the roller, apply paint about 1/2 a roller width from the old wet edge. If the roller is overloaded, roll some paint out to the right. Watch the bubble size and, when it is correct, come back and cover the thin unrolled strip.

with overlapping strokes going lengthwise on the hull. These "tipping" strokes should be made away from the wet edge. If you are moving along the hull from left to right, the tipping strokes go from right to left. The brush must be in motion whenever it is in contact with the hull. The strokes start above the paint then drop onto the paint. The brush is lifted off the paint before the stroke is completed.

At this point it is easy to be overly concerned with the evenness of the paint film. Don't; there are more important matters to attend to. Vastly more important than the film thickness is the state of the leading, or "wet edge" of the paint just applied. Another stripe of paint must be applied to the hull and overlap the old wet edge before it loses enough thinner to thicken or, worse yet, skin over. The time frame here is maybe as long as two minutes.

Swirl the roller pan to spread the puddle of paint across the bottom. Then tilt it to get the excess out of the way. Stick the handle of the foam brush between the ring and pinky fingers on the hand holding the roller tray. Pick up the roller and evenly load it with paint; it will be easier than the first time. Do not over-load the roller. Apply paint to the hull again with vertical overlapping strokes. The first stroke should

be about 1/2 a roller width from the wet edge on the unpainted portion of the hull. Roll towards the wet edge and overlap the wet edge by about half a roller width. Work back away from the wet edge until the freshly painted stripe is about 9" wide. Turn the roller and go over the freshly applied paint with horizontal strokes to evenly distribute the paint. Hang the roller from the tray.

From here on, each stripe of fresh paint will be tipped with the foam brush in at least two sections; the area over the old, now covered wet edge, and the rest of the stripe. Over the old wet edge, make the tipping strokes about 6" long extending back into the previous stripe of paint. The most recently applied paint should have kept the edge of the earlier applied paint liquid. You are trying to redistribute some of the two layers of paint at the old wet edge.

After the old wet edge has been tipped, finish up the rest of the stripe in one or two vertical passes of tipping strokes. As you can see, no paint is being applied by the brush. The brush has two jobs: to redistribute paint already applied by the roller at the old wet edge and knock down the bubbles everywhere else. Only the tip of the brush has to be wet, so it needs be dipped into the paint in the tray very seldom.

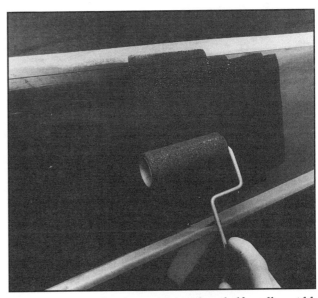

Remember to overlap the new paint about half a roller width over the old wet edge. Move along smartly, alternately rolling and tipping as you proceed around the hull.

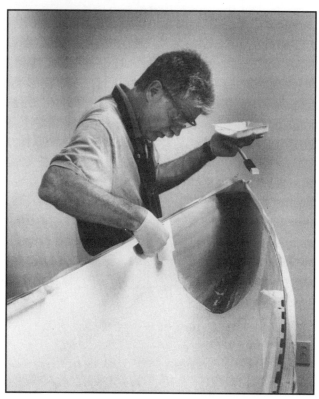

Here is the classic stance of the solo roller and brush painter. When the roller is in use the brush is held between the ring finger and pinky of the hand holding the paint tray. When the brush is in use, the roller hangs from the near side of the roller tray.

Check the tray; it may need more paint. If so, add a few tablespoons from the covered container. Remember that paint in the tray is constantly losing thinner which makes the job of maintaining and then hiding the wet edge harder. Hold only as much paint in the tray as is consistent with proceeding smoothly and quickly around the hull without wasting too much time refilling the tray. Once again, it's a matter of getting the paint on quickly and consistently and it will get easier each time you do it. *Courage, mes enfants.*

Proceed around the hull. Don't get in panic if the color is not perfectly even. On subsequent coats, stagger the wet edges of the paint stripes between the preceding ones and it will be just fine. The third coat of paint will probably go on near perfectly, without a sign of patchiness or uneven color.

In the preceding discussion, I assumed that you will be working alone. If perchance you have an assistant, one person does the rolling, the other the tipping. The tipper should work as closely as possible behind the roller. The tipper must stay out of the roller's way. The biggest danger with two people is that the tipper will overwork the paint while waiting for the roller to finish a section and move on. The person rolling will be continuously busy, the tipper may have some idle moments. A good tipper will point out areas that have been missed or other problems in a supportive, non-confrontational way.

Clean Up

Now it's time to clean up. Clean up will take about 15 minutes and use two to three tablespoons of thinner and all of the remaining paper towels. Do the clean up with your rubber gloves on, they are a lot easier and safer to clean than your hands.

Never return excess paint from the roller tray to the mixing container or to the paint can, throw it out. You can take a chance and try to save extra paint in the mixing container for the next coat. If your mixing container has a screw-on, air-tight lid it is quite possible that the paint will remain usable for the few days needed for the paint to fully dry. When it is time to paint again, add more paint, additives, and thinner to the old paint if it has not skinned over. If it has skinned over, throw it out, clean the container, and start from the beginning.

Start clean up by wiping excess paint from the tray with a paper towel. Leaving traces of paint in the tray is all right. Pour about two tablespoons of paint thinner or mineral spirits into the tray. Remove the roller from the frame. I find this easiest to do by grabbing the end of the roller with a pair of pliers and pulling it off. Discard the roller. Dip a folded paper towel in the thinner in the tray and use it to clean the roller frame and its handle. If you aren't using the lidded container to save excess paint, wipe it out with the dampened paper towel. Discard the paper towel. Dampen another paper towel with thinner and complete the cleaning of the lidded container and its top. Use this towel to complete the cleaning of the tray.

Although the Poly-Brush® brushes are disposable and designed for a single use, after they have been used for tipping there should be paint on only the last 3/16" or 1/4" of the foam brush. This paint is easily cleaned and the brush can be reused. It takes careful cleaning to prevent minute residues from contaminating the brush and causing it to stiffen. Still, reusing the brush for multiple coats of undercoat or primer, or for the first two coats of top coat paint will save a few dollars. I was able to apply seven of the eight coats of varnish to the prototype **Sweet Dream** with a single brush. It is best to always apply the last coat of paint or varnish with a new brush.

Before it is sanded, the first coat of primer or undercoater should be a consistent opaque coating.

In cleaning the brush as much care must be taken not to pull pieces of foam from the chisel edge as to getting the paint or varnish residue out of the foam. Clean the brush in six stages. The first stage is to gently squeeze excess paint or varnish from the brush into a folded paper towel working from near the handle towards the tip. Squeeze the brush between your fingers and do not pull on the brush, especially as you get to the tip. Pour about a quarter of a teaspoon of thinner into the brush and again squeeze the residue out into a paper towel. Again, be careful not to pull small pieces of foam off the sharpened tip. Repeat the application and removal of thinner three more times. The last stage is to work a few drops of Brushing Liquid into the brush. Wrap the brush loosely in a folded paper towel and put it aside for another use.

If you used tape to mask off the rails or cut in a waterline, now is the time to remove it. Pull up a corner of the tape and then pull it off by doubling it back on itself.

Use your last paper towels and a few drops of thinner to clean off your gloves. That's all there is to it.

I just can't keep my fingers out of wet paint. I just have to see if it's dry. For me the best thing to do, once the clean up is finished, is leave the shop, close the door, and come back in no less than four hours. The paint won't be fully dried, but it will have a thick skin. If I'm careful, my fingerprints will be light enough that they'll come out in the light sanding between coats.

Sanding Between Coats of Paint or Varnish

You sand between coats of paint and varnish for at least four reasons: to remove dust and bugs, to flatten very small irregularities, to roughen the surface for the next coat; and to create a non-glossy background so you can see where you're putting the new paint. My suspicion is that breaking the smooth surface

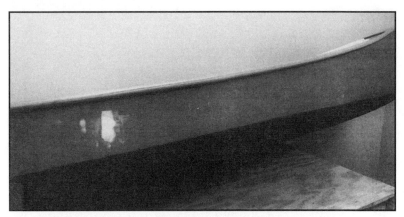

The consistent color of primer makes it easy to find dings or other uneven areas of the hull. Here a depression around the taped butt joint has been filled with surfacing putty. After the surfacing putty is sanded and spot painted with primer, the whole hull will be sanded and a second primer coat will be applied.

of the hardened film helps the thinners in the new paint and varnish melt an infinitely thin layer and thereby turn the two coats into one thick coat.

Sand between coats with the highest grit that will do the job, usually 180 or 220. If the paper clogs or makes little balls or ropes of sanded material, the paint isn't dry enough. Wait 12 hours and try again. Sand with light strokes using a firm foam or rubber/felt backed block. Remember to sand radiused corners very lightly and then only every other coat. Because varnish has no pigmented solids, it shows sanding marks more readily than paint. Use one higher grit of sandpaper on varnish.

Primer and undercoater require special sanding techniques. The first coats of either are meant to fill up the minute holes that are part of the wood grain. The first coat is sanded to "translucency." To me, that means that the grain in the wood is visible but there is a thin, cloudy white layer of primer still there. There will probably be some rough spots up under the breasthooks, and maybe on the interior chines where you will sand through to the wood or epoxy. Touch up these spots, and remember where they are so you can do better on subsequent coats.

Sanding to translucency creates a massive amount of dust. In volume, you sand off more

than you put on! Save yourself a lot of work and do this sanding out of doors.

After the first coat of primer or undercoater, carefully inspect the hull for dings and scratches. The relatively consistent color will show things that were missed earlier. If the dings bother you, this is the last good time to fill them with surfacing putty.

Okume is a relatively porous wood with large pores in the grain. In reality, it will take more than two coats of primer or undercoater to fill the pores. With only two coats, the grain will not be completely hidden, but after all it is a wooden boat. If you must have a mirror finish, keep applying primer and sanding to translucency (make that trans-lunacy) until the pores are filled. I have no idea how many coats that will be: I can live with a little wood grain so I never put on more than three coats.

The role of the last coat of primer or undercoater is to create an even color background for the color coats that follow. It makes no sense to put on the last coat and sand it to the same degree of transparency as the first coat(s). On the last coat of primer, sand with 220 grit paper just to get a smooth surface, then stop. Remember, the goal is to get a smooth, hard, evenly-colored background for the color coats.

Special Bottom Coatings

If you anticipate using your *Sweet Dream* where submerged rocks, stumps, etc. can be reasonably expected, consider increasing the abrasion resistance of the exterior of the hull. Some alternatives are coating the hull below the waterline with graphite impregnated epoxy and cladding either the entire exterior or just the portion below the waterline with 6 or 8 oz. fiberglass cloth. Filling the weave in the cloth with colloidal silica or graphite impregnated epoxy might also be in order. If you anticipate often carrying camping or other equipment in your *Sweet Dream*, you should consider cladding the interior bottom with 4 or 6-oz. glass cloth.

I often put graphite-filled epoxy on the bottom of my canoes. It makes a low maintenance, abrasion-resistant finish with a distinctive slate grey color. The secret is to get as much graphite into the epoxy as possible and still be able to get a relatively smooth surface. Paint-like smoothness is not necessary because the coating will be sanded with 180 grit sandpaper. Still, mixing the graphite with either West System 205 or 206 hardener can result in a lumpy mess. I have found the West System 207 Special Coating Hardener best for this purpose. 207 is intended for coating surfaces to be finished bright. It has enhanced flow characteristics that help get a relatively smooth surface when graphite is added in high proportions.

I put the graphite-filled epoxy on before the hull is painted, but only after at least three coats of varnish are on the rails. Sanding between coats creates a fine black dust that gets everywhere and would otherwise lodge in the grain of the rails.

First put a waterline on the hull (see the following section). Start the coating about 1/4" above the waterline so that it can be feathered

After sanding the first coat of primer or undercoater, the coating will look a little spotty. Not to worry; apply the second coat and sand lightly. You may use a third coat if you're trying to completely fill the grain.

to the hull. Use 2" wide tape to define the edge of the coating. It will take 12 pumps of epoxy to cover the bottom. Do one half of the bottom at a time: two batches of 6 pumps each. Add 1-1/2 scoops of graphite to each batch. Add 1/4 scoop at a time, mixing well between each.

Apply a thick, even coating with the roller and brush. It goes on about three times thicker than paint. Watch around the forefeet and the sides where the coating will tend to run. After the coating has cured it will be glossy, coal black. Sand with 80 or 100 grit paper to get a fairly even surface. A palm sander works well here. A dual action sander requires special care to keep from sanding through around the hollow at the forefoot. Taper the edge at the waterline by hand. Be sure to taper the edge at the water line to the hull. Apply two more coats, one about 1/8" above the intended waterline, and the last right at the waterline. After each coat the surface will be smoother. After sanding the third coat with 100 then 180 sandpaper, rub the surface with a green Scotchbrite pad.

Determining and Marking a Waterline

Where the canoe is still a working craft, waterlines on the canoes are not unusual. They are used to check the trim of a loaded canoe, and are sometimes the boundary between a special bottom coating and the hull paint above. Where the canoe is used mostly for recreation, waterlines are rare. When I put a special coating on the bottom of a canoe, there has to be a dividing line somewhere, so I choose a suitable waterline. Fortunately, determining and drawing a waterline, any waterline, is relatively easy.

Determining a waterline is figuring out where the line must be put on the hull to meet a given loading condition; say a 190 pound paddler and 30 pounds of equipment. Marking a waterline is getting the line itself onto the hull once you figure out where it goes.

You can volumetrically determine a hull's waterline for a certain weight to be carried by going through a heavy duty numeric exercise involving multiple calculations using Simpson's First Rule. For a small hull such as a canoe, it's simpler to just float the hull with the desired weight on board. Presto; if the hull floats, it's on the desired waterline.

It's a little more complex than that, but not much. The waterline can be determined with the hull unpainted.

Starting amidships, run lengths of water resistant tape down both sides of the hull (duct tape works well) from the rail, and around the chine at 1' intervals. Put pieces of tape on the leading edge of the stem and 4" back on either side. On the pieces of tape on the stems, mark and number 1" intervals starting 10" from the rail.

You'll need a carpenter's level, a straight piece of wood that is long enough to span the rails amidships, a pen and pencil, and weights. I use the weighted sacks used in the construction sequence. I put the waterline at the 50 pound increment just below where the expected loading will be. This way the waterline is submerged when the canoe is underway. For up to 200 pounds of paddler and gear, I use 150 pounds or three sacks to determine the waterline.

Now it's off to someplace where there is knee or thigh deep water that is absolutely calm. The shallow end of a swimming pool is fine. You don't need this much water to float the canoe, it gets the hull up to a convenient height. Put the weights in the canoe amidships. Shift the weights fore and aft until the waterline at each stem is identical, measured down from the rails.

Put the straight piece of wood across the rails amidships. Place the carpenter's level on the piece of wood. Adjust the sacks side to side until the hull is level. Check the waterlines at the ends to make sure they haven't changed. If so, adjust the sacks fore and aft to correct. Check the level and adjust the sacks side to side if necessary.

Go around the hull and mark the waterline at each piece of duct tape with which ever of the pen or pencil works on the wet tape. That's all there is to determining the waterline. Now it's back to the shop to mark the waterline on the hull.

Tape a batten against one side of the hull so that it goes through each of the waterline marks on the tapes. With the batten securely taped in place, mark the waterline on the hull with a pencil or pen. Do not use any kind of felt tip marker. Whatever is in the things will bleed through x-teen layers of paint. It's like an atomic melt down, you can't stop it. Remove the batten. Repeat on the other side. The waterline is marked on the hull but there is one more step needed to make it useful over the life of the canoe.

When you are sanding and painting, it's very easy and very frustrating to lose a waterline. To prevent this from happening, mark the waterline with awl punches. Starting amidships, put a deep awl punch every 4" along the waterline. With the japanese saw make a shallow cut on the mark at the leading edge of the stems. Don't worry if the awl goes just through the plywood in places, fill the holes from the inside of the hull with some thickened epoxy.

The holes from the awl are not likely to be sanded nor painted out. At 4" apart, the holes are close enough together to get a smooth curve when applying masking tape. Granted, the holes will show as small depressions even when

You really can do anything you want if you just put your paddle in the water one stroke at a time. You've just got to be willing to invest the time and to give yourself permission."

"And the money," I added.

"Well, no," she said, "if you've got the time, you don't need so much money because you could stop and work along the way..."

Beth Johnson,
Yukon Wild

painting is completed, but that's what you want. When it's time to refinish, you can sand the top coats of paint with abandon. When the hull is ready for the new paint, the waterline marks are still there, ready for taping and repainting.

DO NOT CUT THE WATERLINE IN WITH A KNIFE OR BURN IT INTO THE HULL WITH A WOODBURNING TOOL. In either case you can easily cut through the outer ply. Should the outer ply begin to pucker outward you have a major problem; a crack is developing and it might just unzip the bottom. In the curved sections at the ends, the center ply was bent rather forcefully during construction. The outer ply is restraining the center ply from splitting apart. Cutting through the outer ply would invite the splitting of the center ply. Stick with the awl punches; they work.

Annual Maintenance

There is no avoiding it; a wooden boat needs occasional work to keep it looking fresh. Usually this means retouching the paint and refreshing the varnish annually.

If the scratches and dings in the paint are small and relatively few in number, reapplying paint to the scratch with a toothpick or small brush may be all that's required. For larger blemishes, light sanding with 220 grit sandpaper may be required to smooth the area. Rebuild the coatings that are sanded through to get a smooth surface. Mask around the sanded area and repaint. In the event you repaint the complete hull, sand all over with 220 or 320 grit paper. Try not to sand through the color coats and expose the primer. If you don't sand through to the primer, one new color coat should suffice. If the primer is exposed, you may be able to spot paint the primer and follow with a full color coat.

As a minimum, the varnish should get a new top coat every year. Sand all bright work lightly with 320 grit paper and reapply one or two coats. Ideally, one fresh coat of varnish will replace both the varnish lost over the past year to the sun and the small amount sanded off. If your canoe spent a lot of time outdoors, apply two new coats. The goal in refreshing varnish is to maintain the full thickness of eight coats of varnish without extra buildup or reduction over time.

If dings and scratches extend through the existing varnish to the wood (often shown clearly by dark staining of the wood under the breakthrough) you have to sand through the surrounding varnish to the stained wood. Try to remove the stain with light sanding. Do what you can without creating a deep depression in the wood, or your psyche. Ensure that the exposed wood is dry before applying varnish. The water that caused the staining also lifts the varnish over the stain. There is no sense whatsoever in applying varnish over stained wood; the new varnish traps excessive water under the coating which will lead to further coating failure and staining.

Apply successive coats of varnish to the sanded area to build the varnish thickness up to match the rest of the brightwork. Feather the edges of each dried coat to blend in with the surrounding varnish. Apply one complete coat of varnish to finish the job.

Annual maintenance is an integral part of owning a boat. Any boat, irrespective of what it's made of, will last longer and look better if it gets a thorough going over before each season. For wooden boats, the need is greater and more immediate. The work can be a chore or a source of quiet joy. Revarnishing in a warm workshop on a cold winter night can remind you of the warmth of the summer or of spending time with family and friends. It can kindle a sense of anticipation for the first trip that will come as soon as the ice is out. Here follows a poem by Garrett Conover that integrates the mundane tasks of winter maintenance into the more active outdoors aspects of canoeing. The poem expresses the joy and renewal of spirit that canoeing can create, even as winter lays heavily on the land.

While Readying the Fleet

for Neil McDonald

After the rush of ice
while Bloodroot blooms
and the freshet roars.
That is the time for
renewal.

Each hull is turned
and touched.
Every scratch telling
a truth,
the spell of a season past.

Hands full of love
ask forgiveness with
sandpaper, patch, and glue.
Sing praise where the finish
is yet bright and smooth.
Those surfaces that
keep the tale alive
between the lines.

Fractures in plank and rib
weave the story sharp.
Speak of harder knocks.
Mistakes.
Remember each.
Revive such lessons and every
promise given,
for these are solemn vows.

Varnish bold upon the rails,
bottoms dandy in fresh shellac,
shine with an eagerness to go.
Complete again
the true canoes are free
to greet the Birds-eye Primrose,
surge of water,
reach of sky,
air stretched tight with song.

And do not overlook
a most precious cargo.
Embraced by light and shade,
surrounding the hull,
enfolding the packs.
Invisible, ethereal,
pure paradox it is;
ancient, new,
perfectly female and male.
Chalice
Chariot
Chrysalis
Dream.

There must be no waiting now.
Let invitation
fling us towards familiar mystery.
Let each flash of blade
every tracery of shore
capture us born anew.
Hearts glad
senses tuned to pitch.
Spirits soaring wide,
flying wild.

Garrett Conover, 1995
Used with author's permission,
first published in **Wooden Canoe**,
Vol. 19, No. 1, February '96.

Part 3: Optional Accessories

The building techniques in this part are intended for intermediate and advanced builders. Beginning and first time builders should build their first *Sweet Dream* using the standard techniques in Part I. These advanced techniques add little to *Sweet Dream's* performance. They add considerable time and complexity to the construction. For the most part, the results are in the area of esthetics. They may come close to being gimmickry. I will leave that for you to decide.

Curved Structural Members

Curved structural members can be made in a number of ways:

❧ carving from solid stock,

❧ steam bending on a form, or

❧ laminating thin layers of wood into the desired shape on a form.

Carving is the most difficult way to get curved members. The curved piece is gotten out of a piece of wood thicker than the 3/4" stock that is used elsewhere in the hull. The thicker wood must be bought separately or laminated from the 3/4" stock. Afterwards the curves are achieved by chiseling, planing, and-or cutting on a band saw. This method is unnecessarily difficult, and I won't be discussing it further.

Making a bending form. Both laminated and steam bent thwarts require a form to shape the parts around, so we'll start there.

To get the curve for the form, clamp a metal yard stick or thin wooden batten across the hull to the outer rails at a thwart location. Both the steam bent and laminated thwarts will lose a little of their curvature when they are taken off the bending form. Push inward on one end to get the yard stick to hump up a quarter inch or so above the natural curve. This extra curvature helps minimize the spring back. Even still the curvature will be somewhat less than a segment of a circle that is tangential to the upper surface of the rails. To my eye the tangential circle segment is too high a curve. It looks more like the handle on an Easter basket than a proper thwart.

Put one of the pieces of okume that were cut off the sides of the bottom pad across the the rails standing upright next to the yard stick. Draw the curve on the okume.

> Waking or sleeping, I dream of boats — usually of rather small boats under a slight press of sail. Young feller, if someone can't or won't buy you a boat — a decent one, that is — get anything you can, even if you have to make it.
>
> Eugene Connett,
> *Spirit of Adventure, Tales from the Skipper*

To get an appropriate curve for curved thwarts, clamp a metal yard stick to the outer rails at a thwart location. Transfer the curve to a piece of the cut-off from the bottom pad. This is the unaugmented curve. To get a slightly higher curve, press inward on one end of the yardstick.

It is essential that the bending form is an unbendable piece in the shape of the curve just taken from the hull. Glue two 30" pieces of 2x4 together side by side to get a 3-1/2"x3-1/2" block — carpenter's glue will do. When the glue is dry, tack the piece of ply with the curve on it to the block so that the top of the curve is just below the top of the 2x4s. Cut out the curve on a band saw. A saber saw can't cut both 2x4s at once, and it's impossible to cut identical curves on two separate 2x4s.

Check the capacity of your clamps. For 4" clamps, a 1" strip must be taken off the flat side of the form. Attach the one or two pieces cut off the top of the 2x4s to the bottom of the form with carpenter's glue. This creates identical curves on the top and bottom of the form and the clamps holding either the steamed or laminated thwart blank are stable and don't slip like they do when the bottom surface of the form is flat.

This form is more than stiff enough to resist the tendency of the pieces being bent or laminated to straighten out.

Steamed thwart blanks can be bent on the form as it is.

On the other hand, laminating on the simple form will be difficult and messy. The pieces of the lamination all seem to have a life of their own when they are covered in epoxy and subject to clamping pressure. One edge of all the pieces must be lined up in the stack. With the form as it is, the laminates, slip, slide, and twist until the second clamp is on and tight. There is still a good chance that the laminates are skewed end for end. Add to this the frustration of squeeze-out getting on everything in sight, and you can see that getting a usable blank is going to be the devil's own work.

With just a little more effort, the laminating process becomes a piece of cake. A board screwed to the back of the form adds a significant degree of control over the the individual laminates and the laminate stack as a whole. Controlling the stack becomes just a matter of keeping the pieces from slipping

My bending forms are set up so that either large or small clamps can be used. Small sockets are cut into the form with a drill bit and then squared to accept the clamp jaw. This method does not reduce the rigidity of the form. Note the pressure pads between the clamps and the thwart to prevent the clamps from scaring or staining the thwart.

along their axes until the first clamp is in position. The backing board should be about 10"x40". It will catch and contain all the squeeze-out before it runs onto your work surface, shoes, etc.

A backboard affixed directly to the back of the form does have an undesirable feature; the squeeze-out from the stack has no where to go on the back of the stack. This is easily remedied with standoffs to the backing board only 1/4" or so thick. Attach the standoffs to the backing board on 3" or 4" centers with brads and/or carpenter's glue. Put plastic sheet between the bending form and the standoffs before screwing the two together.

Steam bending is the easiest of the three ways to get curved thwarts and backrest stretcher. It does involve some risk of injury as the steam and the hot wood can cause burns. The risk can be minimized by wearing thick gloves and safety goggles.

[*Author's note:* As I was writing the final drafts of this book, the technique of dry heat bending came to my attention. *Wooden Boat* magazine, March/April 1996, Number 129, has an article, "Bending Wood with Dry Heat" by David Peebles, that explains the process. It appears to be easier and quicker than steam bending. The only drawback appears to be the expense of buying a high capacity heat gun, what looks to be a paint stripping model. If you've already got the gun, you should consider using this method. I'm checking with my friends to locate one of the guns. If I can find one, I'm going to give it a try.]

The curves in the thwarts are relatively gentle. Only a simple press or form is needed to achieve the desired shape. The only problem with this method is scrounging up a way to generate steam, make a suitable steam box, and get the steam from the generator to the steam box.

Steam is elemental stuff of great power. At 212° F as water passes from a hot liquid state into gaseous steam, it absorbs about five and a half times as much heat as it does going from 0° F to 212° F. When steam condenses from a gas back into a liquid, this same amount of heat is released by the steam. Steam bending uses this excess heat energy and an abundance of heated water molecules that are absorbed by the wood. When the wood is in a semi-plastic state it is clamped onto a form or otherwise bent into the desired shape. After a cooling and drying period of at least 24 hours, the wood holds the new shape permanently.

Here is the equipment that I use for laminating thwarts. At the bottom of the picture the plastic that will catch the squeeze-out is turned back to show the standoffs. Immediately above the form are the protective strip and pressure pads discussed in the text. Laminating can proceed quickly when all the required equipment is laid out and ready at hand.

The steam bending process uses the heat given off by the condensing steam to soften the wood. There is absolutely no need for the steam to be under pressure. Steam becomes a

Dramatic lighting creates a picture in keeping with the power of live steam. This is my "Millennium Steambox." With its 6"x6" end opening, it can hold four pairs of thwarts. Despite its impressive name it is made of readily available materials and parts. I have just opened the box after one hour of steaming and steam is rolling upwards out of the box, although you can't see it against the light background. Wear heavy gloves and safety glasses to prevent burns. Get the thwart onto the bending form as quickly as possible.

wickedly dangerous substance when subjected to greater than atmospheric pressure. In the following discussion it is assumed that there will be lots of opportunities for steam to leak out of the generator-hose-box system. Absolutely leak-proof joints are a screw-up. Ensure that there are adequate vents in the steam box for excess steam to escape.

Steaming the thwarts and back rest stretcher is a small job. The size of the parts in the generator-hose-box system can be quite small and yet be effective. The steam generator isn't really a big deal; just about any kettle will do the job.

Getting the steam from the generator to the steam box requires a conduit that won't collapse when subjected to high temperature. The easiest and safest thing to do is buy a length of radiator hose. You don't need much, 12" of hose will do fine. Get hose that fits loosely inside or

outside the pot's spout. As necessary, use a loosely wadded rag to close any gaps.

The steam box need be only big enough to hold two thwarts with enough extra volume that the thwarts can be supported off the bottom and steam can circulate freely. A box 3" square on the ends and 33 inches long is sufficient.

The steam box can be made of wood. Plywood is not a good choice as it tends to delaminate under extremes of temperature and humidity. Four pieces of 3/4"x3"x36" stock can be screwed together to make a more than adequate box.

It is best if the steam is admitted into the box at the center and vented at either end. However, just sticking the hose in one end of the box and filling the crevices with rags will do. At the end(s) of the box farthest from the steam inlet, drill four 1/4" holes for vents. The end(s) of the box can be closed up with a suitably sized piece of 3/4" stock. Arrange the box so that the end opposite the steam inlet is lower and drill a hole in the bottom so that the water that condenses inside the box can drain out.

The pieces of the steam box system are small enough that it can be operated in your kitchen. When steam is put into a wooden steam box, it will give off a distinctive woody smell. Resinous woods like cedar or southern pine give off a strong turpentiney smell which I find not unpleasant, but other members of my family disagree. So you may have to shift operations back out to the shop with a portable heat source. It is best to do a dry run with everything at room temperature.

The bending operation goes like this: Put the parts to be bent in the steam box with supports under them so steam can circulate freely around them. Fill the kettle and bring it to a boil. Attach the hose to the pot. Stick the hose in the steam box. In a few seconds excess steam should vent from the vent holes. If it doesn't, find out why and fix it. Steam the parts for 15 minutes for each 1/4" thickness measured across the widest end grain dimension, one hour for thwarts with 3/4" by 1" end dimensions. Ensure that the pot does not boil dry during the steaming time.

After the required steaming time, put on thick leather gloves and safety goggles. Remove one piece from the steam box . As quickly as possible clamp it to the form. Five clamps is the minimum needed. Put wooden pads between the thwart and metal clamps to prevent permanent staining. Repeat the clamping for additional parts as necessary.

Leave the parts on the form for at least 24 hours, 48 hours is preferred.Cut the thwarts to length and mount them as for the flat thwarts in the building sequence, see page 56 .

Laminating is not so much difficult as it is messy. A lamination is made up of a number of thin strips. The strips can be between 1/16" and 3/16" thick. They can be ripped from 3/4" stock

If you have enough clamps, the bending form will hold two thwarts at once. Here 14 clamps are in use.

although much of the wood ends up in the scrap barrel in the form of sawdust. The faces of the laminates must be relatively smooth. This can require considerable sanding if the table saw or band saw used to cut them is not correctly set up. While it is possible to cut the laminates wide enough to get two thwarts from a single laminate stack, the individual laminates would have to be about 2-1/4" wide: two 1" wide thwarts and 1/4" for the saw kerf to separate them and for trimming. Practically, it is easier to make the thwarts individually from laminates 1-1/4" wide.

The messiness comes in when the laminates are spread with epoxy and clamped to the bending form. Cover the upper surface of the form with masking tape, duct tape, or plastic to prevent its becoming a permanent part of the lamination.

I have found that I don't need a rigid piece on the outer face of the laminate stack. I can get consistent pressure and nearly invisible glue lines with ten or more clamps with individual pressure pads that span the form from side to side. The pads need be no more than 1" wide and long enough to span the laminate stack: 1-1/4" for a single thwart; 2-1/4" for two thwarts laminated in a single piece.

Mark the face of the form with evenly spaced lines, one for each clamp. The last clamps should be right at the end of the stack.

On the outside of the stack, in addition to laminate pressure pads, I use a protecting strip to spread the clamping pressure and prevent the outer ply in the laminate stack from being dented. This protecting strip can be made from a piece of scrap hull material as wide and as long as the laminates. Cover the inside of the protecting strip with duct tape or plastic to prevent it too from becoming part of the lamination.

With your laminates in hand and at least 10 clamps that open wide

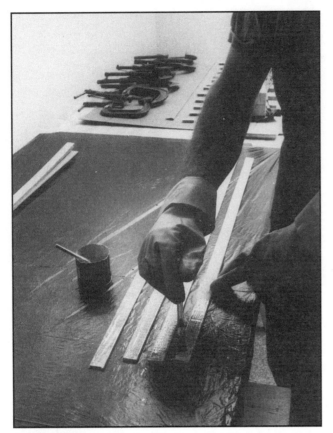

Spreading epoxy on the laminates gets really messy. I cover the work surface with plastic to keep the mess under control. Behind me the laminating equipment is laid out neatly so that clamping can proceed quickly.

enough to span the form, the laminates, the protecting strip, and a pressure pad, it's time to laminate a thwart blank.

Lay out the laminates in a side by side array. Mix 2 pumps of epoxy. (If your laminates are rough, that is if they show saw tooth marks, mix a second 1-pump batch of epoxy thickened with 1 scoop of filler.) With an acid brush, spread epoxy on the exposed face of all the laminates. (If you are using the thickened mixture, spread a layer on the laminate on the left end of the array. You may wish to use a second acid brush for the thickened mixture.) Pick up the laminate second from the left, turn it over, and spread epoxy on its back side. (Spread some of the thickened mixture on this laminate.) Place it on top of the piece on the left end of the row. Continue in this

fashion going from left to right until all the laminates are on the stack.

Place the laminate stack on the form. Place the protecting strip on the outside of the stack. Even up the laminates end to end. Check that each laminate in the stack is in contact with the standoff pieces at the back. Put the first clamp in the center of the form. Place a pressure pad on top of the protecting strip and tighten the clamp. The clamp must be set perpendicular to the curved faces of the form. The clamp must not be skewed sideways or across the stack, *i.e.*, high on the form and low on the pressure pad. In the latter case, the clamp can twist the whole stack off the standoffs.

Recheck the end to end alignment of the stack and that all laminates are still in contact with the standoffs. If there are any problems, loosen the clamp and reset it.

Repeat with the second and succeeding clamps, working outwards from the center of the bending form. After the second clamp is in place, it is less likely that the stack will twist off the standoffs. As the pieces wrap around the form, the inner piece will appear longer than the next and the next, etc. It's fine; the increasing radius of the curve at each laminate in the stack does that. As each clamp is tightened, you

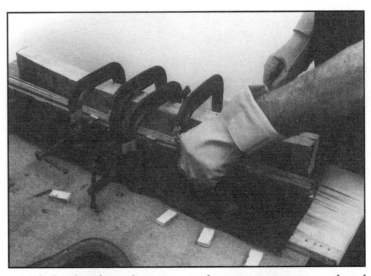

On the bending form, the tape covered protecting strip goes outboard of the laminate stack, then pressure pads under each clamp. I alternate the direction of the clamps so that the screws bars don't interfere with each other, as the clamps are tightened.

should get squeeze-out from all the plies. After all the clamps are in place, wait 20 minutes and check the clamps. As the epoxy squeezes out of the stack, slack can develop in the clamps. Retighten the clamps as necessary

Clean the squeeze-out from the top of the stack. Because the bending form is rigid without the backing board, you can separate them and clean the squeeze-out from the back of the stack as well. Let the laminate stack cure overnight.

In the morning, remove the clamps. With a sharp plane clean up the sides of the blank and trim them to the desired width. If the laminates are wide enough for two thwarts, cut the two thwarts out with the japanese saw, saber saw, or band saw. Cut the thwarts to length and mount them as for the flat thwarts in the building sequence, page 56.

Here the laminate stack is fully clamped down. This stack is only one thwart wide. For a two-thwart stack, the protective strip and pressure pads would have to be wide enough to get consistent pressure across the stack. A corollary to "A boatbuilder never has enough clamps," is "You always need one more clamp than you have," as is demonstrated by the small clamp on the left end of the form. Leave the stack under pressure overnight to get a good hard curve.

Curved One-Piece Backrest Pad

Laminating a curved backrest pad requires a simple press. The press is made of pieces of scrap 1/2" plywood and 2x4. The 1/2" thick backing plate is approximately 7"x11". Two pieces with curved upper faces cut from the 2 x 4 are attached to the backing plate. These pieces are about 10" long; the curve cut in them has an 11" radius. Attach the concave pieces to the backing plate with their outer faces about 7" apart. Before using the press, put masking tape or duct tape on the curved faces so that the press doesn't get epoxied to the pad blank.

Draw the shape of the backrest pad on one of the pad blanks before laminating the two blanks in the press. Spread epoxy on one side of each blank. (1 pump) Put the two blanks together with their epoxied sides together. The uncured epoxy acts as a lubricant and the two blanks must be restrained before they can be clamped in the press. Clamps and clamp pads

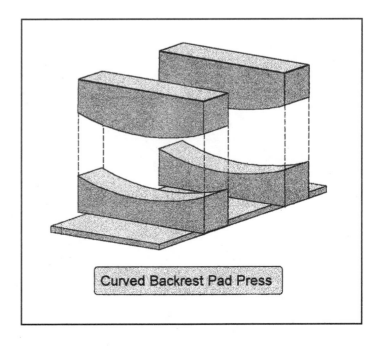

Curved Backrest Pad Press

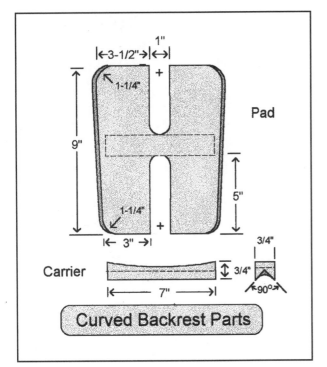

1"

|←3-1/2"→|←→|

1-1/4"

Pad

9"

5"

1-1/4"

|← 3" →|

3/4"

Carrier

3/4"

|← 7" →|

90°

Curved Backrest Parts

the laminated pad with a saber saw or band saw after it has fully cured.

The pad is made as a single piece to simplify aligning the pad with the carrier and to provide a larger gluing surface between the pad and the carrier. When making the carrier, a curved surface is cut to match the curve of the pad in lieu of the two angled faces used for the separate flat pads in the standard building sequence.

Tuffet and Tuffet 2

While I consider myself young of heart and mind, of late my body has begun to insinuate reminders into my consciousness that I am in the second half of my life. More and more often, simple activities cause my joints and muscles to get cramped and stiff. It was difficult to admit that single paddling had become one of these

placed on the centerline of the curvature will work but they are awkward. I drive small brads through the two blanks at the positions marked with pluses "+" in the drawing "Curved Backrest Parts." Put the brads close to the ends of the blank so that they don't foul the convex parts of the press.

Clamp the two breasthook blanks between the upper and lower curved pieces of the press with a 4" screw clamp at either end. Cut out

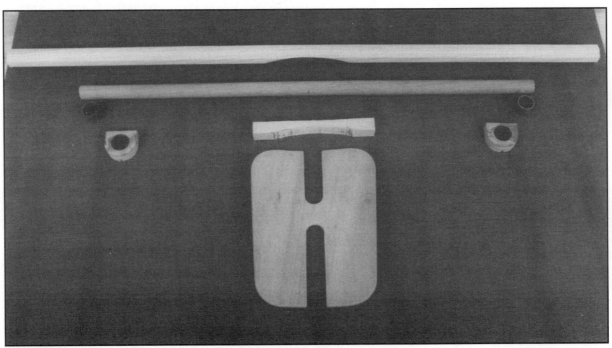

Parts for the curved pad backrest. On top is a custom eight-sided thwart with pad seating area cut in the thwart. Below are the parts for the standard thwart.

Four clamps are used to squeeze the curved backrest pad in the press. The lower pieces of the press are covered with duct tape to prevent squeeze-out from gluing the pad to the press. At the center of the near edge of the pad is one of the two brads used to keep the two pieces of the pad from slipping out of alignment as the clamps are tightened down. Put the brads in before putting the pieces in the clamp.

design something for function and comfort, not looks. I started by kneeling on the bare floor in my paddling stance with my knees 24" apart and resting my butt on my heels. Discomfort began in my insteps where there's no meat to cushion the bones. I shifted my weight onto my toes. Very quickly that became even more painful. I discovered however that by lifting my legs at the shins, I took all the pressure off both my insteps and toes. It was difficult to balance on just my knees so I propped my shins up with paperback books. It was great, no pain in my shins where I guess the nerves are either dead or few and far between. I could rotate my ankles and wiggle my toes. I was going in the right direction.

About this time the pain in my knees had grown greater than my excitement about the

activities. It wasn't the activity of paddling but the required position that was troublesome. I single paddle in the kneeling position. The pressure on my knee joints and insteps caused by the kneeling position would start as an annoyance, and grow ever so slowly into a pain that finally could not be ignored. Getting out of a canoe was agony involving great pain and much stumbling about with the very real possibility that I'd end up on my face in the muck. I loved to single paddle and wasn't going to give it up without a fight.

I decided that a band-aid fix wouldn't do. I would start afresh and

The evolution of the Tuffet. On the right is the first attempt. In the center is the fourth mockup using foam board. The tongue on the mockup anticipates Tuffet II. On the left is the prototype Tuffet. The commercial grade carpet contact cemented to the bottom more than doubled the weight of the simple fiberglass covered foam board structure.

shin rest could hide. I thought that the pain was caused by the acute angle of thigh and lower leg. The only way to open the angle was to raise my butt above my heels. So I started piling magazines up until I was comfortable. By turning the pile so that one corner was between my legs, I didn't lose circulation in my legs. By placing a hard bound volume tilted slightly forward on the top of the magazines there was no pain anywhere. I felt like I was floating, not sitting or kneeling but suspended in space. I felt I was onto something.

A few days later I was on the freeway when I spotted a sheet of 1" foam board in the weeds. Something clicked in my head and I knew this was the material I needed to transform the pile of magazines into something useful. In the shop I reconstructed the pile of magazines and paperbacks. I then tried to visualize the minimum volume and surfaces that would describe the places where my various parts contacted the piles. I began building outlandish shapes from stacks of pieces of foam board which I then carved into the shape I thought I wanted. The foam could be worked easily with japanese saw, Sure Form™ tool, and 100 grit sandpaper. It was crazy. I would sit on this thing and think about guiding its evolution to conform to my needs. I had to keep reminding

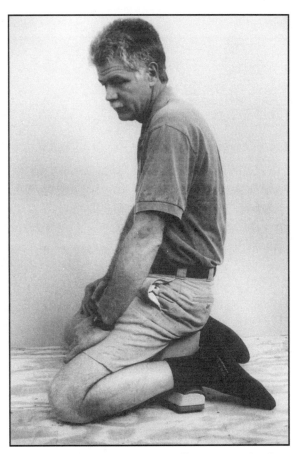

This side view shows how the Tuffet supports the shins and relieves any pressure on the instep of the foot.

myself to forget what it looked like and concentrate on its function. Three or four tries later I had a working model.

When my son Dan found me apparently kneeling on my shop floor with strange pink dust all around and over me, and gazing into the middle distance distractedly, he asked what I was doing. My immediate answer of, "Listening to my butt" was incomprehensible to him. I invited him to take a sit-kneel and see what he thought. Dan is a casual kayaker and canoer, and his opinion would be valuable as a disinterested but knowledgeable observer. He liked how it felt but, well, wasn't it kind of, you know, weird looking. After a few moments he pointed out the certain angles and relationships of

Tuffet and Tuffet II working models. The prototype was considerably refined by focusing on the essential elements and eliminating extraneous volume. Firm foam pads have been added to the shin supports and replaced the carpet on the bottom. Tuffet II on the left looks like something out of star Wars. It too is a minimal design but its dual purpose nature dictates a more complicated shape.

the surfaces didn't quite fit his body. I am 73.5" tall, he was about 71" tall. I wouldn't have thought that the difference was significant. I subsequently had my wife, daughter, and a few friends try the thing, which for lack of imagination and a better word I called a Tuffet. They reported much the same results. The Tuffet was better than either sitting on a conventional canoe seat or kneeling, but for each person it didn't quite fit.

From these experiences I realized the Tuffet fit me exactly, and no one else. The relationship of its surfaces is a function of my lower and upper leg lengths, pelvic structure, and maybe even shoe size. I am excited about the Tuffet but I can't give you a dimensioned drawing, it would do no good. The accompanying photographs show what my final design looks like. To make one you need to start with a pile of magazines and . . . well, I'm sure you

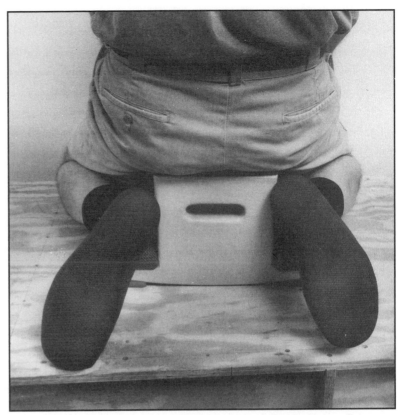

The height of Tuffet's seat is just at the top of my heels. This is why I say the measurements may be dependent on my shoe size. The toes on my right foot are not touching the work surface. The dark oblong between my feet is a hand-hold for carrying.

When turned on its rear side, Tuffet 2 exposes its double paddle backrest pads. Material is removed from between the two squarish foam pieces outboard of the pads to provide clearance for a seat pad that was glued to the bottom of the canoe.

get the idea. To be used in a canoe, the Tuffet's bottom must be contoured to match the shape of the canoe at the paddling position. After the shape is carved out and fitted to the canoe, the Tuffet is covered with 6 or 8 ounce fiberglass cloth and epoxy. Thin dense foam pads are cut to shape and contact cemented to the seat, shin rests, and bottom.

In addition to its comfort, the Tuffet has another improvement over the traditional canoe seat. The typical canoe seat is hung from the rails on thwarts or beams that may be as high as 10" off the bottom; often they are lower. Even if the seat is at the right height and canted forward at the right angle, your feet have to be worked back under the seat. In a narrow beamed solo canoe this process greatly extends those moments of instability before you get your weight settled in when entering and exiting. With the Tuffet, I throw a leg over it and

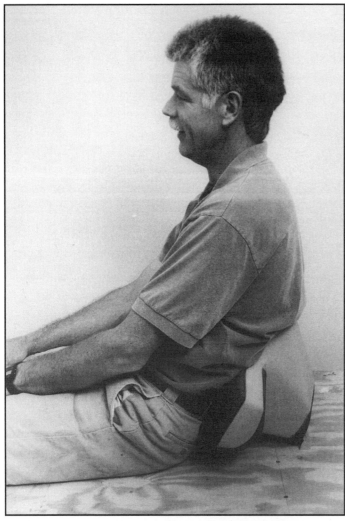

Tuffet II is resting against a small wooden cleat that I've screwed to the work surface. As I lean back, Tuffet II rotates clockwise so that the force vector I'm generating is perpendicular to the backrest pads and passes through the now lower right corner that is supported by the cleat. If I scoot my butt closer to the Tuffet for a more upright position, Tuffet II automatically readjusts its position as well.

drop on; very simple, very quick. Getting out is likewise greatly improved. My joints and muscles aren't stiff and numb to begin with. It is a simple matter to put a leg over the side, and then up and out.

The Tuffet can be used with both legs back under you or with one leg extended. It works with both legs extended, but I don't see that position as being useful. In the Northwoods paddling style the paddle never leaves the water, sides are changed at long intervals, and the torso and pelvis is turned towards the side paddled on. The Tuffet being freestanding can be turned toward your paddling side and is more comfortable than a forward facing seat.

I designed *Sweet Dream* for both single and double paddling. On an outing I like to use a double paddle to get to and from my destination. Once at my destination, I switch to a single paddle for the control it offers. Switching paddles requires a different seat as well. In the past I have perched half on, half off a rotating double paddle back rest. It's a do-able thing but it gets uncomfortable quickly. Sitting on the backrest moves my fore and aft center of gravity aft about seven inches, creating excess trim by the stern and inhibiting maneuverability, which was why I was using the single paddle in the first place.

Tuffet II is a dual function seat for both single and double paddling. It's very nearly self-defeating design criteria were: simple, one-handed operation, minimum number of

*T*here is a special gaze, a sort of hypnotized stare, that men develop as they look at the sail plan or line drawing of a possible boat. It isn't really an examination or analysis, but is more a giving-up of the beholder to the object beheld — a semi-mystical act, producing little that is concrete and especially annoying to people like wives, who speak to you and receive no answer. Sometimes I had moments of guilt. Was this all a waste of time? How serious could a man become about boats and still function and succeed in everyday society? I took comfort in the notion that, in an age which leisure was rarely overtaking work as man's principal preoccupation, boats had a redeeming quality.

Anthony Bailey,
The Thousand Dollar Yacht

moving parts, no shifting of the fore and aft center of gravity in the two paddling positions, and light weight. As difficult as the Tuffet had been to create, Tuffet II was maddeningly more difficult. I gave up in frustration many times. The benefits it promised lured me back after a few days of less strenuous mental work. (I wonder if knowing calculus would have helped.)

In the upright position, Tuffet II offers all the benefits of the standard Tuffet for single paddling. Rotating Tuffet II aft through 110°, onto its former rear side, exposes a double paddle back rest on the Tuffet and a seat pad glued in place to the bottom of the hull. In the double paddling configuration, Tuffet II is constrained from sliding backwards by resting against a 1" tall cleat epoxied to the bottom of the hull. The aft edge of the single paddling seat rests against the cleat. The cleat also serves as a pivot for changes of the angle of the backrest. The double paddle position maintains the same fore and aft center of gravity as the single paddle position. Again, the photographs show what Tuffet II looks like.

(If you are really clever, the after thwart could be moved forward 4" to 6" and Tuffet II would rest against it. In this configuration, you would lose the self-aligning quality that comes from Tuffet II rotating against the cleat.)

If you like to single and double paddle on the same trip, something along the line of Tuffet II is worth considering. In retrospect, Tuffet II may be a design effort gone amuck. The benefits of being able to switch between single and double paddling can be achieved much more simply with a standard rotating backrest and a standard Tuffet. If the double paddling arrangement includes a seat pad glued to the bottom, clearance must be provided for it on the bottom of the Tuffet.

Asymmetric Hulls

I designed *Sweet Dream* as a symmetric hull; that is, the shapes of the waterlines at the two ends of the hull are identical. Most traditional canoe hulls are symmetric. Many contemporary canoe designs have asymmetric hulls. With the three hull plans in **Building Sweet Dream**, there is an opportunity to consider building a *Sweet Dream* with an asymmetric hull. By joining 12' and 13' halves or 13' and 14' halves you get a slight degree of

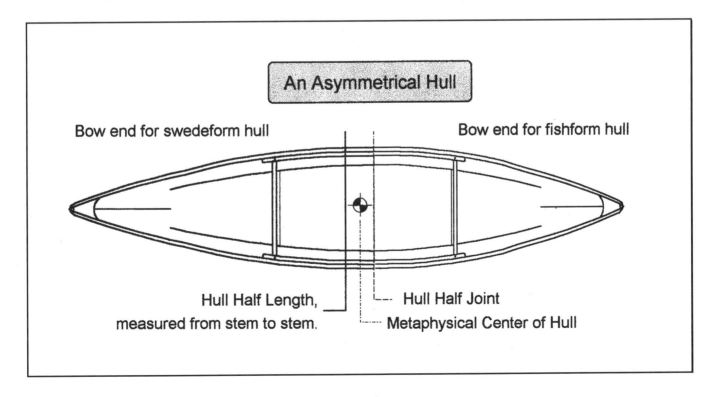

An Asymmetrical Hull

Bow end for swedeform hull   Bow end for fishform hull

Hull Half Length, measured from stem to stem.

Hull Half Joint

Metaphysical Center of Hull

asymmetry, by joining 12' and 14' halves the asymmetry is increased.

There are two forms of asymmetric hulls; the "swedeform" hull with the bow longer and more slender than the stern, and the "fishform" the other way 'round. Today virtually all asymmetric canoe hulls are swedeform.

There are a number of sound reasons for building an asymmetric hull based on proven scientific concepts involving boundary layers, laminar and non-laminar flow, the onset of turbulence, viscosity, and wave making. (What the heck. I'll throw in the square root of tomorrow as an arbitrary constant to add some spice to the soup.)

I believe that if you can't explain a scientific principle to a six-year-old child, then you don't fully understand it yourself. I haven't yet had the opportunity to explain why an asymmetric hull is a good thing to a six-year-old child. I suspect it would take me the better part of a morning, three walls of blackboard covered with drawings, and four colors of chalk. Rather than practice on you, I'm going to save us both a whole lot of time by reducing the entire matter of asymmetric hulls to the statement: While an asymmetric *Sweet Dream* hull may be slightly "cleaner" than a symmetric one in a hydrodynamic sense, most people will build an asymmetric hull just to be different.

I haven't yet built an asymmetric *Sweet Dream*, but I plan to in the near future. After I do some side-by-side testing with a symmetric hull of the same length, I'll be able to say whether the asymmetry produces a better hull or one that is merely different. I'll also be able

to say whether the long thin end or the short fat end is the better "pointy end" or bow.

Building the asymmetric hull should follow right along with the standard building sequence. However, the question of the location of the metaphysical lengthwise center of the hull should be answered before you begin building. Because the two ends of an asymmetric *Sweet Dream* are different versions of the same shape, the metaphysical center of the hull lies between the joint between the two hull panels and the lengthwise center of the hull measured from stem to stem. These two limiting points are at most 6" apart.

When I build my asymmetric hull, I'm going to follow the middle path and put the metaphysical center halfway between the two limiting points, which will roughly correspond with the center of buoyancy of the hull. I will use this point as the center for the rails and bottom pad, and I put the double paddle backrest 13'1/2" aft of it.

If I find it necessary to know the exact location of the longitudinal (fore and aft) center of buoyancy of the asymmetric hull, I'll load a floating hull with three 50-pound sacks piled on top of each other, move the pile to level the hull fore and aft, and athwartships; draw the outline of the bottom sack on the hull; remove the sacks; and draw lines connecting the diagonal corners. Where the diagonal lines cross is the location of the longitudinal center of buoyancy.

When I think how great a part of my life has been spent dreaming the hours away and how much of this total dream life has concerned small craft, I wonder about the state of my health, for I am told that it is not a good sign to be always voyaging into unreality, driven by imaginary breezes . . . If a man must be obsessed by something, I suppose a boat is as good as anything, perhaps a bit better than most.

E.B. White
The Sea and the Wind that Blows, Tales from the Skipper

Part 4: Additional Building Information

Safety in the Shop

A few words about workshop safety. When you are building, concentrate on what you're doing at the moment. Most workshop accidents are the result of inattention. Use safety glasses/goggles whenever you use any power tool. The greater percentage of the rest of the building time that you also wear safety glasses, the smaller the chance that a freak splash, splinter, or speck will injure your eyes. Wear plastic gloves and safety glasses whenever you mix or use epoxy, paint, or varnish. Nicks, cuts, and small splinters are a part of working with wood and sharp edged tools; quick clean-up and first aid will lessen the chance of infection.

Always wear respiratory protection whenever you use a power sander. Consider wearing respiratory protection whenever you sand. If the dust you produce isn't a recognized health risk, it's at least a respiratory system irritant.

Epoxy

Epoxy causes allergic reactions in a very small percentage of the population. To be more specific, the hardeners are sensitizers which can cause a reaction. The typical reaction is a rash on hands, arms, and/or face. In more advanced cases your face puffs up and your eyes and nose run. Sensitization is cumulative. Once you are sensitized, each exposure results in a stronger reaction. A few people are sensitized before they use epoxy the first time. There is no known cure for the sensitization and it cannot be reversed. Prevention is the answer. Once you are sensitized you must stop using epoxy. From that point on you'll have to use more traditional boat building techniques.

Always wear plastic gloves and safety goggles when mixing or using epoxy. When applying large amounts of epoxy, as when coating, encapsulating, or sheathing the outside of a hull, wear an OSHA approved organic vapor mask. Use new filter cartridges every day.

By any standard, epoxy is incredible stuff. Its wide range of applications coupled with its great strength and high degree of waterproofness make it an ideal choice for boat building. It is unfortunate that some wooden boat iconoclasts still drag Herreshoff's comment out of the closet about epoxy being frozen snot. That statement is much like the comments at the turn of the century about the new fangled automobile never replacing the horse. Fifty years ago the resin, more probably it was polyester,

> Canoeing invites exploring. Poking along an unfamiliar shore, each of us is a discoverer in the sense that matters most.
>
> Walter Magnes Teller,
> *On the River*

was crude stuff. It was relatively new and not only was its application still being worked out, at times the quality was irregular.

Today's epoxy is a horse of another color. National brands are consistently high in quality with known characteristics and repeatable cure times. The basic resin is supplemented by a wide range of support products that make epoxy applicable to a broad range of uses, easy to use, and relatively inexpensive when used in moderation.

When you buy epoxy, ask for the manufacturers technical guide, and the Material Safety Data Sheet (MSDS). They are worthwhile reading, if for no other reasons than for you to see the health hazards and how to avoid or minimize them. You will probably have to buy the technical manual. By law the retailer must provide you a copy of the MSDS upon request.

At the risk of repeating what the manufacturers say, here are some thoughts on using epoxy.

If you sand any old piece of wood in your shop it changes color where you sanded. This is because something has reacted with the outer layer of the wood which you have removed. The new wood you uncovered by sanding will slowly darken as the same process affects it. The reaction at the wood's surface is due to moisture, pollution, skin oils, sweat from your hands, and even UV breakdown. It is safe to say that any unsanded wood surface is contaminated to some degree. Glue engineers (there are such people, but I'm not sure that's their job title.) don't really know why glue works. What happens right down at the molecular level where the wood and glue meet, the actual process of adhesion, is still a mystery. Still, it can be determined that some glues or adhesives work better than others in certain applications. Also, the conditions under which a particular glue works best can be determined. In general glues work best when the surfaces they are applied to are clean. This is true for epoxy.

Unlike other glues, epoxy likes a rather thick glue line, about 10 or 15 thousandths of an inch. When using epoxy, an invisible glue line is a screw up. This is not to encourage joints with great gaps to be filled. A close fit is good enough. Always apply epoxy to both surfaces to be glued. Epoxy requires much less clamping pressure than other glues where the pressure is used to squeeze as much glue out of the joint as possible. Moderate pressure is all that's needed. What is moderate? West System® says a firm handshake is moderate pressure.

There is some argument amongst the glue-smart crowd about whether and if so, how much, epoxy permeates into the wood and whether abrading the wood's surface helps get the strongest bond. Well, I don't know. I don't think that any number of little wood fibers being surrounded by epoxy really contribute to the strength of a joint. I suspect that scuffing up the surface may help achieve the less than perfect joint closure that epoxy prefers. Perfect joint closure hasn't been such a frequently recurring failure that I have to guard against it. I do believe that removing surface contaminates by sanding immediately before using epoxy helps achieve higher strength in a joint. The bottom line is lightly sand both parts with 100 grit sandpaper just before gluing.

When used as glue, epoxy is typically applied with a cheap brush, the cheaper the better as it can only be used once. The brushes of choice are "chip brushes" and "acid brushes." Chip brushes have unfinished wood handles and cheap straw colored bristles. (I have been told that chip brushes with black bristles are available in Canada.) They come in various widths from 1/2" to 3". The 1-1/2" or 2" sizes do fine for spreading epoxy over medium sized surfaces as when laminating the breasthook blanks and backrest pads or applying epoxy to the tape covering fillets. For applying epoxy in a long thin area, as when gluing scarphs or attaching the rails, the acid brush is preferred. Acid brushes have a hollow round metal handle and relatively short black bristles. They are available in 1/4" and 3/8" sizes. In the hardware store they are usually in the plumbing section. Get the 3/8" size if possible.

Epoxy cures or hardens by linking lots of EP and OXY molecules into long chains in a process called polymerization. Epoxy polymerizes in an exothermic reaction; that is it gives off heat. The heat in turn accelerates the reaction. Once you mix a batch of epoxy, no matter how large or small, get it out of the container, onto the surface to be glued, and spread out as quickly as possible. Once the epoxy is on the parts, go back and spread it evenly across the surface. In a real run-away situation of rapid polymerization, epoxy will foam up and give off visible fumes that look like smoke. DON'T BREATHE THE FUMES; THEY ARE TOXIC.

It is prudent to have a bucket half filled with water nearby when you're working with epoxy. In the event a batch of epoxy gets too hot to handle, dump the whole container in the water. Epoxy that is excess after a particular operation can be poured into the bucket. This way it can't overheat in the trash barrel.

I use West System® epoxy. I don't know that it is any better or worse than other nationally advertised brands. I've never had a single complaint with it. (Be careful when discussing epoxy with a stranger. Some folks are passionate, even pugilistic, defenders of their favorite brand of epoxy.) I keep using West System® because I am familiar with its characteristics; it works for me every time.

In the building sequence, I note the amount of epoxy needed where it is called for, i.e. (4 pumps, 6 scoops). My unit of measure for epoxy is a "pump." That is, **one pump each of resin and hardener** from the West System® 305 Calibrated Mini Pumps. In real world terms we're talking 0.902 oz. per pump. I use West System® 405 Filleting Blend when a thickened epoxy mix is called for, as in making fillets. The unit of measure for filler material is a "scoop." The scoop I use is from a can of Gatorade® mix. It holds 25ccs. In more familiar terms, that's four teaspoons or 1-1/3 tablespoons. To get a non-slumping mix for filleting takes 1-1/2

scoops of filler per pump of epoxy. If you use another brand of epoxy or other filler these proportions will be different.

In the West System®, there are three common thickeners; filleting blend, Microlight™ and colloidal silica.

Filleting blend is the filler of choice for structural fillets and other uses where strength is a consideration. It cures to a hard, dense, mahogany colored fillet.

Microlight™ should not be used where strength is a consideration. A cured non-slumping mix of Microlight™ has the consistency and strength of foam board. It is useful for making putty for filling small holes, dings in the hull, etc.

Although colloidal silica looks like a white dust in its container, it is a very hard, abrasive silica compound, similar to the basic ingredient in sand and glass. Mixed as a 25% by volume slurry with epoxy, it is an alternative to a layer of fiberglass cloth on the exterior hull for abrasion resistance.

Powdered graphite is a special filler also useful as a bottom coating. See Special Bottom Coatings, page 90.

Although epoxy manufacturers make plastic mixing pots, think twice about using them. They can melt. They are almost always too large for thorough mixing of the relatively small amounts of epoxy needed for most gluing jobs on a canoe or small boat. You are probably throwing out excellent epoxy mixing containers right now. Frozen orange juice cans make excellent containers for mixing straight epoxy. Cut the paper body of the can in half with your japanese saw. The paper sides remain relatively cool even when the metal bottom is too hot to touch. After you've poured any excess epoxy into the water filled bucket, put the can aside

 ractical life or "art" comprehends all our activities, from boat building to poetry

James Joyce

and let the remaining epoxy harden. The can may be reused many times. For mixing thickened epoxy, the largest tuna fish cans are suitable containers. They will hold up to 6 pumps of epoxy and 9 scoops of filler.

When making a thickened mixture, first mix the resin and hardener well, then add the filler. Add about half the filler, and then half again. I devise a mixing schedule that has a single scoop left to add at the end; for nine scoops the scoop schedule is 5-3-1. This way I can do some last minute correction if the mix is too stiff. If the proportions don't give a thick enough mix, add a little more filler.

Under certain combinations of temperature, humidity, atmospheric pressure, and maybe the phase of the moon, epoxy produces a by-product as it cures that collects on the outer surface. This "amine blush" as it's called has a waxy texture. Usually it is a very thin coating that can be felt but is hard to see. Occasionally it forms a thick coating with a whitish tint. The blush is formed after the first hours of polymer-ization. Epoxy won't stick to the blush; the blush must be removed before more epoxy can be applied. It can be removed in two ways; by sanding or by scrubbing with a green Scotchbrite pad and a weak solution of ammonia and water. After scrubbing, rinse with clear water. Wait until any dampened wood is dry before applying more epoxy.

It is most efficient to plan work involving epoxy so that a whole epoxying sequence from beginning to end can be gotten through in one session: preglue, fillet, taping, recoating. It will take about four hours including the waiting for the fillet and epoxy on the tape to partially cure.

Uncured epoxy can be gotten off with vinegar. If you clean your gloves and tools while the epoxy is still runny, vinegar will whisk the obnoxious stuff right off. In my experience vinegar won't get epoxy out of clothing. If you get epoxy on your skin, **Do Not Clean It Off With Acetone** or any other solvent. The solvent drives the unpolymerized hardener through the pores in your skin. A lot of the epoxy is gone from your skin but you've just given yourself a walloping large internal dose of the very stuff you're trying to avoid. First wipe this epoxy off, then wash with vinegar, follow immediately with soap and water, and then some hand lotion to provide protection in the absence of the natural skin oils you just washed away. If you religiously wear gloves when using epoxy, this will only rarely be a problem.

The Work Surface

In the folded plywood construction method, the work surface is more than just a table. As the hull is formed, the work surface and small blocks placed on it determine the rocker, the end to end curve of the hull; and the degree of arc in the bottom running from chine to chine amidships. While a table or bench can be used as the work surface, it is essential that it be 8' long. Two smaller tables can be used but they must be arranged such that the tops are in the same plane.

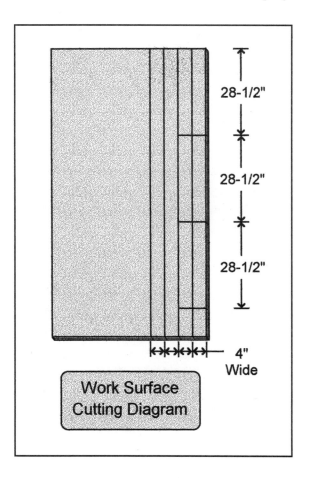

28-1/2"

28-1/2"

28-1/2"

4" Wide

Work Surface Cutting Diagram

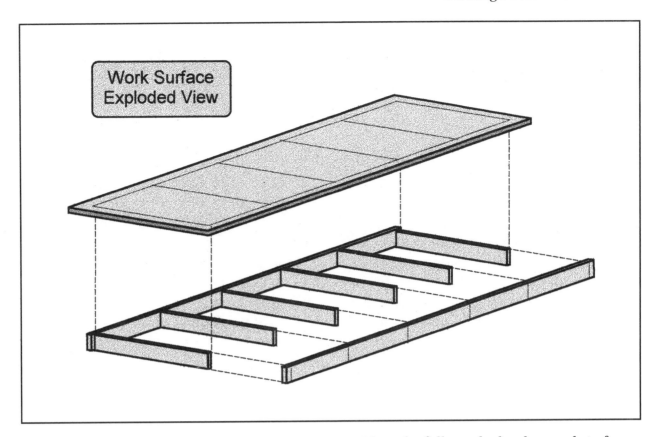

Work Surface
Exploded View

Eight foot long tables are not easy to come by. In most homes only the dining room table is likely to be eight or more feet long. Although it's probably been months since your dining room table was used, I am not seriously suggesting that it be considered. (Perish the thought!) If you're lucky enough to have an 8' work bench, that will do fine. If you can't beg, or borrow an 8' table, it would be foolish to buy one just to build *Sweet Dream*.

It is easy to build a suitable work surface. A suitably rigid work surface can be made from a single sheet of 5/8" interior fir plywood and about 100, 1-5/8" deck screws. Deck screws differ from drywall screws (sometimes referred to as "the Maine State Fastener" by boat builders Down East) in that their threads are larger and coarser. Drywall screws are not an acceptable alternative as they will not hold tightly when driven into the edge of a piece of plywood. What follows are directions to build a simplified version of the work surface I use and can be seen in many of the pictures in the building sequence.

Have the folks at the lumber yard rip four 4" pieces off one side of a 4'x8' sheet of 5/8" plywood using their panel saw. See the figure, "Work Surface Cutting Diagram" on page 112 . Usually they'll perform this service for you, their valued customer, at no charge. At home, cut two of the 4" wide pieces into 28-1/2" long sections. The resulting six short pieces and the two 8'-long pieces are used to form the stiffening structure under the work surface. The approximately 31-1/2" wide piece is the work surface itself.

On a side of one of the 4'x8'-long pieces, draw lines at right angles across the piece at 1-1/2", 20", and 39" from each end. Mark each of the six lines 1" from the edges of the piece and at its center. Clamp the two 8' long pieces together and drill 3/16" holes at each mark through both pieces. Turn the pieces on edge and with 2" deck screws, build a ladder-like grid by attaching one of the short pieces at each set of holes on the two long pieces. Try to get the screws into the center ply of the short pieces. (*See the figure "Work Surface Diagram" on page 112.*)

Using a carpenter's square, square the grid. Place the work surface on the grid and center it both lengthwise and crosswise. Put marks on the edge of the work surface at the center of all the pieces in the grid. Connect the marks with lines running from side to side and end to end of the work surface. Drill 1/8" holes on 3" centers on all the lines. Carefully position the work surface on the grid. Align the marks on the edge of the work surface with the centers of the pieces in the grid. With a torque driver, drive 1-5/8" deck screws through the four holes nearest the corners of the work surface and one in the middle of each 8' long piece in the grid to keep everything from moving. Go back and drive 1-5/8" deck screws through the remaining holes and into the grid below.

Because there is no plywood attached to the bottom of the grid, the work surface is bendy from corner to corner diagonally across the top. This will be controlled by the saw horses or other means of supporting the work surface. All that you need is a surface that is stiff enough end to end not to sag in the middle during construction, and this will work nicely. The grid is set back from the edge of the work surface to allow clamping pieces to the work surface when shaping thwarts, etc. during construction.

While building **Sweet Dream**, it is not absolutely necessary that the work surface be level. All that is required is that the opposing sides be parallel. Leveling the work surface is best and easy to do, but if it can't be done, parallel opposing sides are sufficient.

Sturdy Sawhorses

If you wreck your back bending over to build **Sweet Dream**, you may never get to use her. That would be a crying shame. I find that a work surface at a height between my wrist and first knuckles when I am standing with my arm at my side puts the work at a comfortable height. Here is a design for some sturdy sawhorses that put the work surface at the right height for me at 6' 1" tall. If you change the height, don't forget that the work surface is 4+" thick.

The accompanying figure, "Sturdy Sawhorses'" gives all necessary measurements, angles, and locations of parts. The diagrams are not strictly to scale but all measurements are accurate. Number 2 common lumber will do fine. The parts are held together with 2" boat nails or 2" galvanized deck screws. The screws are driven within a half an inch of edges or ends of pieces and predrilling will prevent splitting. Begin by setting a bevel gauge and a saber saw to 107°. Whenever a saber saw is called for, it is understood to be set at 107°.

The heart of the sawhorses is a crossbar made from a 2x6 cut to a trapezoidal cross section. Begin construction by cutting the 2x6 as shown in the first drawing. Make the cuts on a table saw or with the saber saw and a straight board for a cutting guide. Cut two 36" crossbars to length.

Cut the taper in the leg blanks. Do not cut the legs to length just yet. Measure back 5" from each end of the crossbar, and mark a line square across the top. (This distance is the setback for the legs. It gives lots of room for clamping at the end of the crossbar and puts the crossbar ends inside the lower ends of the legs for stability.)

started building boats in the early 1970s, and I guess I've built about a hundred of them over the years. Yet each completed boat gives me the same thrill as the first one, the same deep satisfaction. The process itself – creating from lines drawn on sheets of paper an object that is not only beautiful but perfect for its intended use – is no less fascinating now than when I started.

Tom Hill,
Ultralight Boatbuilding
International Marine, 1987

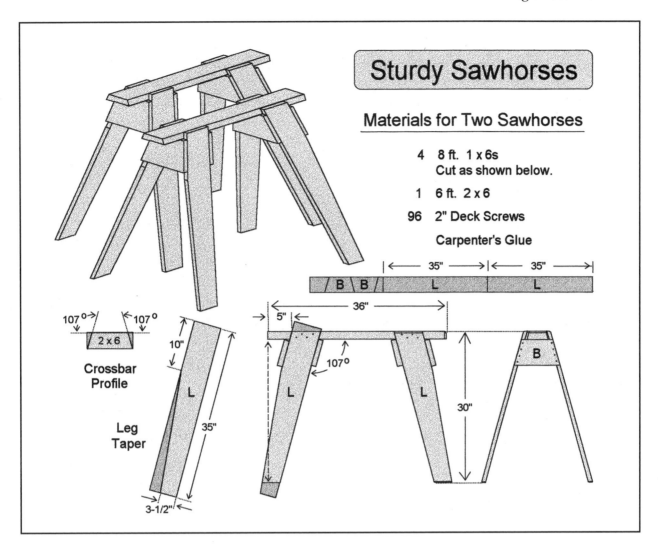

Sturdy Sawhorses

Materials for Two Sawhorses

4   8 ft. 1 x 6s
Cut as shown below.

1   6 ft. 2 x 6

96   2" Deck Screws

Carpenter's Glue

|← 35" →|← 35" →|

| B | B | L | L |

107° →| |← 107°

2 x 6

Crossbar Profile

10"

35"

Leg Taper

3-1/2"

|← 36" →|

5" |← →|

107°

107°

L   L   L   B

30"

With the bevel gauge set at 107°, draw lines from each end of the setback lines, down the angled side of the crossbar and angled towards the end of the crossbar.

Attach the legs with the taper facing toward the end of the crossbar and aligned with the angled lines just drawn. The top inner corner of each leg should stand 1/4 inch or so above the top of the crossbar. Use carpenter's glue and four 2" deck screws driven parallel to the upper surface of the crossbar. The screws should be staggered and set well down from the upper edge of the crossbar so the legs can be trimmed flush with the crossbar later.

Once the four legs are attached to the crossbar, trace the shape of the leg braces from the actual construction. Cut the braces about 1/4 inch long. Although the braces do not lie flat against the legs or the cross bar, with 2"

screws the joint is more than strong enough. Attach the braces to the legs with four screws in each leg.

Rough-cut the top of the legs with the saber saw. Trim the legs flush to the crossbar with a block plane. With the plane, cut small cambers in the outer edge of the leg tops, and the tops and sides of the crossbar ends. Trim the ends of the leg braces flush with the legs with the block plane.

Getting both the compound angle and leg length correct the first time on all four legs can be difficult. Here's a simple method that works for me. Temporarily screw or securely clamp a small board or piece of scrap to a vertical surface so that its upper edge is 30 inches above the floor, and it extends three or four inches horizontally into open air. (If you change the height of the horses, set the board at the new height.) The vertical surface can be on a door frame, cabinet, bench leg, or whatever. There must be enough clear floor space in front of it to put a sawhorse on its crossbar, with the legs sticking upwards. The floor needs to be relatively flat without large bumps; a well-worn plank floor won't do. Turn a sawhorse on its back and position it so that the outer corner of one leg touches the end of the board. Stand on the crossbar to ensure it firmly contacts the floor.

Mark the outer corner of the leg where it and the upper edge of the small board touch. Make just a small mark. Don't extend the mark across the leg. Repeat these steps for the other three legs. Align a straight edge across the marks on the two legs on the same side of the crossbar and draw a line across each leg. Before cutting the excess off the leg blanks with the saber saw, make sure that the saw cuts are made in the right direction to get a cut surface parallel to the crossbar. With the saber saw, cut across the leg keeping the base plate of the saw firmly against the leg. With the block plane, cut small cambers in the edges of the lower leg ends to prevent spit-offs.

Milling the Parts for the Hull

Ideally, the rails and other parts for *Sweet Dream* are cut from a single 3/4" thick board that is at least 8" longer than the hull you are building. If full length stock is not available, a long board can be made by scarphing shorter pieces together. The scarph should be at least 8:1; 10:1 is better. Scarph pieces should be of sufficient length that the scarph in the rails can be offset from the joint in the middle of the hull sides by at least a foot.

Although the thwarts, rails, etc. can be gotten out with a saber saw, they are most easily and accurately cut on a table saw. If you don't own one, see if a friend will let you use his or hers. The work will take less than an hour. If

you are unfamiliar with the table saw, be sure to get thorough instruction in its use. On a table saw things can go very wrong in a hurry. A severed finger or mangled hand can be the price of inexperience or inattention. Always wear eye protection. Always use a push stick to finish each cut.

Batten. Inspect the grain of the board closely. Look for the edge with the longest, straightest grain. From that edge, cut a piece 1/4" wide to be used as a batten. The batten will be used to draw smooth lines between points when laying out the hull. The batten must not have any bends or wiggles. If the first batten cut from the board is unacceptable, cut a second. If that one is unacceptable too, you'll have to make a batten out of other stock.

Outer Rails. The outer rails are nominally 3/4" x 3/4" in cross section. You can substantially lighten the appearance of the rails without significantly affecting their stiffness by beveling their undersides. In this case, the rails remain 3/4" wide but are 7/8" thick at the hull and 5/8" at their outer edge. (*See the figure "Outer Rail Cross Sections".*) Cut two rails of the desired cross section that are at least 8" longer than the hull you are building.

Inner Rails. There are three ways to do the inner rails. See the figure, "Inner Rail Profiles." The easiest inner rails to make are solid 3/4" x 3/4". Other than cutting the rail to length, no further work is involved. The drawback to the solid rail is the difficulty its stiffness can cause when bending it into place in the hull. For this

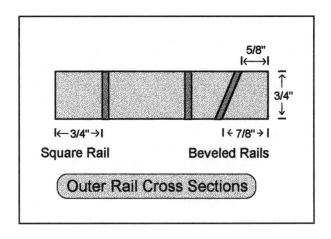

Outer Rail Cross Sections

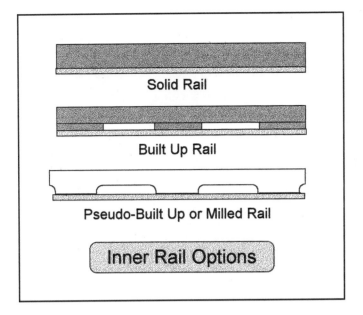

Solid Rail

Built Up Rail

Pseudo-Built Up or Milled Rail

Inner Rail Options

option cut one 3/4" wide piece from the board. Whichever configuration you opt to use, the inner rails are 5' long.

A built up rail that is 3/4" wide will have nearly the same stiffness as a solid rail once installed. The rail itself is 1/2" wide and 3/4" deep. Between the rail and the hull there are many 1/4" thick standoff blocks. Many people think the built up rail is so much better looking than a solid one that the extra effort required to make it is worthwhile. When being bent into place, the built up rail is only as stiff as the 1/2" rail itself. Once glued to the hull it acts much like a 3/4" thick solid rail. For this option, cut one piece from the board 1/2" wide for the rail and one piece 1/4" wide for the standoff blocks.

The blocks in the built up rail should always be longer than 1". Draw a few options full size. Fiddle with the measurements until you find an arrangement that you like. I prefer short blocks and long spaces. It is also helpful if the blocks are spaced 3" apart with a space at the center of the rail. This way when the inner rail is attached, the blocks cover screw holes left from attaching the outer rails. The blocks can be epoxied to either the hull or the rail first, and then epoxied to the other. When attaching built up rails to the hull, ensure that the inner side of the rail, the ends of the stand off blocks and the entire length of the hull behind the rail

is coated with epoxy. This will seal these areas preventing water intrusion, and simplify finishing later on.

A third inner rail option is to simulate a built up rail by milling slots in a solid rail with a router. This method is easier to build than the true built up rail. Its major drawback is that it requires a router. See Builder Made Tools, page 129, for a router guide that considerably simplifies the job of milling the slots. The slots should be 1/4-5/16" deep. Again the size of the openings and the pseudo-blocks are a personal choice, and the blocks should be longer than 1". I prefer a small radius at the top of the slot. I use a 3/16" round nose bit to rout out the slots. For this inner rail option, cut one 3/4" wide piece from the board.

Thwarts. The thwarts are 1"x3/4". After the thwarts are cut to length at the end of the building sequence, they can be eight-sided with a spokeshave. Eight siding reduces the apparent size of the thwarts while maintaining most of the stiffness of the original dimensions. The rails look very smart done this way. Cut one 1" wide piece from the board. From it rough cut two 28" long pieces for the thwarts.

Single Paddling Seat Beams. The beams are 1"x3/4". Rough cut two 32" long pieces from the piece the thwarts were taken from.

Double Paddle Backrest Stretcher. The materials list calls for a 7/8" diameter hardwood dowel to be used for the backrest stretcher. Some people find the look of a cylindrical stretcher unacceptable. Alternately the stretcher can be made from the same wood as the rails, and thwarts. Laminate two 30" long pieces of 3/4"x1" stock together. Plane the resulting blank to 1"x1" keeping the joint between the two halves in the center of the blank. After the stretcher blank has been planed square, you may wish to eight side it. The cut-to lines for eight siding are 5/16" from the corners of the blank.

Joining Plywood Sheets

There are three ways to join plywood sheets in order to make longer or wider panels. These are the:

〜 Butt Joint

〜 Fiberglass Tape Butt Joint

〜 Scarph Joint

Each joint has its advantages and its disadvantages.

Butt Joint. In the butt joint, two sheets of plywood are brought together end to end. A butt block is then glued and fastened with nails or screws across the joint between the two sheets. The butt block is the same thickness as the plywood being joined. The butt joint cannot be used in building *Sweet Dream*. The butt block would interfere with the bottom pad which is put in the center of the hull later in the building sequence.

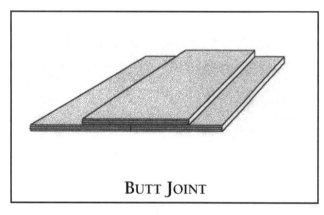

BUTT JOINT

Fiberglass Tape Butt Joint. In this joint, fiberglass tape takes the place of the plywood butt block. This joint is also called the "Dynamite" Payson Butt Joint after its popularizer. When properly made this joint is far stronger than the plywood it joins. It can be made nearly invisible too. The thin fiberglass tape can be hidden quite well by sanding long tapers on its edges. The tape does not materially interfere with installing the bottom pad. (If the surface plys are hollowed slightly at the joint before the fiberglass tape is applied, it becomes an "invisible butt joint".)

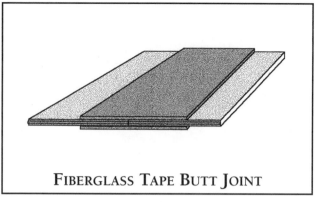

FIBERGLASS TAPE BUTT JOINT

The joint is simply made on the floor or work surface. Center a strip of plastic wrap under one end of a sheet of the plywood to keep the joint from being glued to the floor or work surface. Butt the second sheet firmly against the first. Ensure that the edges of the sheets are aligned in a straight line. As necessary, weight the sheets so the ends to be joined are flat. Apply epoxy 1-1/2" out on either side of the joint with a chip brush (2 pumps). Cut a piece of 3" fiberglass tape 50" long. Center the tape over the joint. Apply epoxy to the tape working out any bubbles. Bubbles in the crack between the panels are acceptable. Let the epoxy cure at least four hours; overnight is better.

With at least one helper, carefully turn the panel over. Be especially careful not to bend the panel so that the joint is flexed towards the tape. With the panel flat again, apply tape to the second side of the joint. Let cure. The joint is finished.

Scarph Joint. In this joint, the two sheets of plywood are joined with bevels across the ends of the sheets. The two ends of the panels overlap each other by the width of the bevels. The slope of the bevel is between 8:1 and 12:1.

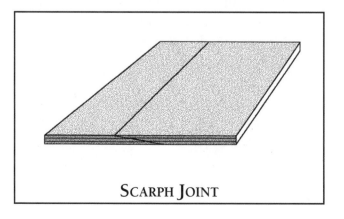

SCARPH JOINT

Properly made this joint is as strong as the plywood. Often the joint cannot be seen, except at the edge of the panel.

There are two ways to cut scarphs. The first uses power tools; either a belt sander, an electric hand plane, a router, or a circular saw. In addition to the power tool, a very accurate and fairly expensive fixture is needed to guide the tool and control the cut.

The second method is to cut the scarphs using hand planes. Scarphing plywood using hand planes has an unjustifiably bad reputation. It is true that scarphs in relatively hard woods with a pronounced grain like fir, or in thickness more than 1/4" are a real bear. Scarphing course grained plywood like luaun can also be difficult. However, okume is a relatively soft, virtually knot free wood that has a very subdued grain pattern. Okume plywood also has very thin glue lines which plane easily. Scarphing 4mm okume is not a difficult task. To be more precise, scarphing 4mm okume with razor sharp plane irons is simple.

At this point you must be honest with yourself. Either you can already consistently get an edge on your plane irons sharp enough to shave the hair on the back of your hand, or you can't. There's no middle ground here. If you can't, you'll have to learn how to do it. Get a friend to show you how. If your friends don't know, visit a local wood working, wood turning, or decoy carving club. Someone there is eager to help you. As soon as they start talking about honing to a mirror finish or micro-bevels, it's time to leave. Razor sharpness requires neither of these.

As a last resort, have your chisels and plane irons professionally sharpened. When you use them you will be amazed at what they, and you, can do. Once you see the bill, you'll have sufficient incentive to learn how to do it yourself.

Cutting the Scarphs

The Goal: An even, flat surface planed at a 10:1 bevel across the 4' ends of two sheets of 4mm okume plywood.

This is most accurately and quickly accomplished by cutting the bevels in the two sheets simultaneously. Before starting to cut the scarphs, read this entire section through a few times. None of the work is difficult; it just takes a while to explain. Take the time to thoroughly understand the process and cutting the scarphs will proceed with few problems. Once you start to cut the scarphs, it will take 45 minutes or so to complete them.

Required Equipment:
Work surface or bench
50" x 2" x 1/8" aluminum straight edge
3/4" x 1-1/2" x 50" wood clamping bar
2" or 3" x 4mm (or 1/8") x 50" spacer
Four, 2" or larger spring clamps
Two, 2" screw clamps
Three 2" deck screws
Razor sharp plane(s). Block and low
  angle block planes are preferred. Two
  planes speeds the work.

Before setting up the equipment, draw a line 1-1/4" from one end of each sheet of okume. This is the set back line and it determines the bevel of the scarph. 1-1/4" gives a roughly 10:1 scarph.

There is no more perfection in canoes than in wives, there are only convenient compromises . . .

An ideal canoe is a bundle of compromises, yielding something of her paddling speed to be able to sail fairly, sacrificing a portion of her sailing lines to secure reasonable lightness and sharpness, losing somewhat of her steadying weight and momentum for the sake of portability and being less portable because she must be strong and stiff.

Edwin Fowler,
Field and Stream, December 6, 1883

The general arrangement of the required equipment is shown in the figure, "Setting Up to Scarph," see page 121. Note the location of the straight edge, spacer, and pressure bar.

In a perfect world, the top of the work surface is perfectly flat. In the real world, the top of the work surface has dips and bumps in it. Set up the scarphing equipment at the place on your work surface that has the fewest and smallest bumps. As you will be setting up along one of the long sides of your work surface, the okume sheets will have to be supported at their far ends where they overhang the work surface by about five feet.

The aluminum straight edge serves a number of important purposes. First, it serves as a hard surface to plane the bottom sheet of okume down to a feather edge against. Second, as aluminum is softer than the tempered steel of the plane iron, should the sharpened edge of the plane iron cut into the straight edge, the plane iron will be dulled but not nicked or gouged. Third, the forward overhanging edge of the straight edge can be lifted with the fingers of the non-planing hand to compensate for dips in the work surface. The aluminum straight edge is not absolutely essential to get a good scarph. However, it makes the job of scarphing so much easier that I won't scarph without it.

Put the straight edge in position and put a spring clamp on each end to hold it in place. Put the spacer roughly in place with its forward edge about 5" from the front edge of the work surface.

The spacer lifts the okume sheets off the work surface to a height roughly equal to the thickness of the straight edge. The pressure bar holds the okume sheets firmly against the straight edge and spacer so that they don't slip as they are scarphed. Look at the location of the pressure bar relative to the spacer in the enlarged side view. The pressure bar overhangs the spacer to the front. In fact, the pressure bar has only 1/4" or so overlapping the spacer.

As the deck screws at the end of the pressure bar are tightened, the pressure bar rocks forward and causes the two sheets of okume to bend slightly between the spacer and the straight edge. This serves to keep the sheets squeezed tightly together and against the straight edge at their forward edges. This is important as wood dust or small chips between the plywood sheets or the straight edge will cause premature tear-out of the forward edges as the scarph nears completion.

Put the two sheets of okume on the work surface with their set back lines at the forward end and facing upwards. Align the upper sheet of okume so that its forward edge is on the lower sheet's set back line. Be sure that the upper sheet lies directly above the lower sheet with no overhang at either side. Go to the far end of the sheets and align the sides of the sheets so that there is no overhang. Clamp the sheets together with a spring clamp at either corner. Return to the front of the sheets, check the side alignment. Check that the upper sheet is still on the lower sheet's set back line.

Sometimes when the sides of the two sheets are aligned front to back, the front edge of the top sheet is at an angle to the set back line on the lower sheet. Confirm that the set back lines are perpendicular to the side of the sheets. If they are, the misalignment of the set back line and the end of the plywood sheet results from one or both of the ends not being cut at 90° to the sides of the sheet at the factory. Check both front edges with a carpenter's square. As necessary, square the end(s) of the sheet(s) and redraw the set back lines. Realign the sheets on the straight edge.

When the two sheets are aligned with the straight edge and parallel along the length of their sides, check and correct the position of the spacer as necessary. Drill two 3/16" holes through the pressure bar 49-5/8" apart so that the deck screws pass through it freely. The two screws at the ends of the pressure bar should be just outside the two sheets of plywood. Put the pressure bar in place so that its rear edge overlaps the spacer by 1/4". Screw the pressure bar down loosely.

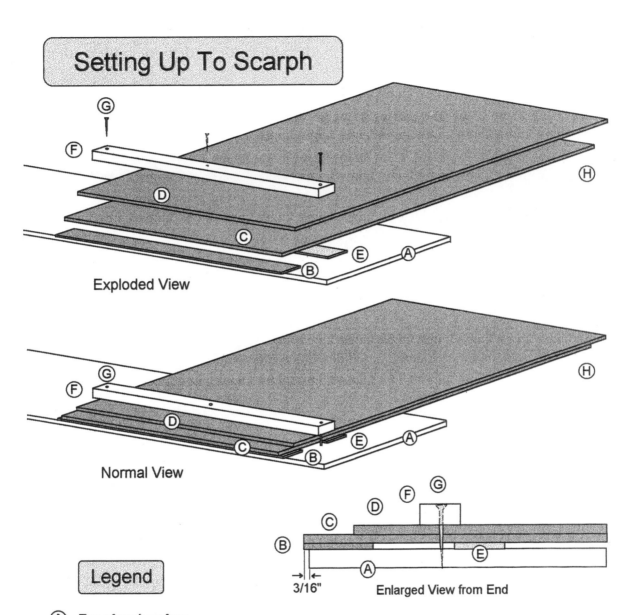

Setting Up To Scarph

Exploded View

Normal View

3/16"

Enlarged View from End

Legend

(A) Top of work surface

(B) 2" x 1/8" x 50" aluminium straight edge; extends 3/16" beyond front edge of work surface.

(C) Lower sheet of 4mm 4' x 8' okume; 4' width across front edge of straight edge.

(D) Upper sheet of 4' x 8' okume; front edge set back 1-1/4" from front edge of lower sheet.

(E) Spacer; 4mm or 1/8" thick scrap wood; 50" long and 2" or 3" wide.

(F) Clamping Bar; 3/4" x 1-1/2" x 52" wood; extends beyond front edge of spacer.
Front edge of clamping bar is set back 4" from front edge of upper sheet of okume.

(G) 2" Deck Screw

(H) Far ends of okume sheets supported at height of work surface on sawhorses.

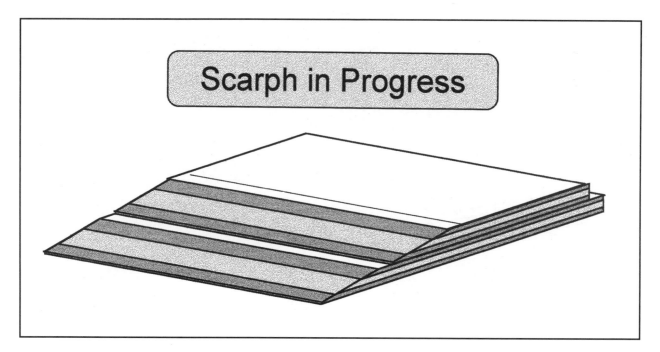

Scarph in Progress

Check that the two sheets are squeezed together and against the straight edge at their center. If necessary, use a third deck screw in the center of the pressure bar to close up the sheets and the straight edge in the middle. Clamp the two sheets to the back edge of the work surface with the two screw clamps. Put pads between the clamps and the okume to prevent scarring. Recheck the alignment of the sheets. Make corrections as necessary. Remove the spring clamps at the ends of the straight edge.

While care should be taken during the entire beveling operation, things don't get critical until the bevels are cut all the way through the two upper plys. Take your time as you go. As the bevels are cut through the sheets, the glue lines between the plys will be used as guides to maintain the angle of the bevel. Very small inconsistencies in the thickness of the three plys that make up each sheet mean that the location of the glue lines on the bevels on the two sheets will most likely not be identical. Understanding this fact is important if you want to avoid having a nervous breakdown as you cut the bevels.

The three plys in 4mm okume plywood are not equal in thickness. The center ply is usually thicker than the two edge plys. It is also impor-

tant to note that the two edge plys are usually not the same thickness. I would guess that the center ply is typically about 1.5mm thick and the edge plys average 1.25mm each. The practical ramifications of these small differences is that the beveled faces of the plys in the scarph will never be exactly the same width. Trying to get them to be the same width will drive you crazy. It can't be done and also keep the face of the bevel flat and in the same plane. Cutting the bevels is proceeding nicely when the glue lines run straight or nearly so across the beveled face.

In the figure, "Scarph In Progress," a representative scarph has been cut down into the third ply. For simplicity's sake the various pieces of equipment have been omitted from the figure. The bevels are not finished as can be seen by the thick forward edge of the bottom plys, and the remaining flat area on the upper surfaces of the two sheets. The different widths of the beveled faces of the plys reflect the different thicknesses of the plys. What is significant is that the glue lines run straight across the width of the bevel, parallel to the forward edge. This scarphing operation is going along quite nicely. Notice also that the as yet unplaned areas on the upper faces of the two sheets are roughly equal in width. You will be doing well if at this stage your scarph looks like the figure.

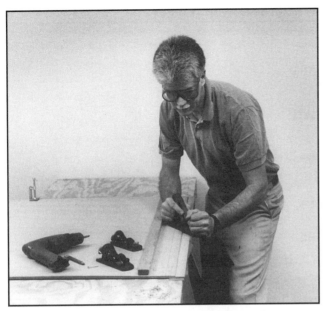

Start the scarph with your steepest angle plane. Save your low angle planes for the final cuts.

If you have more than one plane, save the lowest angle one to finish the final stages of the scarph. If you have only one plane, you'll need to resharpen as you cut into the third ply of the sheet.

To begin cutting the scarph, set the plane iron for a very shallow cut and square across the sole of the plane. Put the front of the plane on the lower sheet with the body of the plane at an angle so that the iron will cut only the upper sheet. As the cut is made, the heel of the plane rides along the front face of the pressure bar and helps keep the cut on the upper sheet. By having the sole of the plane in contact with

The sceret to using a plane is to get your body behind it. Move the plane with your arms and legs!

both the upper and lower sheets, the 10:1 bevel is maintained throughout the beveling operations. Some part of the sole of the plane should be in contact with each of the sheets at all times as the bevels are cut. For the most part, cuts are made with the plane skewed 30° to 45° to the direction of the cut.

Take three or four full length cuts on the upper sheet. Shift to the lower sheet and take three or four full length cuts. Check to see if you have cut through the upper ply and into the center ply on either sheet. If not, alternate pairs of cuts on the two sheets until the center ply begins to show along the front edge of one of the sheets. In a perfect world, the cuts made by the plane are all identical in depth. In the real world, some of the cuts are deeper than others and the center ply begins to show in some places before others. Take a few reduced length cuts with the plane to get down to the center ply along the full width of the front edges of both sheets. Take a minute and check what's happening to the bevels.

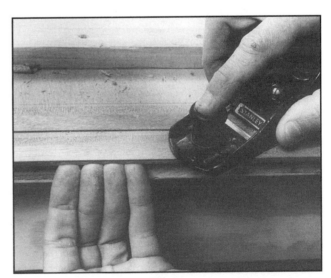

Lift the straight edge and make short cuts to remove high spots in the scarph that coincide with dips in the work surface.

It may be that in places along the front edge of the lower sheet you can't get the second ply to show. Check the top of the work surface under the straight edge. There is probably a dip directly under the places where the center ply won't show. With the fingers on your non-planing hand, carefully lift the straight edge at the dip and plane down into the center ply. Be careful not to plane off the tips of your fingers in the process. Even up the bevel so that the center plys show an equal amount on each sheet.

As you plane through the center ply, use the glue line between the top and center plys as a guide. The glue line should run in a nearly straight line from side to side of the sheet. The glue lines on the two sheets should be at roughly the same distance from the front edge of their sheets. Where the glue line curves towards the front of the sheet, not enough wood has been taken off, which usually is the sign of a dip in the work surface. Where the glue line curves away from the front of the sheet, too much wood has been removed. As necessary use short cutting strokes to take off high spots.

Sometimes parts of the grain in the center ply will tear out. This means that there is a grain reversal in the center ply. By narrowing the throat of the plane (if your plane has this feature) and retracting the iron ever so slightly this can often be overcome. If the reversal is severe, the only thing to do is cut that portion of the bevel coming back the other way. If you

Finish the bevel with a razor sharp plane iron set very shallow. Here a low angle block plane is being used to take the last cuts. Note the straight feather edge, no tear outs this time!

are strongly single handed, this can be done easily by pulling the plane towards you as opposed to the typical pushing cut.

Stop planing as soon as the bottom ply begins to show. Resharpen the plane iron to razor sharpness. When the bottom ply shows, the scarph is a little more than half finished. It is best to go slowly and deliberately as the bevel proceeds through the bottom plys. Frequently check the glue lines and unplaned area on the top of the sheets to ensure that the bevel is being cut flat and straight. Often the unplaned area showing on the top surface of the lower sheets is wider than the one on the upper sheet.

This is a sign of there being a slight crown in the face of the bevels. Work out the crown by cutting the bottom ply on the upper sheet and the top ply on the bottom sheet on the same cut. As the bevels approach completion, more and more cuts will be made on both sheets at the same time.

Work the two bevels down into the bottom plys until the forward edges feather out to nil or until the leading edge begins to tear out. Use the side of the plane body as a straight edge to check for flatness of the bevels from feather edge to setbackline. Reduce the depth of the plane iron so that it just barely cuts, and go over the entire face of the now continuous bevel across

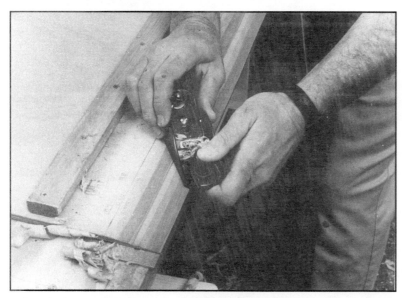

When the bottom plys show, change planes or resharpen the plane iron. Here a block plane is being used.

both sheets to take off even the smallest bumps. If you feel so inclined you can clean up the bevel with 100 grit sandpaper on a hard sanding block.

Joining the Two Scarphed Sheets into a Single Panel

The Goal: To glue the scarphed sheets together with consistent pressure across the scarph while ensuring that the sides of the two sheets form straight lines from one end of the panel to the other.

Required Equipment:
> Backing Bar; a 50+ inch long piece of 2x4 does fine.
> Pressure Bar; the pressure bar used to cut the scarphs will suffice.
> 4 ea. 1" Brads
> Hammer
> 8' straight edge, or
> Roll of thin string or wire
> Pencil
> Measuring tape or yard stick
> 18, 1-5/8" or 2" deck screws
> Torque driver or phillips head screw driver
> Plastic wrap, duct or masking tape
> Epoxy mixing pot and stirring stick
> One pump of epoxy
> Acid brush

To join the two sheets you need a space at least 20' x 8'. If you don't have such a space indoors, join the panels on a relatively flat place out of doors. The sheets can be joined on the work surface or on the floor.

Prepare the pressure bar by drilling 3/16" holes at 3" intervals along the centerline of the wide face.

On one of the okume sheets, carefully mark the center of the ends on the side of the sheet with the bevel facing upwards. Mark the center of the sheet just outside the bevel and again at the far end of the sheet. On the other sheet, mark the center of the sheet on both ends with the bevel facing downwards. The figure, "Scarphing Fixture," on page 126 shows the center marks connected with a center line for clarity. Using the japanese saw, make a 1/8" deep cut on the center marks on the unbeveled ends on both sheets.

Secure the backing bar to the center of the work surface with two 2" deck screws. Put a piece of the plastic wrap over the backing bar. Place the scarphed end of the sheet with the bevel and centerline marks facing upwards over the backing bar. The bevel should be centered on the bar in both length and width. Pin the sheet to the backing bar with two 1" brads. Put the brads about 1" from the sides of the sheet, and set back 1/2" from the bevel to allow clearance for the pressure bar.

Flip the other sheet so that its bevel is facing downwards. Place the second sheet so that the feather edge of the bevel is even with the set back line on the first sheet. Prop up the ends of the sheets so that they are roughly at the level of the work surface and lying in the same plane. Ensure that the center marks on the two sheets line up. There should also be no overhang on either side of the two sheets. Pin one corner of the second sheet to the backing bar with a brad.

It is important that the two sheets be aligned in a straight line from end to end. Stretch a thin wire or string between the two

Spreading epoxy on the scarphs.
ALWAYS wear plastic gloves when using epoxy.

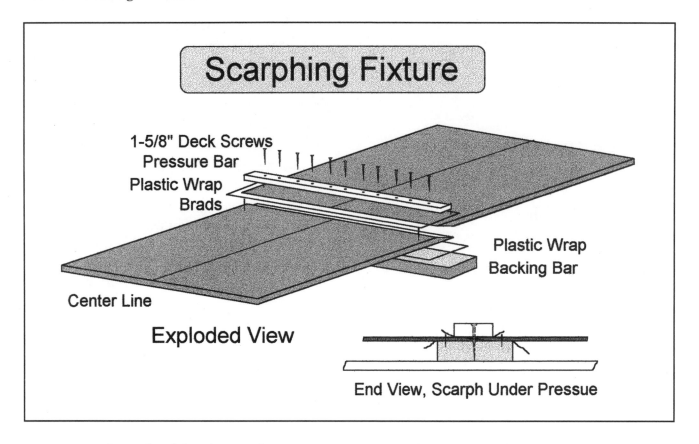

Scarphing Fixture

1-5/8" Deck Screws
Pressure Bar
Plastic Wrap
Brads

Plastic Wrap
Backing Bar

Center Line

Exploded View

End View, Scarph Under Pressue

saw cuts on the ends of the sheets. The string or wire should pass directly over the two center marks on the ends of the sheets at the backing bar. If it doesn't, something is out of alignment. Check that all the center marks on the sheets are correctly positioned. Make corrections as necessary. When the string between the two cuts at the outboard ends of the sheets passes

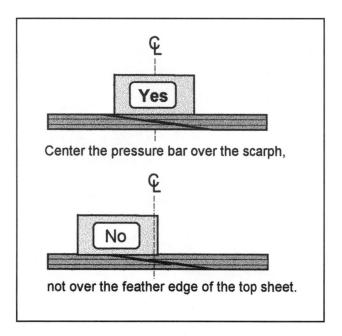

Center the pressure bar over the scarph,

not over the feather edge of the top sheet.

over the center marks at the backing bar, drive the second brad into the second sheet of plywood. The brads will be used to register the sheets in alignment when the pressure bar is screwed down.

Remove the two brads in the sheet with its bevel facing downward. Flip the sheet over so the bevel is facing upwards. Mix one pump of epoxy. With an acid brush, apply epoxy to both bevels. Wait a few minutes and then look at the epoxy on the bevels; it is probably smooth and wet looking on the center ply and rough looking on the outer plys. The outer plys on the sheets are end grain. The end grain acts like a sponge and soaks up the epoxy. Reapply epoxy to the bevels. Wait a few more minutes and do it again. You should have applied just about all of the epoxy at this point.

Flip the unpinned sheet over so that its bevel is facing downward and its center marks face up. Place the sheet over the backing bar and put brads through the two holes at the sides. The sheet should be adjusted so that the brads pass through the sheet and into the holes made earlier in the backing bar. Drive the brads into the backing bar so that about 1/8" stands proud of the sheet. Place a piece of plastic wrap over the scarph.

Place the pressure bar so that it is centered over the scarph. The holes in the bar should be over the center of the scarph which is 5/8" behind the feather edge of the sheet. Starting at the center of the pressure bar, drive 2" deck screws through the scarphed sheets and into the backing bar. Just set the screws with light pressure. If you are using a torque driver, use the lowest torque setting. Alternate putting in the screws on each side of the center of the sheet. When all the screws are in place, there should be some epoxy squeeze-out along the feather edge of the upper sheet.

Go back and tighten the screws starting in the center and alternating sides. If using a torque driver, use the 3 or 4 torque setting. There should now be squeeze-out along the entire scarph. Using a small square ended stick, clean the squeeze-out off the top of the scarph. Leave the sheets in the scarphing fixture for at least four hours, over night is better. If you leave the screws in place for more than 12 hours you risk them being epoxied into the backing bar. It is no real problem as their heads will torque off and when the pressure bar is removed (Remember that the holes in the pressure bar are oversized.) there is 3/4" of shaft to grab with pliers and screw out.

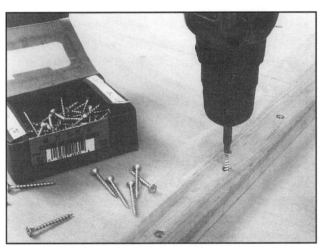

Remember to put plastic wrap between the plywood and backing bar and pressure bar.

Remove the scarphing fixture and clean up the scarph with 100 grit sandpaper on a hard sanding block. It is relatively easy to sand off only the excess epoxy if the sanding is done with the panel resting on the backing bar turned on edge under the scarph. This bends the panel slightly and it is easy to avoid sanding the relatively soft okume. The side of the panel with the smoothest scarph should be used as the exterior of the hull.

How Many Clamps?

It is an axiom that a boat builder never has enough clamps. In building *Sweet Dream*, a minimum of twenty four clamps is required. Ten of the clamps are screw clamps, ten are spring clamps, and four are bar clamps.

Two of the screw clamps should have a 5" opening across the throat, two at least 4" throat opening. The other six screw clamps can be rather small, 2" throat will do. With screw or "C-clamps," the upper limits of the force they can apply are very high. In all but the smallest screw clamps, the force is limited by the pain experienced in trying to turn the short handle. This ability to apply great force on the relatively small surface area of the jaws means that two pieces can be securely held without fear of them moving.

It also means that pieces being clamped together can be crushed. This is especially true if the wood is soft, as is okume. Crushing rarely results in the piece being flattened. More typically, it results in round depressions being forced into the wood. This disfigurement is very difficult to remove. To prevent these marks, pads made of the wood being clamped or of a softer wood, should always be used between the clamp jaws and the pieces being clamped.

The four small bar clamps are used to reach across the breasthooks when epoxying the rail to the hull. They must be able to open at least 8". Huge pipe clamps aren't needed, just some of the smaller bar clamps.

The ten spring clamps are the 2" size or larger. Don't get the 1" size. The clamps will be operating near their maximum opening, and the little plastic protectors on the jaws and handles will keep slipping off the 1" size.

Spring clamps have a relatively narrow operating range. The pressure they can generate is limited by their spring. Even when the spring is strong enough to hold two pieces in contact, the pieces tend to creep when there are strong shearing forces or vibrations present. Nonetheless, spring clamps need only one hand to manipulate, are light weight, and are suitable for many applications. At the point in the building sequence when the hull is aligned, the spring clamp's tendency to slip when sheer forces are applied to the pieces being clamped is actually beneficial.

In addition to the twenty four basic clamps, it would be nice to have about 50 screw clamps with a 2" throat. These would be used to clamp the two outer rails to the hull at 3" intervals when they are epoxied in place. In the absence of such riches, low cost alternatives are available for generating the needed clamping pressures.

The lowly drywall screw can be used to hold parts together when at least one of the

parts is quite thick. This is the situation with the 4mm hull and the 3/4" thick rail. By using two 4mm thick, 1" by 1" pressure pads under the head of a 1" drywall screw, there is no marking of the okume hull except for the screw hole. After the screws are removed, the 100 or so holes can be filled with thickened epoxy and sanded flush to the hull.

The Stem Bevels

Small 1/16" x 1/8" bevels cut in the inside edges of the stem sides create roughly parallel opposing surfaces as the forefoot and upper stem are closed up. See the figure, "The Stem Bevels." The surface of the bevel should be a flat plane. A radiused edge is little better than the original square corner and will lead to considerable frustration. The relatively broad surfaces of the bevel prevent the sides from slipping past and digging into each other when they are misaligned. They also allow relatively easy alignment as the sides are brought together. Small misalignments can be corrected by pushing the sides into place. If the pressure on the joint is such that the sides strongly resist being moved, inserting the blade of a thin 1-1/2" putty knife creates a low friction surface to align stems.

These bevels, while physically small, play a significant role in the trueness of the hull. As the sides of the hull are pulled together at the stems, the forefoot closes up first. As the stems are pulled together, the plywood must bend across its width back in the body of the hull. This bending is resisted by the center ply in the plywood between Station Lines 4 and 6. Curves are formed in the bottom and in the sides at the ends of the hull by bending the plywood around the forefoot. At the forefoot, the two sides exert considerable pressure against each other as they are pulled together to form the upper stem.

Square Edges

Beveled Edges

Nearly impossible to align

Easily Aligned

The Stem Bevels

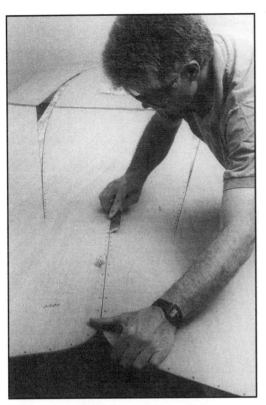

On the lower chine, the bevels go all the way to the lower face of the plywood..

As the upper portion of the stem closes up, at the forefoot the sides are under such pressure as to be immovable. This is not a bad feature as long as the two sides are in perfect, or at least near perfect, alignment. If the ends of the sides are cut at a 90° angle, correct alignment requires that the infinitely small edge of the angles on the two sides be in contact. Even the smallest misalignment results in the sides slipping past each other. One sharp edge digs into the opposing sides and prevents further movement. To realign the end, it must be disassembled.

On subsequent and even repeated reassembly, there is a great likelihood that the same problems will reoccur. The small slippage at the forefoot results in a misalignment that causes gross distortions of the hull and cannot be overlooked or wished away. If the slippage is below a 45° line through the forefoot, the hull is twisted from top to bottom around a horizontal axis. Above the 45° line, the slippage results in a hull twisted to one side lengthwise.

Builder-Made Tools and Fixtures

It was once held that humans are the only tool using creatures. Later it was discovered that certain species of birds and primates use twigs to fish ants, termites, and grubs out of their holes. Currently, we are told that humans are the only creatures to use tools to make other tools. Some builder-made special tools are required to build *Sweet Dream*. Here are some opportunities to get out your tools and show your humanity.

Aluminum Straight Edge

The 50" x 2" x 1/8" aluminum straight edge is cut from a 6' length of 2" x 1/8" aluminum flat bar available at hardware stores. Drill a 1/4" hole at one end to permit hanging the straight edge from a nail.

Router Guide

(Optional) The router guide is used when cutting the slots between the pseudo-blocks on a false built up rail. (*See the figure "Router Guide" on page 130.*) The guide is made of scrap 3/4" stock. The width between two long parallel runners is 2". Use this formula to determine the width between the short cross members with the router and bit to be used:

$$X = \text{Desired cutout width } +$$
$$\text{router baseplate width - router bit diameter.}$$

Fasten the cross members perpendicular to the runners with 1" drywall screws and carpenter's glue. Mark the center of the distance between the cross members on the longer runners. Make a register mark 1" to the left of the center mark. This mark will be used to align the guide with the rails as the cutouts are made.

Lightly mark the lengthwise centerline on one inner rail. Make a register mark 1" to the left of the center mark. Using the register mark as a proxy center line, mark off distances at

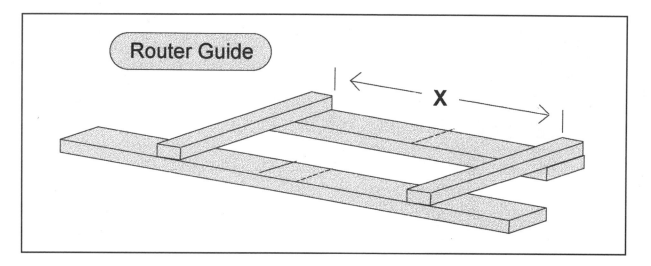

intervals equal to the sum of your chosen slot length and standoff width. (I recommend that the sum of slot length and standoff width equal 3".)

Clamp the router guide to the front edge of the work surface. Slide the pair of inner rails under the cross members. Align the rails end to end and clamp them together with screw clamps at both ends. Align the register mark on the guide with one of the cut out lines on the rails. Clamp the pair of rails to the front runner of the guide. Set the router bit to the desired depth of cut between 1/4 and 5/16". Rout out

Here the two rails have been removed from the router guide for clarity. The side rails on the guide are set for 2" wide slots. On the forward router guide rails, the offset register mark is just outside the area removed by the router bit in getting a flat surface all the way across the rails..

the slot. Unclamp the rails from the guide. Slide the rails under the cross members and line up the next cut out mark with the register mark on the guide. Clamp the rails to the guide. Rout the cutout. Continue in this manner making the rest of the cutouts.

Dragon's Teeth

Dragon's teeth are a set of angled steps that are positioned outside the rails and create parallel surfaces for the clamps to work against as the outer rails are epoxied to the hull alongside the breasthooks. A set of two is used at each breasthook. See figure on page 131.

The steps are made of 3/4" scrap. The flat bar that the steps are fixed to is a piece of 1" wide scrap 4mm hull material. The steps are glued and screwed to the flat bar. The figure gives the required measurements. Make up four pieces.

Filleting Tools

The filleting tools are used to smooth and shape a thickened epoxy mixture that is put in the inside of the chine and stem joints. The shaped thickened epoxy mixture is called a fillet. I've found that a total of six tools are required to get correct sized fillets. Three of the tools are made from scraps of 4mm okume. The other three are cut from a 6" wide plastic squeegee.

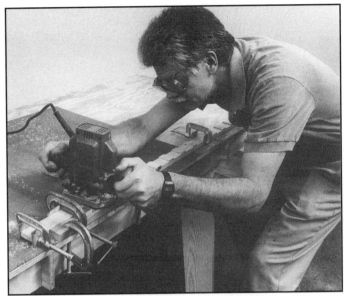

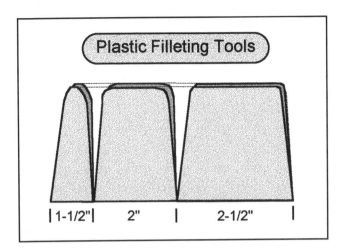

The three clamps in the lower left each have a different job. The first is clamping the two rails together. (Another clamp doing the same can be seen under my chin.) The second clamp is holding the router guide to the work surface. (Another clamp at the other end of the guide is hidden by my left hand.) The third clamp holds the rails securely in the guide.

The three wooden tools are 6" long with one square end and one rounded end. Tools are required that are 5/8", 1-1/4", and 2" wide. Sand the tools with 150 grit sandpaper and round all edges slightly. Wipe some epoxy on the tools with a cloth. Let it cure, and sand again lightly.

The three plastic filleting tools are cut from a single 6" wide plastic squeegee. The

Under all the clamps you can just see the dragon's teeth lying outside the rails as they pass along the breasthook.

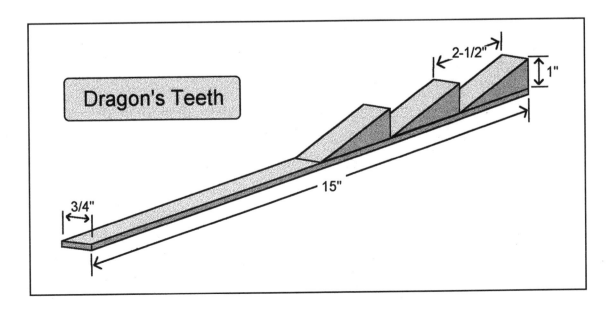

squeegees are sold by epoxy retailers. The figure, "Plastic Filleting Tools," page 131, shows how the three filleting tools are cut out. Cut them out with a sharp knife. Round the cut edges with fine grit sandpaper. After each use, wipe the tools clean with a paper towel. Wipe again with a paper towel wetted with vinegar.

Rail Tapering Fixture

At the ends of a double ended canoe, all the hull lines are converging. Although the outer rails are only 3/4" wide, tapering their ends makes the hull ends appear considerably smoother and lighter. If the rails were cut with a bevel on their lower side, the taper must be cut on the side of the rail that goes against the hull. If the rails have a beveled underside, tapering the rail width will also produce a slight taper in the height of the rail. Planing the taper is a bit of work but the results are worth the effort.

There are two ways to plane the taper; straight and curved. In a straight taper, the line of the taper runs in a straight line across the rail. When a rail with a straight taper is clamped to the sheer, there is a perceptible angle or break in the line of the outer edge of the rail where the taper begins. If the rail is beveled on the underside, planing or sanding the angle off the outer face of the rail will produce a noticeable wide spot on the outer face of the rail. For this reason the straight taper

should only be used on rails with square or rectangular cross sections.

On the curved taper, the entire length of the taper is slightly curved. When epoxied to the hull, the curved taper shows no angle or break in the outer face of the rail. A second advantage is that it is easy to make a fixture to assist in planing the curved taper. A third feature of the curved taper is very subtle.

If the grain on the top of the rail runs parallel to the sides of the rail, when the curved taper is clamped to the hull the grain curves into and ends at the hull. This is a subtle touch that complements the converging hull and rail lines at the ends of the hull. If the grain in the rails is curved outward slightly, after the rails are clamped to the hull, the grain will at least be straight, which will look better than it did before tapering.

Since the curved taper can be used on rails with any cross section and its fixture is simple to make, there is no need to further consider the straight taper.

The fixture for cutting the curved taper consists of two guides made from two pieces of scrap 3/4" thick stock about 36" long, a 3/8" thick wooden shim, and eighteen 1-5/8" dry wall or deck screws. (*See the figure "Rail Tapering Fixture" below.*)

The fixture guides the plane in cutting a straight taper in a curved rail. When the rail is released from the fixture it reverts to being

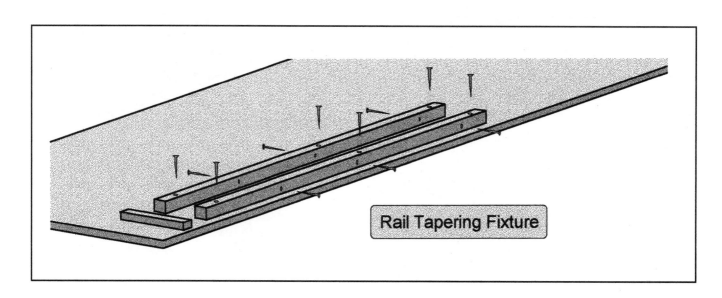

Rail Tapering Fixture

Here the rail in the fixture is ready to have its top planed even with the top of the guides. Use the shim under the end of the rail to adjust the rail height which determines how much wood is removed from the rail. Make sure that the screws fastening the guides to the work surface are well countersunk so that the heads can't come in contact with the plane iron.

straight, and the planed surface becomes curved. It really works too. The rail is held down against the top of the work surface by a pair of opposing screws threaded through the guides where the taper is to begin The shim is put under the end of the rail lifting it off the work surface and setting the amount of taper. The rail assumes a smooth curve between the screws holding the rail against the work surface and the shim. The two other pairs of opposing screws in the guides are then tightened against the rail to hold the curvature during planing. As the taper approaches completion the plane is prevented from cutting too deeply by the guides.

The pieces of the fixture are easy to make. The two pieces of scrap which serve as the guides are 3/4" thick and can be any width. Drill and countersink holes about 1" from their ends and at their centers for 1-5/8" deck screws. The screw heads must be sunk below the top surface of the guides so they do not contact the sole of the plane or the cutting edge of the plane iron. The wooden shim can start out being any thickness greater than 1/4". It will be

trimmed to get the desired rail end thickness once a rail is clamped in the fixture.

The fixture is simple to set up. At one end of the work surface, the left end for righties, screw the pair of guides to the work surface 4" or 5" from its long edge and about 7/8" apart. Put a rail in the fixture with the side that goes against the hull facing upwards. At this point in the building sequence the rails have assumed a curved shape from being clamped to the hull. When the side of the rail that goes against the hull is facing upward, the rail will curve upwards at the far end of the work surface. Align the cut at the base of the lap joint on the end of the rail with the left end of the fixture. Push the rail down firmly against the work surface and tighten the opposing screws on the right ends of the guides. Clamp the rail to the work surface at the far end. (This clamp ensures that the rail doesn't slip as it is planed.)

I remove the bulk of the wood from the rails with a bench plane. I take the last few cuts with a low angle block plane to get a smooth surface on the rail which will make a tight joint with the hull.

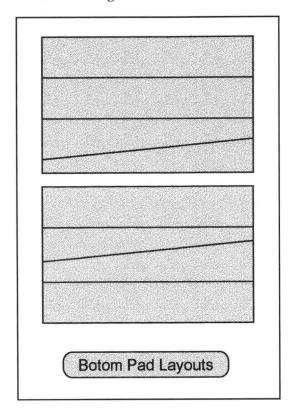

Botom Pad Layouts

has the bending and torsional rigidity generated by a full width bottom pad.

There is enough wood in the panel cutoffs to get a full size bottom pad, but it requires some extra work. The two pieces at the end of the scarphed panel have been reduced to 8" wide. Allowing 1" for an 8:1 scarph, they can provide 15" of the required 25". Two long triangular cut off pieces will provide the width that is missing. The two pieces shown on the Hull Layout Plan are roughly 9" and 3" at their ends. Allowing 1" for scarphing, joining them along their sloping sides makes a piece about 11" wide.

The two pieces, one 15" wide, and the other 11" wide, give a total of 26". As you

On the left end of the rail, make a mark 3/8" from the bottom of the rail. Place the shim under the rail at the ends of the guide. Trim the shim so that the mark on the side of the rail is in the same plane as the top of the guides. Tighten the remaining sets of opposing screws only enough to hold the rail securely.

Plane off all the wood on the sides that is standing proud above the upper surfaces of the guides. Sharpen your plane iron and have at it. If you have ash or mahogany rails it will take some effort. Consider resharpening the plane iron after doing two ends. A bench plane is better than a block plane for this work because it has a large handle at its back to push against.

Bottom Pad for the 14 foot Sweet Dream

The 14' version of the hull gets the most canoe possible from the joined plywood panels. In maximizing the hull length, the bottom pad halves are reduced until when joined along their long edges they don't reach from chine to chine. It is important, however, that the hull

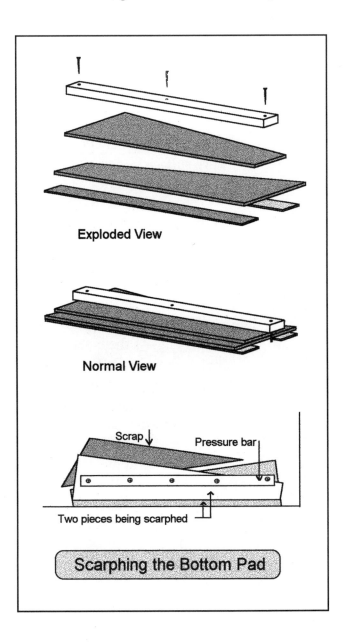

Exploded View

Normal View

Scrap ↓   Pressure bar

Two pieces being scarphed

Scarphing the Bottom Pad

might guess, when these pieces are joined, another inch is lost. That leaves a single piece 25" wide, which is just enough. No matter how you approach it, there are three joints to be made. The pieces can be joined in either of two patterns shown in the figure, "Bottom Pad Layouts," page 134. If you use epoxy-fiberglass tape joints, the panel will be about 28" wide.

If you use scarphs to join the two trapezoidal pieces, the scarph should be cut along the sloping sides of the pieces. To set up to cut the scarph, align the pieces as shown in the figure, "Scarphing the Bottom Pad," page 134 . Make a thin pressure bar from scrap okume to hold the pieces in place. Slip some scrap okume under the end of the upper piece that is unsupported by the lower piece. Screw through the pressure bar and both pieces to be scarphed. Put the pressure bar back far enough from the edge that it does not interfere with the plane.

Making Filleted and Taped Joints

Filleting is simply putting thickened epoxy in the angle of a joint to create a smooth curved surface across the joint. The fillet is completed by a layer of fiberglass tape that spans the fillet from side to side and is firmly anchored to the structural members that form the joint. In general, a filleted joint is more pleasing to the eye than the sharp angle. A fillet might be included in a hull design on those grounds alone. In fact, a fillet inside a joint in the hull also serves as a means to fasten the two parts of the joint, and it can function to restore thickness and strength lost when material is removed from the outside of the joint.

When two thin panels meet at an angle, any forces being carried by or in the panel tend to focus at the joint. If the joint is improperly designed or built, flexing of the panels can lead to rapid joint failure. A good way to help dissipate and redirect forces at a joint is to add a fillet. No matter how good it looks, the fillet's role as a part of the hull structure is far more important than cosmetic considerations. Of course, if the fillet looks good that's a plus.

Making A Fillet

The fillet is formed by putting the thickened epoxy into the joint with a putty knife or other flat or spoonlike tool. This is a pretty messy operation and it pays to use a little too much mixture so that it will fill the joint without voids or bubbles. After the material is in the joint, the inner face of a fillet is given a smooth circular cross section by pulling an appropriately shaped tool along the joint. It is important to get a smooth inner surface on the fillet to make it easier to apply the fiberglass tape.

Fillets are made of a mixture of epoxy resin and a filler. The mixture has the consistency of peanut butter. In the West System®, the preferred filler is their Filleting Blend. It makes a strong, hard fillet when mixed to the ratio of 1-1/2 scoops of filler to one pump of epoxy.

Man is an animal, a primate. When you think that the primates have been about 2 million years emerging, and the latest theory is that Homo sapiens has only been around for 100,000 years, and only in just the last 100 years has he been living in these huge megalopolises, I don't think you can expect a complete change to these new conditions. A large number of us are still wild. We're not domesticated animals. Unconsciously we search out areas where our nomadic feelings and our need to be around nature are satisfied. Boats are one of those areas

The small personal boat goes back into prehistory, and therefore the concept of the small boat is imprinted in the human brain. This is why it has such a deep emotional meaning to so many people.

James Wharram, "Out Of England,"
WoodenBoat Magazine #122

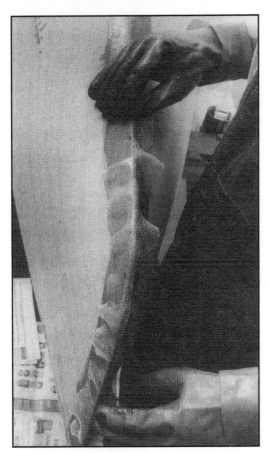

Here, presaturated bias cut tape has been laid around the forefoot and upper stem. If it were regular tape, each one of the bights in the tape would have to have a dart cut in it.

When applying epoxy to the tape covering a fillet, it is best to put the epoxy on in short strokes at a medium speed. If long quick strokes are used, tiny bubbles get entrained in the epoxy and these can be subsequently worked under the tape. Once there they are difficult to remove. The tiny bubbles appear as a hazy white blur. They weaken the tape to fillet bond. Large bubbles under the tape can be worked to the edge of the tape by lightly tapping the end of the brush next to them and moving them to the edge. If there are bubbles which won't move, it is probably a hole or depression in the face of the fillet. Put a little epoxy on it and with a tapping motion with the end of the brush, work the epoxy through the cloth. Hopefully the bubble will disappear as the hole is filled.

Regular vs. Bias Cut Fiberglass Tapes

In regular fiberglass tape the strands of the weave run parallel and perpendicular to the length of the tape. In bias cut tape the strands run across the tape at more or less a 45° angle. This difference gives the two types of tape vastly different qualities.

Think of the wide horizontal line passing through the two tapes in the figure, "Types of Fiberglass Tape," as being a joint. In the regular tape, only those strands running at a right angle across the tape resist forces tending to open the joint. The strands running the length of the tape make no contribution to keeping the joint closed. In the bias cut tape, every strand runs across the joint and resists its opening.

On a flat or nearly flat surfaces, and on a joint that is a straight line or is a very large radius (say 10' or so) both tapes will lie flat. In *Sweet Dream,* regular tape does fine on the chines, inside and out. When regular tape is asked to bend in two directions, as at the forefoot, it cannot follow both curvatures. It stands away from the surface in waves or bights. To get it to lie down, you must make relief cuts or darts across the tape. On the other hand, bias cut tape easily conforms to both curves. For

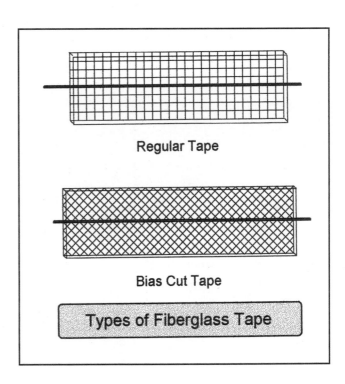

Regular Tape

Bias Cut Tape

Types of Fiberglass Tape

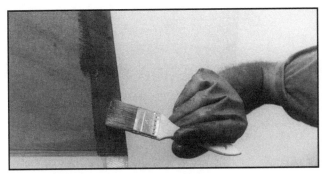

Bias cut tape lies down smoothly without having to cut darts.

good looks and ease in sanding, bias cut tape is preferable on at least the outer stems.

The major drawback to using bias cut tape is that it is not generally available. (West System® has bias tape that has all the strands running in one direction at 45° to the length of the tape. Unfortunately, it is very heavy and quite stiff. It will not follow the tight radius curves on either inside or outside of *Sweet Dream's* stem.) If you want to use bias cut tape you'll have to make your own. It's not hard to do.

You'll have to buy some fiberglass cloth in 8 or 10 oz. weight. Be sure to specify that you'll be using it with epoxy. You won't need much cloth. One yard of 52" wide cloth will produce quite a few approximately 4' long pieces of 2" and 3" wide tape.

It is easiest to make bias cut tape with a straight edge and a rotary cutter. (Hint: before cutting, check that there aren't any screw heads under the cut. They wreck havoc with the cutter edge.)

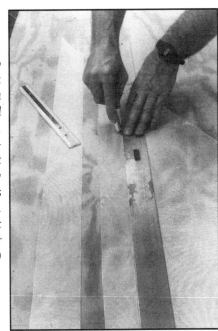

Cutting bias tapes with scissors is possible but difficult. The scissors must be very sharp. With scissors it is especially hard to keep the cuts running straight and not distort the tape. The tapes can also be cut with a razor blade and a straight edge. The easiest way to cut the tapes is with a circular cutter such as the X-Acto® 7770. The cutter works by pressing its sharpened wheel against the cloth on a hard surface; the top of the work surface works fine. When used with the aluminum straight edge as a guide, a circular cutter cuts cleanly and effortlessly without distorting the tape.

Bias cut tape must be handled very carefully. Very little force applied either lengthwise or across the tape will cause it to distort badly. As the tape stretches in one dimension, it shrinks in the other. As soon as a bias cut strip is cut from the cloth, gently roll the piece up without stretching it lengthwise. Secure the roll with string or an elastic band. Do not use sticky tape of any kind to secure the roll.

Using bias cut tape on the fillets on the internal stem joints is quite difficult. The confined spaces in the ends of the hull make it hard to manipulate the tape into position without serious distortion. For this reason I use bias cut tape only on the external stems. When applying the tape to the exterior stem joint, apply epoxy to the hull and then gently unroll the tape into the epoxy. Again, do not tension the tape along its length; it will neck down to a point and then pull apart. Follow with more epoxy applied from the inboard end of the stem joint towards the forefoot, and on to the sheer.

Determining the Sheer

For most of us, a boat's sheer, or upper edge of the side, is its dominant visual line, both on paper and on the three dimensional hull. A sheer that is smooth and lively is said to be "sweet." Drawing a fair curve on the side view of the hull during the design process is fairly simple. Getting a sheer that was drawn on a two-dimensional sheet of paper to come out sweet on the three dimensional hull is another matter.

A profile or side view of a hull is drawn as if viewed from amidships, with the viewer's eye at the level of the rail. The hull is level both fore and aft, and amidships. This is not how a hull is usually viewed in the real world. Therein lies the reason why sweet design sheers can turn sour.

Sometimes we see a hull in a position that closely approaches the profile view on the drawing board. The boat is off aways, and we are standing or sitting at water level. Most often however, we view a hull and its sheer from above the level of the rail and in a quartering view. This viewing position is most likely to display a sheer gone to vinegar.

The eye and brain have evolved a set of paradigms for quickly analyzing visual data. Sometimes the paradigm doesn't work, optical illusions are an example. In the figure, Optical Illusion," the vertical lines are straight. The eye-brain wants to see them otherwise.

Visually there are a lot of things happening at the pointy ends of a hull. Lines are converging inward from the sides and upwards from the bottom. At the ends of a boat the eye-brain wants to see smooth convergence in predetermined, unconsciously accepted curves. Even the slightest deviations from those curves are immediately perceptible. I can't get sheer curves on the drawing board that stay sweet in quartering views on the hull. But I can sneak up on them in increments in the real world.

A sheer is most likely to go sour on a relatively wide hull that carries broadness at its rails well toward the ends before converging to the stems. *Sweet Dream's* hull is one of those hulls. A natural sheer is drawn on paper simply by springing a batten between the top of the stems and a point at the desired freeboard height amidships. On the three-dimensional hull, a natural sheer is closely approximated by letting the rails act as a batten between the top of the side amidships and the tops of the stems.

On a *Sweet Dream* hull, the near natural sheer, when viewed from the quarter and above, has a distinct swelling at about Station Line 6, about 2' inboard of the stems. You can't miss it either when standing beside the boat, or when paddling. It bothers me, and since I spend as much time paddling *Sweet Dream* as I can, it bothers me a lot. I think the sheer should be at least appealing to the paddler as to a viewer ashore. Fortunately, it's not a great distance from sour to sweet, a matter of 3/8".

The building sequence uses a method to cut the sheer that produces a sweet sheer directly. If you have the time and inclination you can mark, cut, and then observe the near natural sheer and then the corrected sheer. The following procedure shows how to do this. It ends up with the same final sheer as the build-

Optical Illusion

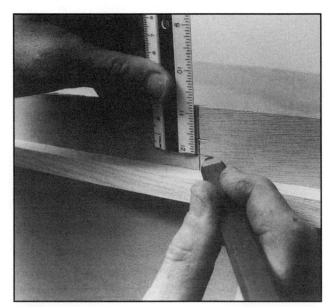

Mark the "natural" and depressed sheer on the adjustment line.

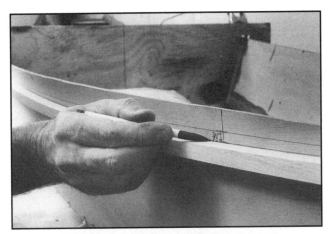

The "sweet" sheer runs flatter amidships and curves up to the top of the stem more steeply than does the "natural" sheer.

ing sequence, it just takes longer to get it. The compensation for the extra work is getting to see the sheer go from sour to sweet.

When it comes time to cut the sheer in the building sequence (page 41), clamp the rails so their tops intersect the top of the stem and the top of the hull amidships. Clamp the rails amidships with their upper faces 1/32" below the top of the side. Place the clamps about 8" apart. At the stems, the rails should be even with the top of the sides.

At Station Line 6, the rail will be about 7/8" below the top of the hull. Go around the boat and equalize measurements at Station Lines 6 and 4. Run a pencil along the top of the rail to transfer its position to the hull. This line is the near natural sheer.

Unclamp the rail ends at the stems and move them downward 4 or 5". Midway between the point where Station Lines 5 and 6 meet the top of the hull side, draw 2" long lines on the outside of the hull perpendicular to the top of the side. As a convenience, I will call these lines the "adjustment lines."

Make a mark on the adjustment lines 3/8" below the near natural sheer line. Clamp the rails to the hull with their upper face even with the lower mark on the adjustment line. Hold the rail in position with the clamps at the adjustment lines in addition to those amidships and at the stems. Mark the upper surface of the

rails from end to end onto the hull. Unclamp the rails and move them down out of the way.

Stand back a ways and look at these two sheer lines. Each starts at the same height amidships and end at the same point at the top of the stems. However, when the sheer is depressed 3/8" at the adjustment line, the sheer runs flatter across the middle of the hull and turns more sharply upward to end at the top of the stem.

The natural sheer seen in the side view on paper is lively, buoyant, bouncy, or whatever. However as I've already said, it is not sweet in three dimensions. The sheer line that is depressed 3/8" is sweet to my eye in profile, quartering, and rear views.

With the japanese saw, cut just above the uppermost of the two sheer lines. Reinstall the rails. Go off a ways and view the hull from directly amidships with your eye at rail height. Look at the sheer while standing at one end of the hull. Look at the rail in the area around the Station Line 2 at the far end. There is the bulge and the sheer is anything but sweet. Remove the weighted sacks from the hull and place the hull on the ground. When the hull is viewed from above and from a quartering position, there is even less sweetness. Unfortunately, this is the position from which a canoe is most often viewed.

Return the hull to the work surface, replace the weighted sacks, and move the rails down out of the way. Cut the sheer 1/32" above the lower sheer line. Remount the rails. Again look at the sheer from a ways off and

---

Perhaps the one single line that crowns or dams the whole creation is the sheer line. It may look well in plan view on paper, and it may look well in profile view on paper, but be careful – some peculiar effects can happen in the three-dimensional view.

Francis S. Kinney,
Skene's Elements of Yacht Design

amidships. The flattening in the sheer amidships is barely detectable. Look at the sheer from the end and quarter views. There's a big difference; the swelling is gone or nearly so.

My eye sees this sheer as sweet. It strikes a balance between flattening the sheer in the side view and getting rid of the swelling around Station Line 6 in the end and quarter views. Sometimes I think that I can just see traces of the swelling. If you are a very critical appraiser of sheers and you can still see the swelling, you may wish to depress the sheer another 1/4". I haven't felt the need to. Perhaps you should depress the sheer by only 1/8" and see how that looks first.

To the technically inclined or tradition-burdened reader, let me say that I know that what I am doing here is inversely related to "augmenting the sheer." Further, I will admit that my method of determining a sweet sheer may have only its nose in the tent of accepted methodology.

My method departs from accepted practice at least in that the ends of the rails are pinned together. As a result they, and the sheer, are constrained to a fixed length. When the rails are depressed, a zero-sum game begins. The new path described by the rails along the side of the hull is longer than the "natural" sheer line. (As an extreme example of this, remember that the arc of a semi-circle is longer than the diameter of the circle.) In the real world, the sheer is three-dimensional. When the rails are depressed to the new sheer when viewed from the side, at the same time the rails squeeze inward when

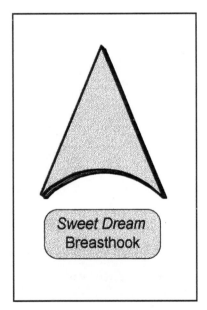

Sweet Dream Breasthook

viewed from above. As luck would have it, the rails squeeze the sides of the hull together around Station Lines 5 and 6.

Broadness of the hull carried into the ends is one of the conditions already identified as a cause of a sweet sheer gone bad. The squeezing reaction of the pinned rails reduces the broadness in just the right places. I don't know which action, lowering the sheer or reducing the broadness of the hull, is primarily responsible for the resulting sheer which I see as sweet. I don't think it matters; the combined results are better than the beginning condition. I just want you to know that, to misquote Bob Dylan, "Something strange is happening here and I don't know what it is. Do you, Mr. Jones?"

Breasthook Options

In traditional boat building, installing the breasthooks is one of the more difficult operations confronting the builder. The difficulty arises from having to cut a compound bevel along the slightly curved sides of the breasthook where they meet the hull. When the breasthooks are finally fitted, they are attached with screws through the planking from the outside. The screw heads are covered by the rail. The rails are held in place with countersunk screws that are covered by plugs.

Since *Sweet Dream* is hardly a traditional hull, there would be little sense in going through the tedium of mounting the breasthooks in the traditional manner. It would be nice though to use a method that preserves the sweep of the sheer and has the clean lines of the traditional breasthook. An epoxy/fiberglass

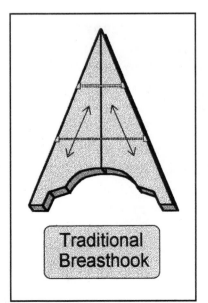

Traditional Breasthook

taped fillet beneath the breasthook can provide a strong connection between the breasthook and the hull. Three ways of installing the breasthooks come easily to mind:

✑ Breasthooks sitting on top of the outer rails and hull. This method is quick and easy. Its disadvantage is that the breasthooks break up the sweep of the sheer. After the rails are epoxied to the hull, the breasthooks are attached to the rails with epoxy and screws driven down through the breasthook and into the outer rail. At their ends the rails are canted slightly outwards. Before installing the breasthooks, the rail tops must be trimmed flat in way of the breasthooks. Alternately, the gap along the outer edge of the breasthook can be filled with thickened epoxy.

✑ Breasthooks inset into the outer rails and hull. After the rails are epoxied to the hull, cut-outs are made in both the rails and the hull to accept the breasthooks. Getting a clean straight cut in the rails is difficult. The breasthooks are attached to the rails with epoxy and screws driven through the breasthook and into the outer rail. The upper surface of the breasthooks are flush with the line of the top of the rails. After a lot of hard work, the end grain on the sides of the breasthooks still shows.

✑ Breasthooks inset into the hull with rails running alongside. This method looks very much like traditional breasthooks and is relatively easy to do. In this method not only are compound angles not cut, but not a single angle is measured. The breasthooks are fitted to the hull before the rails are permanently attached. After the breasthooks are attached with a fillet and tape joint inside the hull, their sides are trimmed flush with the hull. The outer rails run alongside the breasthooks to the stem preserving the sweep of the sheer and covering the end grain on the breasthook sides. This method is described in detail in the building sequence beginning on page 42.

Traditional breasthooks are made of two mirror image pieces with the joint running down the centerline. The grain in the two pieces runs parallel to the rails. At the joint there is some degree of end grain which tends to weaken the joint if it is glued. To overcome this weakness, sometimes the breasthook is drilled through from side to side and through bolted. At the inner end of the breasthook there is considerable fitting to be done. The tabs must be the same size as the spacers in a built up rail and they must be cut at a compound bevel to land the inner rails.

Sweet Dream's laminated plywood breasthooks do not suffer from weakness at the centerline. The cross grain plys serve the positive function of continuous cross bolting.

To the question of what shape should the inner breasthook edge take, there is no correct answer. Anything will do so long as there is about 6" of solid breasthook aft of the stem. Most traditional shapes are a portion of a circle or ellipse. One fanciful traditional design incorporated a heart shaped cutout. It is up to you.

I prefer a segment of a circle of about 4" radius. When viewed from the opposite end of the hull, the eye interprets the smooth curve of the inner edge of the breasthook as a crown in the breasthook's upper surface The breasthook you are standing

A canoe is a poor man's yacht. In common with nine-tenths of my fellow citizens, I am poor — and the canoe is my yacht, as it would be were I a millionaire.

George Washington Sears,
"Nessmuk," 1885

Sand smart, not hard. The hull is being held upright by one of the 50lb weighted sacks placed on the hull side behind me. I'm letting gravity pull the sander into the work as opposed to sanding the tape with the hull upright and having to support the weight of the sander.

next to is flat but the one at the other end of the hull appears to be crowned. When you walk to the far end, again it is the breasthook at the far end that appears curved.

After you have selected a shape for the inner edge of your breasthook, return to the building sequence at page 42 for details on mounting the breasthooks.

Tapering the Edges of Fiberglass Tape

There is much less tape to be sanded on *Sweet Dream* than on other stitch and glue boats of her length. This is good because sanding the tape edges is a demanding job. Depending on the level of finish that you are striving for, sanding the tape will take between 10 and 20 hours.

How long the sanding takes is partly a function of the size of sander used. I use a 6" dual action sander; with 40 grit paper it

removes material in a hurry. I've used a friend's 5" sander. The 6" was considerably faster in removing material. At the edge of a 6" disc spinning at 3500 RPM, the paper is moving at a linear motion equivalent of 5500 feet per minute or 62.5 MPH. It's only 52 MPH for the 5" sander. With the 5" sander, doing the ends of the inside chines and the inner end of the stem joint was easier if slower than the 6" sander.

Two additional factors contribute to the 10 to 20 hour range for sanding; degree of cure of the epoxy, and how the inside stems are handled.

Sanding a seam within 24 hours of applying the tape and epoxy goes much quicker than if you wait longer. The epoxy is hard and shows no sign of tackiness, yet the sanding residue is not dust but little balls. When the epoxy is fully cured it is very hard and sands into dust. Sanding the fully cured tape edges proceeds much more slowly.

Sanding the inside stems to an invisible transition to the hull requires a lot of time because a rotating sander can't get into the confined space in the stems. As a result, the tape edges must be sanded by hand or with an electric detail sander. Either way, it's a lot slower than using a dual action sander. When was the last time you moved your hand in 62 MPH oscillations? If you are bound and determined that none of the seams will show, it's a good idea to sand the tape edges inside the stems before you put the breasthooks on.

An electric drill with a disc sander attachment can be used for sanding the tape edges. I've tried it, and it worked, but I'll never do it again. With the disc sander the opportunity to

> We live in a society where the guarantee of not starving to death is purchased at the price of dying of boredom.
>
> Raoul Vaneigem

The inside chines and lower stems are not much more difficult to sand than the outside ones. Around the inside chine ends, the sander has to be held at an elevated angle to prevent cutting the plywood on the side opposite to the one being sanded. If you successfully overcome the chine ends, you might wish to address the lower stem seams. Here, too, but to an even greater degree, the sander is held at an elevated angle. With care and concentration

Taper the double layer of fiberglass tape so that the surface is smooth and flat. Avoid sanding depressions in the hull just beyond the tape and sanding through the tape at the chine.

correct a situation going bad just passed. With the dual action sander, there is a second or two to recognize a problem developing and avoid it.

It is important that the outside seams be really smooth to reduce parasitic drag on the hull. Smoothness of the seams inside the hull is a matter of aesthetics and ego. Sand the outside seams first, then see how you feel about the inside ones and especially the stems.

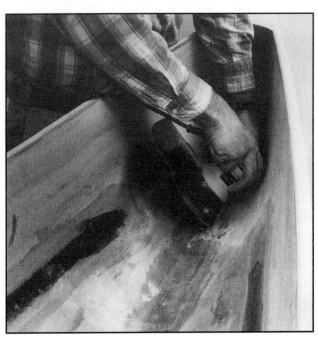

I have to steel myself to sand the lower stems with the dual action sander. It can be done and it is faster than hand sanding, but it's hard to keep the sander at the right angle and sand at the right point on the tape.

the tape edges can be tapered almost up to the forefoot. As to the upper stems, to hand sand or not hand sand, that is the question.

Do not sand epoxy that is even the slightest bit tacky to the touch. Wear a dust mask and safety glasses when sanding the tape edges. You will create a large volume of dust. If at all possible, sand the tape edges out of doors. Support and weight the hull so that it cannot shift. Sand smart, not hard. Turn the hull on its side so that gravity pulls the sander onto the work. Let the sander do

It takes some care to sand only the tape at the chine ends without gouging the adjacent hull.

the work; you should be the brains and guiding hand. The sander works best when it spins freely. Leaning on the sander slows down the work and leads to rapid and unnecessary clogging and wearing out of the sandpaper.

On the outside of the hull, be especially careful when sanding near the ends of the chines and around the forefoot. It is very easy to cut right through the tape to bare wood here. Consider hand sanding in these areas.

There is an alternative to sanding for the interior. If you feel that the tape on the interior does not need to be invisible, the edges can be given a short steep taper with a special carving tool.

The gouge, unlike the chisel, is sharpened on the side of the blade that contacts the wood. Gouges are available with blades curved across their width. The curvature is designated by number with higher numbers signifying greater curvature. I use a 3/4" #7 gouge. (I suspect a #5 or #6 might work even better. But at almost $30 each, I'll stick with my #7.) A curved chisel requires a special sharpening stone to get inside the curvature of the blade. A gouge can be sharpened on a flat stone. Gouges are not

easy to come by. Two sources for gouges are Garrett Wade, 1-800-221-2942; and Woodcraft, 1-800-535-4482. Call and ask for their catalog.

As epoxy cures, there is a period of time when it is quite firm, but not yet really hard. Just when this time occurs after application, and how long it lasts are a function of many factors. These include brand of epoxy, hardener, temperature, and humidity. I can't say when it will occur on your hull. You have to check the epoxy every 30 minutes or so. But it can be worth it to hang around for a few hours and with a few minutes work avoid hours of sanding later on.

The condition you're looking for is just the slightest tackiness to the epoxy. At this point, you can cut a triangular sliver off the edge of the tape with the gouge. The gouge must be razor sharp. The center of the gouge contacts the hull directly under the edge of the tape. As the gouge is advanced, it cuts off a sliver about 1/8" wide. If the gouge is at all dull it will lift the edge of the tape as it cuts and the taper will be greatly reduced in width.

Seating Options

Sweet Dream is designed for either single or double paddling, For double paddling, you sit on a pad or cushion on the bottom of the canoe and lean against a backrest. For single paddling, you sit on a seat at, or just below rail height. You can also kneel with your knees wide spread on the bottom for support and control, and your butt perched on the front edge of the seat or supported on your heels.

If you are a newcomer to solo canoeing, you will find double paddling a good introduction. Seated on the bottom of the canoe your butt is below the waterline. I tell people that you have to fall up to fall out of a solo canoe. A slight exaggeration, but not wholly untrue. Seated on the bottom, your center of gravity is as low as it can practicably be, and the canoe is as stable as it will get. *Sweet Dream* is about 26 inches wide at the waterline when carrying 150 pounds. Barring some of the high dollar, high-

Backrest Parts

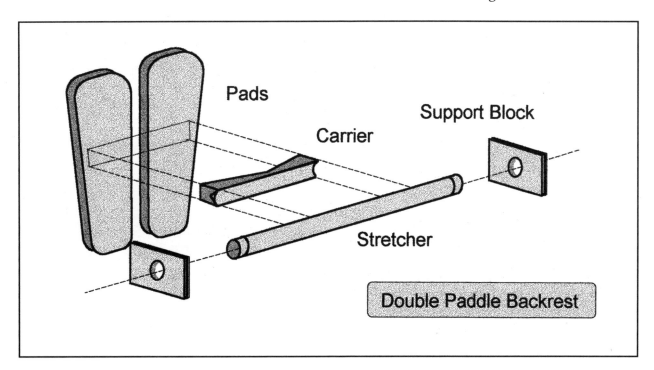

zoot, near custom hulls, most store bought, 13' long, solo canoes will have a waterline width in excess of 30 inches. For comparison, two person, tandem, canoes have waterlines starting at about 36 inches.

Waterline width is only one of the factors contributing to a canoe's stability. Other factors are hull cross section amidships, draft, rocker, hull length, and the proficiency of the paddler. Stability in canoes is like stability in people, it's a relative thing. Once you get used to the responsiveness of *Sweet Dream*, soloing a tandem canoe will feel like paddling a bathtub in a lake of molasses.

When double paddling you sit on the bottom and lean against a backrest. The backrest I've designed for *Sweet Dream* is shown in the figure, "Double Paddle Backrest." Dimensions for the various parts are given in the figure, "Backrest Parts." It has features in common with the backrest designs of L. Francis Herreshoff and Tom Hill. Overall it strikes a nice balance between its predecessors. Like theirs, it rotates to accommodate different paddler positions. It gives up a little comfort to Herreshoff's because its pads are fixed to the stretcher. But then it is considerably less fiddly to build. Because *Sweet Dream* has two fixed thwarts, the backrest stretcher does not have to do double

duty as a thwart as does Tom Hill's. So again it is easier to fit. The backrest pads are fixed to a carrier which in turn is fixed to the stretcher. The face of the carrier that mates with the pads is cut at 160° which places the flat of the pads against the muscle masses that parallel the spine.

The stretcher is hung in support blocks that hang just below the inner rails. With the thwarts bolted in place the stretcher is locked into the blocks. When the thwarts are removed, the hull sides can be pulled apart enough to insert and remove the stretcher. To avoid the difficulty of drilling the hole in the support blocks at the correct compound angle for the end of the stretcher, I've devised a procedure that laminates four pieces of okume together with slightly oversize holes for the stretcher. The pieces are laminated on the hull and the compound angle is arrived at easily.

The stretcher support blocks can be mounted in different ways. The easiest is to epoxy them to the hull and rails. Alternately they can be bolted or screwed to the rails without epoxy. In this case a block shape like that in the lower left of the figure "Backrest Stretcher Support Block Shapes," page 146, is in order. Use a single carriage bolt or two #10 screws in each wing of the block. The okume plys do not much like having screws driven into them parallel to the glue lines. Be sure to drill a pilot hole of the right diameter into the block, it will prevent splitting the block. Remember to finish the back and upper edge of a support block attached with bolts or screws.

After you have gotten comfortable with your *Sweet Dream* by double paddling a while, try moving up to the single paddle seat. After the relative stability of sitting low in the hull, sitting on the single paddle seat will make the hull feel somewhat unstable. The hull hasn't changed, your center of gravity is about 10 inches higher. Small sideways shifts of weight that had little perceptible effect when sitting on the bottom result in larger angles of heel. Moving up to the single paddle seat also involves having to learn and become adept at using a repertoire of single paddle strokes. It is challenging but rewarding. With a single paddle, *Sweet Dream* can fairly dance. She's a nimble performer and rewards the effort of becoming a proficient single paddler many times over.

When you move up to the single paddle seat other things change as well. Because you sit higher, you can see more clearly down into the water. Here in Tidewater Virginia there are uncountable logs, and other debris lurking below the surface. The water is often coffee-colored from a high concentration of tannic acid, and it's rare to be able to see things six inches below the surface. Getting up high helps you see some of what's down there . . . maybe even in time to avoid it.

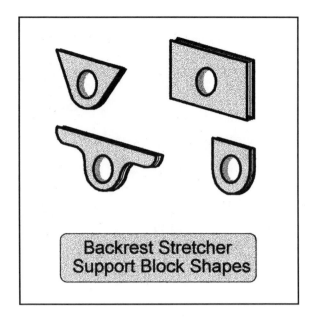

Backrest Stretcher Support Block Shapes

Sitting on the single paddle seat changes your perception as well. First, the canoe seems smaller. After a while you notice, I do anyway, that there is an indefinable difference in how things outside the canoe look and feel. I'm certain it has something to do with height of eye above the reference plane, in this case the water. I suspect the feeling is linked to the experience of learning to stand up and walk when the eye went from crawling height to standing. Sitting or kneeling up high I feel more on top of things, physically and mentally as well.

Which ever seating arrangement you choose, you can retrofit the other at a later time. The building sequence details the steps in building both the backrest and the single paddle seat. See Install the Seat, page 61, for the single paddle seat. Instructions for the double paddle backrest begin on page 62.

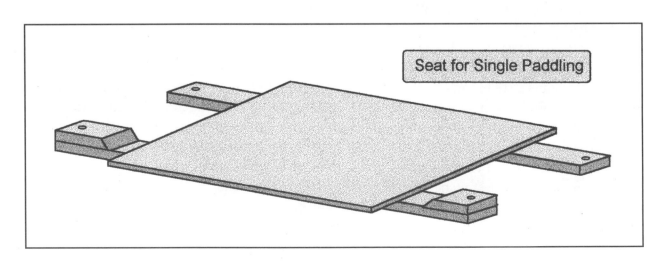

Seat for Single Paddling

Part 5:

Supplemental Reading

Paddle Styles, Shapes, and Lengths

*He who walks in the middle of the road
gets hit by cars going both ways.*
Anon.

I designed *Sweet Dream* for use with both single or double bladed paddles. (Some people mistakenly call the double bladed paddle a kayak paddle.) The single paddle is typically used in a sitting or kneeling position. (See The Tuffet, page 102, for a discussion of a seat-like arrangement for a position in between sitting and kneeling.) While the double paddle is traditionally used by a paddler sitting on the bottom of the boat, it is every bit as effective when used kneeling.

As a solo canoeist, just about everyone else on the water using a paddle (and absolutely everyone using oars) will find something wrong with what you're about. Kayakers say that using a single paddle is highly inefficient, and by sitting above the bottom your stability is greatly reduced; and your body acts like a sail in the wind; and they are right. Canoeists who use a single paddle will say that by using a double paddle you give up considerable maneuverability and you use far fewer muscles as you paddle, and they too are right. The single paddle folks will also think you somehow unmanly-unwomanly if you admit to not

understanding how to do some of their more esoteric strokes. (Because the solo canoe is quite narrow, a lot of the single paddle strokes which cross over the hull, and are considered difficult to do, are quite simple. Discretion being the better part of valor, it is usually best not to say so.) Unfortunately there seems to be an unbridgeable gap between die-hards in the two camps; double paddle kayakers, and single paddle canoeists. Each feels that theirs is the only way. Most likely, each group will consider you suspect for not using their techniques and equipment exclusively.

Using a double paddle while kneeling is a relaxed way to move along at a pretty good clip. I am sitting on a Tuffet and paddling the canoe backwards so that I don't have to put my feet under the backrest stretcher. With a symmetrical hull, from the water's point of view, there is no difference which end of the hull goes first.

Paddling in *Sweet Dream* you can pick and choose your paddle, paddling style, and seating position to best suit a particular situation and your preference at a given time. You can have the best of the two arbitrarily defined worlds.

Double Bladed Paddles

Buying a double paddle for a solo canoe can be a frustrating experience. Although the double paddle was in use in recreational canoes long before the single paddle, few people now know it. Today just about everyone associates the double paddle with the kayak, and the single paddle with canoes.

A student of mine had a difficult time when she went to buy a double paddle for her solo canoe. The "local expert" argued so energetically with her that she left the store empty handed and doubting that she had really wanted a double paddle in the first place. She went home and paddled around having a great time sitting on the bottom of her double paddle solo canoe and using a single paddle from an inflatable dinghy.

Later she asked me if I too got sore from paddling like she was. I asked how on earth she chose such an ungainly and uncomfortable method of paddling. She told me about her trip to the expert. I let her try one of my double paddles and she took to it right away. She steeled her nerve to go back to the store and buy a double paddle. She would get one even if she had to lie and say she was a kayaker to get it! She got her double paddle but the kayaker ruse was unsuccessful. A 7' paddle is longish for a kayak; she needed one about 8' from tip to tip.

In his book, *Canoes & Kayaks for the Backyard Builder,* Skip Snaith has an extended discussion of building double paddles. The book put me on to how easy it is to make good looking paddles with excellent paddling characteristics. Skip has an excellent in-depth discussion of the many factors and considerations that are part of a better paddle. It is a must-read for all beginning double paddle builders, no matter the techniques or materials used. (See pages 166 to 173 in his book.)

Sitting on the bottom of the canoe is the most stable paddling position. If this is your first experience with solo canoes, I recommend you start out double paddling and sitting on the bottom, leaning against the backrest.

In his book *Low Resistance Boats*, Thomas F. Jones also presents a closet pole-based double-paddle design that uses a laminated blade.

Other books with information on double-paddle making are:

Boats, Oars, and Rowing by R. D. Culler; p 117
More Building Classic Small Craft by John Gardner; p. 72.
Sensible Cruising Designs by L. Francis Herreshoff; p. 9.
Wood and Canvas Kayak Building by George Putz; p. 5.
Building Lapstrake Canoes by Walter J. Simmons; pp 79 - 81.

When building your double paddle, remember that paddle weight is a major consideration. A barely acceptable weight is 2-1/2 pounds, 2-1/4 pounds is good, 2 pounds is excellent. Closet pole and okume bladed double paddles are intended for use where you don't expect to routinely encounter rocks. While the plywood blades are highly resistant to splitting, the paddle won't survive long on a steady diet of rocks.

Single Bladed Paddles

Over the past century there have been any number of formulas used for predicting what length single bladed straight shaft paddle you should use. Strangely enough, most of them try to predict the paddle length by taking some segment of a person's height when standing upright. Over time canoe adventurers have moved into faster and faster moving waters. In these situations quick, powerful maneuvering comes to the fore and a shorter paddle with a short compact blade is preferred.. The "preferred" paddle length has gone from the ground to the top of the head, to eye brows, to nose, to the chin, to the shoulder. At times even the thickness of one's footwear is taken into consideration. I find such methods strange because they gloss over very real differences between any two paddlers in arm, leg, and torso length; height of the seat above the water, and the length of the blade on the paddle. There has to be a better way.

Fortunately there is one, and it is simple and accurate. To get the correct length paddle, you have to sit in your canoe holding a paddle, or broom stick, etc. The correct length for this paddler in this canoe is the sum of three segments: the distance between the paddler's hands, the distance from the lower hand to the water, and the length of the particular blade style the paddler favors.

The distance between the paddler's hand is gotten simply. Sit in your canoe. Holding a paddle, broom stick, or whatever, (from here on I'll call it the "shaft.") drop your lower hand until it is straight down, and at an angle so that your hand clears the hull. Adjust the length of the shaft so that your upper hand which is across the top of the shaft is at chin height. The length of the shaft between your hands is the first segment.

Without changing where your hands are on the shaft, hold the paddle at your side, so that it sticks straight up out of the water. Your upper arm should be extended across your body, and your upper hand is out over the water. Look down and see how much distance there is between your lower hand and the water on the shaft. This distance is the second segment of your preferred paddle length.

The third segment has to do solely with the shape of the blade. Older traditional blades tend to be longish and thin with a well rounded tip. More contemporary shapes tend to be squarish, wider and shorter. Pick out a shape and blade area, typically between 100 and 120 square inches, that you like.

Add the length of your preferred blade to the two other segments, and there you have it. Make (or buy) a paddle to these specifications and give it a good work out for a while. You will probably find that you prefer different paddle shapes and lengths for different situations. No problem, make paddles with as many shaft lengths and/or blade shapes as you like.

As far as making a single paddle, Gil Gilpatrick has a nifty design in his book, *Building a Strip Canoe*. He also has a number of tricks for toughening the blade, especially the blade tip. The one modification to Gil's procedure that I would suggest is to make the paddle blade out of doubled 4mm okume. (Gil also does an excellent job of explaining how to cane a seat. A caned seat would add a distinctive traditional touch to any of the *Sweet Dreams*.)

Gil doesn't say clearly what wood to use for the shaft. Store bought paddles are made of spruce, ash, maple, cherry, you name it. So even if you don't have enough ash left over, just about any wood will do. All told the wood in the paddle will cost about $10. Your first paddle, like your first canoe, may turn out a little rough. That's fine, you'll do much better on your second. At $10 for materials, you can make quite a few paddles for the $60-$100 you'll pay for a good to very good store bought one.

Using a single paddle requires that you master a number of technical strokes. It's not really hard; it just takes time and practice. In my opinion, the rewards far outweigh the effort required.

Hull Numbers & The *Sweet Dream* Registry

Sweet Dream feels like a part of me. To track of all my various parts, I have established the *Sweet Dream Register*. To have your *Sweet Dream* entered into the register, send me a picture of your completed *Sweet Dream*. On receipt I will enter your hull in the register and assign it a unique hull number. Hull numbers will be assigned in the order that I open the mail. Listing in the register and assignment of a hull number is free. Please send the following information:

Sweet Dream
Hull Number 0001-1
Built by Marc F. Pettingill
September 1995

Builder's Name: _____ Age: _____

Street: _____

City: _____

State: _____ ZIP _____ Phone: _____

Month & year completed: _____ Length: _____

Optional Information:

Original Owner: _____

Canoe's Name: _____

Distinguishing Features or Custom Details: _____

_____

Comments on *Building Sweet Dream* "folded ply" construction, or *Sweet Dream:* _____

_____

For the record, the prototype *Sweet Dream*, which made its debut at the 13th Mid-Atlantic Small Craft Festival in October 1995, has been assigned Hull Number 0000 and is registered to me as builder and original owner. The first "production" hull, a 13-footer that I built in September '95 is assigned Hull Number 0001-1. The original owner is Winslow Womack of St. Michaels, MD. (The suffix, "-#" is reserved for my use; it is the sequential number of the *Sweet Dreams* that I build.) The address of the registry is:

The *Sweet Dream* Registry
c/o Tiller Publishing
P.O. Box 447
St. Michaels, MD 21663

Many classic canoes have a hull number and builder's name displayed on a small brass plate. My hope is that in time *Sweet Dream* will come to be considered a classic of sorts. When you register your *Sweet Dream*, you may elect to purchase a Hull Number Plate. If you include a postal money order or cashier's check for $30 made out to The *Sweet Dream* Registry, I will send you a brass hull number plate and mounting screws. I envision something along the lines of the plate shown above: an ellipse about 3" across, to be mounted in a conspicuous place such as on the forward breasthook. I will also send you a brass plate with the "Paddle Your Own Canoe©" logo.

Safety on the Water

Sweet Dream is designed for use on flat water lakes, ponds, swamps, rivers, etc. It is not intended for use on large, open bodies of water such as large lakes, bays, or sounds, the oceans, etc. *Sweet Dream* is not designed for use on fast running or white water.

When underway in your *Sweet Dream* always, **ALWAYS**, wear a Coast Guard approved personal floatation device (PFD). Put it on and buckle/zipper it up before you go aboard. Wear it throughout the entire outing. Take it off only after the trip is over. Insist that everyone who uses your canoe, and anyone with whom you canoe does likewise.

If you are a beginning canoeist, check around your area for a canoeing course. There is no better or faster way to learn basic canoeing skills and water safety procedures. Courses are often offered by the American Red Cross, YMCA and YWCA's, municipal recreation programs, canoe and outdoors clubs, and outdoor equipment stores. As a last resort, call a local Boy or Girl Scout Troop. Very often one of the leaders will be a canoe fanatic and can connect you with a course.

Solo canoeing does not imply canoeing alone. It means having only one person in each canoe. Build two solo canoes and go solo canoeing with a friend.

FLOATATION. In its basic arrangement, *Sweet Dream* will float just below the surface when filled water. If you can swim; and know how to right and empty the canoe in deep water, this need not be a problem on short trips on familiar waters. However, if you let others use your canoe, especially children, go on long trips, or explore unfamiliar waters, it is best to install floatation in the ends of the hull. The floatation can be in the form of foam blocks, inner tubes, pre-made floatation bags, even empty plastic gallon jugs.

In every case the floatation material must be securely fastened to the hull. Foam blocks can be cut so that they match the inside shape of the hull and then covered with a layer of 8 oz. fiberglass cloth and painted. The blocks should be secured with straps or sealed in a closed compartment. The other forms of floatation should be securely lashed down with strong cord secured to eyes fastened to the breasthook and the sides of the hull inside the outer rails. There are some nice glue-on D-rings with large pads made for plastic-fiberglass canoes that should work well too.

Although not required by federal boating safety regulations, carrying a flotation cushion is safer than not doing so. If it serves no other function, it can be very useful in reboarding a swamped canoe in deep water.

The first thing that you must learn about canoeing is that the canoe is not a lifeless, inanimate object; it feels very much alive, alive with the life of the river. Life is transmitted to the canoe by currents of air and the water upon which it rides.

Bill Mason,
Path of the Paddle

Canoeing Safety Tips

⁓ Put your PFD on before entering the canoe, and keep it on and properly fastened throughout the entire trip. Ensure that others whom you let use your canoe do the same. Children weighing less than 75 pounds should wear a child sized PFD, not one sized for an adult.

⁓ Carry a Coast Guard approved throwable floatation device in your canoe in addition to the PFD worn by the paddler.

⁓ Never use alcoholic beverages or illegal drugs before or during activities on or near the water. Boating while under the influence of alcohol or drugs is an offense under both state and federal statutes.

⁓ Always provide first time users with some instruction on entering and exiting your canoe, and using a double paddle.

⁓ Check your canoe for damage before and after each use. Fix structural damage immediately.

⁓ Be alert to danger from unseen hazards below the water surface or behind obstructions.

⁓ Get a copy of the Navigation Rules: International and Inland. (Available from the Government Printing Office, Washington, D.C. (202) 783-3238. Ask for publication CG-16672.2B) Read it and be familiar with its pertinent parts.

⁓ Always assume that the person operating other watercraft can't see you, and if they do see you they don't know or won't follow the Navigation Rules. While it is the law that human powered watercraft have the right of way over all other watercraft, some recreational power boat operators concede this point grudgingly. Don't knowingly get caught in situations where you are endangered by someone else's ignorance, obstinacy, or outright negligence.

⁓ Never obstruct or hinder the passage of deep draft vessels in narrow or obstructed waterways. (This is a notable exception to the human powered watercraft right of way.)

⁓ Remember that a collision at sea will ruin your whole day, and many days following. In virtually all collisions involving injury or death, responsibility and financial liability is established on a case by case basis in costly civil or criminal court cases.

⁓ Never rely on the Coast Guard or other water safety patrols to get you out of trouble. Be proactive to anticipate and avoid trouble. If you're using your canoe on the quiet protected waters it is intended for, it is unlikely they can even find you.

⁓ Always fill out a FLOAT PLAN and leave it with your spouse, a friend, or a neighbor before going on a canoe trip, no matter how short. See the sample FLOAT PLAN on the next page.

⁓ If you are harassed or endangered by someone negligently using a watercraft, report it as soon as possible to the nearest Coast Guard, marine police, or water patrol station. Get the names, addresses and phone numbers of any witnesses. Enforcement action can be initiated only if you can identify the other vessel. To do this you need the registration number of the vessel. It appears on each bow; it has eight characters; two letters followed by four numbers, and then two more letters. A description of the vessel and the operator may be required. As a last resort, in many states a watercraft owner can be identified through motor vehicle or trailer license numbers.

⁓ LAST & ALWAYS, **ALWAYS wear a Coast Guard approved Personal Floatation Device (PFD) when using your canoe.**

F L O A T   P L A N

ALWAYS WEAR A LIFE JACKET OR PFD WHEN IN A SMALL BOAT.
Never mix drugs or alcohol with small boating.

Name: _____ Age: _____ Date:_____

Address: _____ City: _____

Phone numbers: Home: _____ Work: _____

Color of outer clothing: Jacket/shirt _____ Pants/shorts: _____

TRIP INFORMATION:

Location of Boating Activity: _____

_____

Place where vehicle will be parked: _____

_____

Time to depart home: _____ Time to arrive at put-in: _____

Time to return to put-in: _____ Time to return home: _____

Other persons in the group: _____ Phone: _____

BOAT INFORMATION:

Hull Type: _____ Manufacturer: _____

Propulsion: _____ Length: _____ Beam: _____ Depth: _____

Color: Outside of Hull: _____ Inside of Hull: _____

Trim: _____ Bottom: _____

Equipment carried on this trip: _____

_____

VEHICLE INFORMATION:

Make and Model: _____

Color: _____ License number: _____ State: _____

Trailer license number: _____ State: _____

NEXT OF KIN INFORMATION:

Name: _____ Relationship: _____

Address: _____ City: _____

Phone numbers: Home: _____ Work: _____

If I am not back or have not called you by _____ **, please call**

Coast Guard Search and Rescue at: _____

Further Canoeing Adventures

Sweet Dream is but one of many canoe designs. The folded ply construction is but one of many building methods. There are many "good reads" about canoes and canoeing. The folowing volumes, mostly about canoes, along with those quoted throughout this book, will give you many hours of interesting reading.

Birch Bark
Adney, Edwin T. and Chappelle, Howard I. *The Bark Canoes and Skin Boats of North America.*

Traditional Wood on Canvas
Stelmok, Jerry, and Thurlow, Rollin. *The Wood and Canvas Canoe.*

Traditional Lapstrake
Simmons, Walter J. *Building Lapstrake Canoes.*

Plywood Lapstrake
Hill, Thomas J. with Stetson, Fred. *Ultralight Boatbuilding.*

Cedar strip
Gilpatrick, Gil. *Building a Strip Canoe.*
Moores, Ted and Mohr, Merilyn. *Canoecraft.*

Skin on Frame
Putz, George. *Wood and Canvas Kayak Building.*
Dyson, George. *Baidarka.*

Design
Buehler, George. *Buehler's Backyard Boatbuilding.*
Herreshoff, L. Francis. *Sensible Cruising Designs.*

Jones, Thomas Firth. *Low Resistance Boats.*
Gardner, John. *More Building Classic Small Craft.*

Stitch and Glue
Devlin, Samuel. *Devlin's Boat Building.*
J. Gengler Boat Design. *Stitch and Glue Construction Guide.*

Laminated Wood
Miller, Hub. *The Laminated Wood Boat Builder.*

Composite
Moran, James. *Building Your Kevlar Canoe.*

Solo Canoeing
Foshee, John H. *Solo Canoeing.*
Jacobson, Cliff. *The Basic Essentials of Solo Canoeing.*

Literature
Burroughs, Franklin. *The River Home; A Return to the Carolina Low Country.*
Johnson, Beth. *Yukon Wild.*
Mason, Bill. *Path of the Paddle.*
McPhee, John. *The Survival of the Bark Canoe*

History
Brennan, Dan, Editor. *Canoeing the Adirondacks with Nessmuk.*
Manley, Atwood with Jamieson, Paul F. *Rushton and His Times in American Canoeing.*
Quirke, Terence T. *Canoes the World Over.*
Teller, Walter Magnes. *On The River; A Variety of Canoe & Small Boat Voyages.*

The number of boating men who find pleasure merely in sailing a boat is small compared with those who delight not only in handling, but as well in planning, building, improving or "tinkering" generally on their pet craft, and undoubtedly the latter derive the greater amount of pleasure from the sport. They not only feel a pride in the result of their work, but their pleasure goes on, independent of the seasons. No sooner do cold and ice interfere with sport afloat than the craft is hauled up, dismantled, and for the next half year becomes a source of unlimited pleasure to her owner — and a nuisance to his family and friends.

W. P. Stevens,
Canoe and Boat Building, 1885

Paddle Your Own Canoe ©

"Paddle your own canoe" is an aphorism for independent thought and action, and personal integrity that came into wide use in the mid 1800's. What is believed to be its original cite in literature had a clear spiritual context:

"When the form of worship and creed is simple, it is difficult to make converts, and the Indian is a clear reasóner. I once had a conversation with one of the chiefs on the subject. After we had conversed some time, he said,
'You believe in one God — so do we, you call him one name — we call him another; we don't speak the same language, that is the reason. You say, suppose you do good, you go to the land of Good Spirits — we say so too. Then Indians and Yangees (that is, the English) both try to gain the same object, only try on not the same way. Now I think that it much better that as we all go along together, that every man paddle his own canoe.'"
Fredrick Marryat,
Settlers in Canada, 1844

In common usage, "paddle your own canoe" lost much of its original connotation of living a just and upright life while journeying to an ultimate goal. In the character of the time, its meaning was reinterpreted as guidance for daily life. Still, it carried a strong message.

In the parlor and drawing room, it was used genteelly:

Voyager upon life's sea,
To yourself be true.
And whate'er your lot may be,
Paddle your own canoe.

Anon.

On the back porch and in the woodshed, a rougher version was often heard:

IF YOU WANT TO GET RICH,
YOU SON OF A BITCH,
I'LL TELL YOU WHAT TO DO:
NEVER SIT DOWN
WITH A TEAR OR A FROWN,
AND PADDLE YOUR OWN CANOE.

Anon.

I have adopted "Paddle Your Own Canoe" as an identifying mark for what I hope to be a series of books on ultralight canoes. I have three or four folded plywood designs in mind, and I also have a new design for a "tidewater cruising canoe" and a radical method of cedar strip building that is begging to be published. With or without a paddle, up or down the creek, I'd better get busy.

What's in a Name?

After you've put a lot of time and effort into building your *Sweet Dream*, it seems right to give it a personality by giving it a name. Usually, the name is meant to evoke a state of mind or say something special about the boat or its owner/builder. Here, arranged in no particular order, are some general categories of names:

🙿 Someone or something special; a family member, someone you admire, your dog.

🙿 Wildlife, especially a fish or bird.

🙿 Words describing water or waves.

🙿 Flowers, especially a wild flower or water plant.

🙿 A heartfelt sentiment, ambition, or goal.

🙿 A catchy word or phrase.

🙿 A word meaning something small, light, or ethereal.

A good name is original, classy, and catchy without being rude, hostile, trite, or pretentious. Here are a few possibilities:

Antidote	Daze	Fingerling
Arrow	Delight	Finis
Apogee	Dipper	Flea
Back Eddy	Dite	Flicker
Bee	Dragonfly	Flinder
Big Enough	Dream	Fling
Boom!	Dreamer	Flitter
Breeze	Drifter	Flittermouse
Button	Eager	Flyer
Cat-tail	Echo	Foam
Chip	Eddy	Folly
Click	Enough	Freedom
Conceit	Escape	Freshet
Cricket	Eureka	Frisky
Cruiser	Explorer	Glimmer
Curlew	Fantasy	Gnat
Cypress	Feather	Go Lightly
Dance	Felix	Gossamer
Dancer	Fiasco	Gypsy
Dart	Fidget	Hard Rain
		Harmony
		Heartsong
		Heron
		Hornet
		Impulse
		Inevitable
		Interlude
		Jingle Horse

I believe a name, like a title, should be a touchstone indicating some of the qualities one hopes the named object will possess, and at the same time perhaps recreating or at least recalling a moment past.

Anthony Bailey,
The Thousand Dollar Yacht

Jot
Jubilant
Juniper
Just So
King Fisher
Kip
Lark
Least Ripple
Lily
Linger
Lucky
Meander
Minnow
Mippet
Mischief
Mist
Mite
Moot Point
Mosquito
Mote
Mouse
Muskrat
No Matter
Nonesuch
'Nuff Said
Nubbin
Odyssey
Oriole
Osprey
Patience
Pearl
Penny
Penultimate

Pickerel
Plunge
Prime
Prize
Promise
Prophet
Psyche
Quiver
Racer
Rambler
Ranger
Rhythm
Riddle
Ripple
Roamer
Rogue
Sandpiper
Scoot
Scooter
Scout
Serene
Serenity
Shadow
Sigh
Skeeter
Skookum
Slipper
Slippery
Smirk
Smoke
Snag
Snap
Snippet

Snug
Solitaire
Spark
Speck
Splash
Splinter
Squeak!
Storm
Success
Surprise
Swan
Swift
Swish
Thrill
Tickle
Traveler
Trifle
Triumph
Two Step
Vagabond
Victory
Waltz
Wasp
Wave
Which-a-Way
Whirl
Whisper
Willow
Wisp
Wood Drake
Zenith
Zephyr

The word canoe has two distinct meanings, having been applied, for how long a time no one knows, to boats of long narrow proportions, sharp at both ends and propelled by paddles held in hand, without a fixed fulcrum, the crew facing forward. The members of this great family vary greatly in size and model, from the kayak of the Esquimau, to the long war canoes, 80 to 100 feet long, of the islands of the Pacific. Within the past twenty years the word has been applied in England and America in a more limited sense, to small craft used for racing, traveling and exploring, as well as the general purposes of a pleasure boat, the main essentials being those mentioned above, while sails and a deck and usually added, the double paddle being used exclusively. In Canada the term has for a long time been applied to a similar boat, used for hunting and fishing, without decks, and propelled by a single paddle.

W. P. Stevens
Canoe and Boatbuilding, 1885

Often a single word in a different language can encompass a whole idea. You'll come across good candidates for names in books and in songs, especially their titles.

Here are a few examples from the book *Maybe (Maybe Not)* by Robert Fulgum:

Aro Ne - Japanese; "Hey You."

Forsan - Latin; "Maybe."

Forwursteln - Viennese; the ability to cope and muddle on, to function between maybe and maybe not.

Timshel - old Hebrew; "You will, you shall." The modern translation is "It may be," or just "Maybe."

Ver Llagar - "To watch them come;" to plant your feet just so, to hold your ground and see calmly the charge of the bull knowing that you have what it takes to maneuver the bull safely by; dynamic stability.

From random sources:

Aristos - Greek; "the best." Aristin, "the best thing."

Cielito lindo - Spanish/Mexican; "Pretty little heaven."

Prasadam - Sanscrit, "The Joy of God."

Sousan - Iranian, "lily."

From Sanskirt:

Dakini - "female wisdom brings"

Karuna - "sensitivity to the suffering of other beings"

Nadi - "channels in the body through which subtle energies flow"

Samatha - "calm abiding"

Sunyata - "emptiness"

Tathata - " 'suchness,' the final nature of phenomena"

A vessel with a humble name is likely to pass unnoticed by the elements; one with a haughty name is bound to land in trouble.

Fredrick Tilp,
The Chesapeake Bay of Yore.

Possible Boat Names from Native American Vocabularies

(Ojibway unless otherwise noted)

Ahmeek'	Beaver
Amik	Beaver %
Ai	Heart
Akkee-waizee	One who has been long on the earth #
Annemee'kee	Thunder
Apuk'wa	Bullrushes
Awasees	Catfish #
Cheemaun'	Birch Canoe
Chetowaik'	Plover
Dahin'da	Bullfrog
Dush-kwo-ne'she	Dragonfly
Ewa-yea	Lullaby
Ienawdizzi	Wanderer %
Ishkoodah	Fire, Comet
Ishkwon Daimeka	Keeper of the Gate of the Lakes
Jee'bi	Ghost, Spirit
Joss'akeed	Prophet
Kabeyun	West Wind $
Kabibonok'ka	Northwind
Kayoshk'	Seagull
Kee'go	Fish
Keeway'din	Northwest Wind, Home Wind
Keno'zha	Pickerel
Ke-ske-mun-i-see	Kingfisher
Kwo-ne'she	Dragonfly
Mahnahbe'zee	Swan
Mahng	Loon
Maskeno'zha	Pike
Minneha'ha	Laughing Water, Hiawatha's Wife
Monedo Kway	Female Spirit, Prophetess
Mudjekee'wis	West Wind, Hiawatha's Father
Nah'ma	Sturgeon
Nawbesah	Foolishness
Nee-ba-naw'baigs	Water Spirits
Nee Sheema	Younger Sibling

Nemesho . . . . .Grandfather $
Nenemoosha . . . . .Sweetheart
Neshomiss . . . . . . .Grandfather
Noko'mis . . . . .Grandmother,
                Wenonah's mother
No-noskau-see . . . .Humming Bird
Nosa . . . . .Father %
Odah'min . . . . . . .Strawberry
Okahah'wis . . . . . . .Fresh-water herring
Onaway' . . . . .Awake
Owais'sa . . . . .Bluebird
Pah'-puk-kee'wiss . . .Grasshopper
Pe'boan . . . . .Winter
Pone'mah . . . . . . .Hereafter
Sah'wa . . . . .Perch
Sebowish'a . . . . . . .Rapids
Segwun' . . . . .Spring
Sha'da . . . . .Pelican
Shah-shah . . . . . . .Long ago
Shawonda'see . . . . .South wind
Shaw-shaw . . . . . . .Swallow
Shesh'ebwug . . . . . .Duck
Shin'gebis . . . . . . .Grebe

Shuh-shuh'gah . . . .Blue Heron
Soan-ge-ta'ha . . . . .Strong Hearted
Sugge'ma . . . . .Mosquito
Tau-wau-chee-hezkaw
                White Feather @
Ugudwash' . . . . . . .Sunfish
Wa-bun . . . . .East Wind
Wa'bun An'nung . . .Morning Star
Waupee . . . . .White Hawk *
Wa'wa . . . . .Wild Goose
Waw-be-wa'wa . . . .White Goose
Wah-Wah-Taysee . . .Fire-fly
Weno'nah . . . . . . .Hiawatha's Mother

Name Origins:
* Shawnee   @ Sioux
# Chippewa $ Ottowa   % Muskeg

From Schoolcraft's *Algic Researches, Indian Tales and Legends,* Vols. I & II, and Longfellow's *The Song of Hiawatha*

Post Script

There wouldn't be a *Sweet Dream* if I hadn't found Phil Green. The story goes like this…

In November 1994, I read an article in the small boating magazine *Messing About In Boats* about an English ultralight canoe designer-builder named Phil Green. (Phil Green Designs, 2 Keep Cottages, Berry Pomeroy, Totnes, Devon TQ9-6LH England) The article included descriptions and pictures of six or eight of his nifty lightweight plywood designs. Some of the designs seemed to be just the thing for adult and youth boat building classes.

I wrote to Phil, telling him about my small boat building, writing, and teaching activities, and included a list of his plans that interested me and some money. In a surprisingly short time I received a thick package of plans. Phil was very supportive of my efforts and encouraged me to keep in touch. Over the following months we exchanged ideas and philosophies on small canoes, their construction, their appeal, our hopes and dreams, etc.

In one of his letters, Phil sent an updated catalog of his plans. One of the plans was for a 10' 10" canoe named *Dream*. It used the then unknown to me "folded plywood" construction technique. I was intrigued and wrote back to Phil for the plans. When the plans arrived I was fascinated by the folded plywood concept. It offered a simple, low tech construction technique that would do well in boat building classes. I immediately traced and cut out some hull shapes on thin plastic sheet and started to play with them to discover their possibilities.

While I was entranced by the folded plywood technique, I felt that *Dream* was just too small to safely carry me and others who weigh more than 185 pounds. For lack of a more objective standard, I consider my weight to be average for adult males. If a canoe is too small for me, it's too small for more than half the potential builders, men and women included.

I wrote back to Phil and told him of both my interest in the folded ply technique and reservations about *Dream*'s capacity. I told him of making the plastic sheet models. I also told Phil how I would change the *Dream* design to better fill my requirements. In addition to modifying the *Dream* hull design, I would change many of the structural members; rails, thwarts, breasthooks, and bottom pad, and I would substantially restructure and reorder parts of the construction sequence to accommodate the structural changes. Even with all these changes, I acknowledged that Phil's *Dream* had played an instrumental role in my design and its basic construction technique. I asked that I be allowed to call my design *Sweet Dream*.

Phil wrote back saying he had no problem with either the name *Sweet Dream*. He also encouraged me to stop spending my time on models and build a full size hull incorporating my design changes. At the first opportunity I built the *Sweet Dream* prototype. Although I can't claim to be a disinterested observer, *Sweet Dream* has proven to be all that I hoped for; she's easy to build, shapely, and is a pleasure to paddle.

I met Phil Green in person in October 1995. I was his host at the Thirteenth Mid-Atlantic Small Craft Festival at the Chesapeake Bay Maritime Museum in St. Michaels, Maryland. It was no coincidence that I presented the main workshop at the festival. The subject of the workshop was building *Sweet Dream*. Phil was with me for five days and I wish that I could remember every second that we shared. I now wish that I had a tape recorder running the whole time.

From the moment we first met at the airport we got on famously. Phil has a much greater creative talent than I do; I am more technically inclined. Phil found my building techniques instructive; I fed on his ideas for new designs. Phil candidly discussed his many successful designs. We pored over photos of designs that didn't get past the initial on the water testing phase. One morning at breakfast we discovered that at three o'clock we had each awoke, sat up in our beds, and made notes about the ideas that we had discussed during the day.

It was pure joy to watch Phil paddle *Sweet Dream* or any canoe. As a veteran white water kayaker and canoeist, licensed instructor, and ex-outdoor adventure provider, his use of a paddle is masterful. As a self taught paddler, I splash around a bit and if I find something that works I continue to use it. Seeing the precision of Phil's paddling technique which included subtle weight shifts and various hull attitudes was a real eye opener. Compared with Phil, my paddling looks like I use a garden spade. Phil was delighted with *Sweet Dream*'s responsiveness. In Phil's hands *Sweet Dream* was as nimble as a ballerina. Together they were a spirited pair dancing across the harbor.

At the festival I put *Sweet Dream* down by the launching ramp where anyone who wanted to could give her a try. It pleased me to no end to see paddlers of all ages and sizes taking her out. When they came in they couldn't hide their smiles. I couldn't hide mine either.

The *Sweet Dream* building demonstration was enthusiastically received by the folks at the festival. The speed with which the hull takes shape and the painless method of fitting the breasthooks occasioned especially favorable comments. The high level of interest at the festival cemented my conviction to get this book finished and in print as soon as possible.

Building *Sweet Dream* started out as a manuscript for a building article in one of the boat building magazines. When I started to write, I never would have believed that I would end up with more than a hundred pages. Looking back I can see that I would not have been satisfied had I been forced to tell *Sweet Dream*'s story in only ten or fifteen pages. I hope that in these pages I have been able to convey some of the excitement that I find in canoeing and canoe building in general, and with *Sweet Dream* in particular. I also hope that if you've ever wanted to build your own boat that you've found enough information, inspiration, and encouragement to order two sheets of okume and build *Sweet Dream*.

At the beginning of this book in the Acknowledgements, I recognized the canoe builders and teachers who were part of the inspiration for the my approach to small canoe design and construction. Inspiration alone will not build a canoe or publish a book. A number of friends have provided me with invaluable help along the twisting path that has led to this book becoming a reality, and not just a dream. I'd like to thank sincerely:

Bill Tanous, Yukon Lumber, Norfolk, VA
Richard Popkin, Eastern Burlap & Trading
   Company, Norfolk, VA
John Hodges, Virginia Beach, VA
Bob Frick, Virginia Beach, VA
Nancy Lekberg, Virginia Beach, VA
Bob Ander, photographer, Norfolk, VA
Joe Filipowski, Flagstaff Marine, Norfolk, VA
Anne and Jim Sommers, Chesapeake Rent-All,
   Chesapeake, VA
Terence Young, artist, Young's Studio and Gallery,
   Jay, NY
Garrett Conover, poet, North Woods Ways,
   Guildford, ME
Jerri Anne Hopkins, editor, Edgewater, MD
Jay and Dona Benford, Tiller Publishing,
   St. Michaels, MD

-mfp-

Phil Green shows some advanced single paddling techniques in Sweet Dream.

Photo by Marc Pettingill

Bibliography

Adney, Edwin T. and Chappelle, Howard I. *The Bark Canoes and Skin Boats of North America*. Washington, DC: Smithsonian Institution Press, 1983.

Bailey, Anthony. *The Thousand Dollar Yacht*. First printed in 1967, reprinted by Sheridan house, New York and Seafarer Books, London, 1996.

Burroughs, Franklin. *The River Home; Boats, Oars, and Rowing A Return to the Carolina Low Country*. Boston: Houghton Mifflin Company, 1992.

Chapelle, Howard I. *American Small Sailing Craft*. New York: W.W. Norton & Company, Inc., 1951

Culler, R. D. *Boats, Oars, and Rowing*. Camden, Maine: International Marine Publishing Company, 1978.

Culler, R. D. *Skiffs and Schooners*. Camden, Maine: International Marine Publishing Company, 1978.

Dyson, George. *Baidarka*. Seattle: Alaska Northwest Books, 1986.

Fulgum, Robert. *Maybe (Maybe Not)*. New York: Ivy Books,1993.

Gardner, John. *More Building Classic Small Craft*. Camden, Maine: International Marine Publishing Company, 1984.

Gilpatrick, Gil. *Building a Strip Canoe*. Freeport, Maine: De Lorme Publishing Company, 1985.

Herreshoff, L. Francis. *Sensible Cruising Designs*. Camden, Maine: International Marine Publishing Company, 1973.

Hill, Thomas J. with Stetson, Fred. *Ultralight Boatbuilding*. Camden, Maine: International Marine Publishing Company, 1987.

Jacobson, Cliff. *The Basic Essentials of Solo Canoeing*. Merrillville, Indiana: ICS Books, 1991.

Johnson, Beth. *Yukon Wild*. Stockbridge, Massachusetts: The Berkshire Traveller Press, 1984.

Kesselheim, Alan S. *Water and Sky, Reflections of a Northern Year*. Golden, Colorado: Fulcrum, Inc., 1989.

Kinney, Francis S. *Skene's Elements of Yacht Design*. New York: Dodd, Mead & Company, 1962.

Mason, Bill. *Path of the Paddle*. Minocqua, Wisconsin: NorthWord Press, Inc., 1984.

Payson, Harold H. "Dynamite," *Instant Boats*. Camden, Maine: International Marine Publishing Company, 1979.

Schoolcraft, Henry Rowe. *Algic Researches: Indian Tales and Legends*, Vols I & II, 1839. Baltimore: Clearfield Company, with new introduction by McNeil, W. K., 1992.

Simmons, Walter J. *Building Lapstrake Canoes*. Lincolnville Beach, Maine: Duck Trap Press, 1981.

Snaith, Skip. *Canoes and Kayaks for the Backyard Builder*. Camden: International Marine Publishing Co., 1989

Stelmok, Jerry, and Thurlow, Rollin. *The Wood and Canvas Canoe*. Gardiner, Maine: Tillbury House, 1987.

Stephens, W. P. *Canoe and Boat Buildings*. New York: Forest and Stream Publishing Co., 1884.

Teller, Walter Magnes. *On The River; A Variety of Canoe & Small Boat Voyages*. Dobbs Ferry, New York: Sheridan House, Inc., 1988.

Tilp, Fredrick. *The Chesapeake Bay of Yore, Mainly about the Rowing and Sailing Craft*. Richmond, Virginia: Chesapeake Foundation, Inc., 1982.

Wooden Canoe, journal of the WoodenCanoe Heritage Association (WCHA). Published bi-monthly. John Quenell Editor, PO Box 225, Paul Smiths, NY 12970

All small water craft have their excellent qualities but the canoe makes them all seem heavy and cumbersome by comparison. Your launch is all right in its way, but there is the noise and vibration of the engine and the odor; about your row boat there is the rattle of the oars or the creaking of the oar locks; but your canoe takes to the water with a whisper indistinguishable from the whispered greeting of the leaves along the bank or the whispered good-bye of the running water. Pushing out into a swift running stream you seem at once to become a part of it, and if you are wise you will not at once disturb the impressive stillness but listen to "the voice of the Great Creator, that speaks to the heart alone." It is impossible to describe the joy of the sensation of being carried along the surface of a fine stream in a canoe.

James R. Hile, *Riding the Judicial Circuit in a Canoe*,
Superior Wisconsin Evening Telegram, Sep. 30, 1908

Biography

MARC PETTINGILL was born in Baltimore, Maryland, in 1948. He is the second of ten children. Through high school Marc divided his time between the school year around Baltimore and for a short while in Waldwick, New Jersey, and summers on Bear Pond in Hartford, Maine. When not working in the woodlot, Marc's activities centered on the beach: fishing, swimming, and messing about with anything that floated — canoes, rowboats, logs, or sections of floating dockthat had gone adrift.

Marc earned a B.S. in Engineering from the Coast Guard Academy, Class of '70. In the service his professional specialty was merchant vessel safety with emphasis on wooden boat construction and repair. Marc "graduated" from the Coast Guard in 1993.

Since then, Marc has pursued a multi-dimensional second career designing, building, and writing about ultralight canoes and teaching boatbuilding. Marc has: taught boat building at youth camps in Virginia and on Long Island, New York; conducted a building class at his local community college; designed two solo canoes; had articles published in *WoodenBoat*, *BoatBuilder* and *Messing*

About in Boats; won blue ribbons for three canoes that he built; conducted canoe building demonstrations and boat building skills workshops in Washington, DC, on "successful Camp Boat Building"; and been involved in many other small craft related activities.

Marc works out of his home in Chesapeake, Virginia, where he lives with his wife, Ann Harriman Pettingill, and their children, Liz and Dan.

Building Sweet Dream, Marc's first book, is the first volume in a series called *Paddle Your Own Canoe©*. The planned second volume in the series, tentatively titled *Building Merlyn*, will detail the building of an advanced design ultralight canoe, again using the "folded plywood" construction and two sheets of 4mm okume marine plywood. *Merlyn* features a 3' radius rounded chine, a lapped sheer strake, and curved breasthooks, and weighs about 30 pounds. *Building Merlyn* will also include the design details and building sequence for Marc's *Widgeon* paddle blade, a force-balanced asymmetric double paddle intended for touring and cruising solo canoes and kayaks. An eight-foot *Widgeon* double paddle weighs two pounds.

The canoe is built, the photos are taken, and the text is written. At last the book is in the hands of the editor. It's a beautiful day, and I think I'll head into the swamp to revisit my favorite spots and see how the first spring flowers are looking. Maybe that pair of otters has a new brood of kits again his year. "Bye, I'm outta here!

Index

A

Acceptable hull material,18

Acetone, don't use it, 112

Adhesive backed sanding discs, 17, 70

Additional Building Information, 109

    Bottom pad for the 14' Sweet Dream, 134

    Breasthook options, 140

    Builder made tools and fixtures, 129

    Determining the sheer,137

    Epoxy, 109

    How many clamps?, 127

    Joining plywood sheets,118

    Making filleted and taped joints, 135

    Milling the parts for the hull, 116

    Regular *vs.* bias cut fiberglass tapes, 136

    Safety in the shop, 109

    Seating options, 144

    Stem bevels, 128

    Sturdy sawhorses, 114

    Tapering the edges of fiberglass tape, 142

    Work surface, 112

"Adirondack Swirling", 15

Adjustment Lines, 42

    Used in determining sheer, 139

Algic Researches, Indian Tales and
    Legends, Vols I & II, 159

Aligning the hull, 34, 37

    Before filleting chines, 38

    Forefoot, 30

    Stem bevels, 28

Allergic reaction to epoxy, 109

Alternatives to metal clamps, 128

Aluminum straight edge.129

    Used in scarphing, 119

    Used to make bias cut tape, 137

    Making, 129

American Red Cross, 157

American Small Sailing Craft, 57

Amidships frame, 37

    Alignment, 34

    Building, 32

    Diagram, 32

Amidships, defined, 25

Amine blush; epoxy, 111

Ammonia; used to remove amine blush, 112

Annual Maintenance. 93

Asymmetric Hulls, 107

    Diagram, 107

Athletics and Manly Sport, 70

Attaching the inner rails, 54

Attaching the outer rails,

    Permanently, 51

    Temporarily, 32

Automotive acrylic enamel paint, 75

Awl punches to mark the waterline, 92

B

Backboard for laminating form, 97

Backing plates for taped butt joint, 35

Backrest

    Arrangement, diagram, 145

    Pad carrier, 62

    Parts, dimensions, 144

    Resilient spacer, 65

    Stretcher, 62, 145

    Stretcher support blocks, 62, 64, 145

    Alternate shapes, diagram, 146

Stretcher, hardwood dowel, 63, 117

Bailey, Anthony, 106, 156

Bar clamps, 53, 127

Batten, 116

Bear Pond, Hartford, Maine, 11

Beston, Henry, 44

Beveling the stem cuts, 127

Bias cut fiberglass tape, 50
    vs. regular, 136
    diagram, 136
    making, 137
Bibliography, 162
Boat nails, 114
Bottom arc, setting, 31
Bottom pad, 37
    Halves, 28
    Installing, 36
    Layout, 134
Bottom pad for the 14' Sweet Dream, 134
Boy Scouts, 151
Breasthooks
    Blanks, 42
    Inner edge shape options, 141
    Installing, 42
    Laminated plywood, diagram, 140
    Methods for installing, 141
    Options, 140
    Traditional, diagram, 140
    Trimming, 46
Brightsides® one part polyurethane paint, 76
Brightwork, 74
Bugs, 83
Builder Made Tools and Fixtures, 129-134
    Aluminum straight edge, 129
    Dragon's teeth, 130
    Filleting tools
        Plastic, 132
        Wood, 131
    Rail tapering fixture, 132
    Router guide, 129
Building a Strip Canoe, 149
Building Lapstrake Canoes, 34, 148
Building Sequence, 26
Building the steam box, 98
Burroughs, Franklin. 11
Butt joint, diagram, 118

*T*he desire to build a boat begins as a little cloud on a serene horizon. It ends by covering the whole sky so that you can think of nothing else.

                Arthur Ransome

Canoe
    Birch bark, 10
    Canadian or tandem, 10, 24
    Dugout, 10
    Folded plywood, 10
    Lapstrake, 10
    Paper, 10
    Strip built, 10
    Wood and canvas, 10
Canoe and Boat Building, 154, 157
Canoe as first recreation vehicle, 25
Canoeing safety courses, 151
Canoeing Safety Tips, 152
Canoes and Kayaks for the Backyard Builder, 29
Capacity limits, hull, 19
Carving curved hull parts, 95
Cautions on saving weight, 95
Celebrate Your Accomplishment, 66
Center of hull, defined, 25
Centering the pressure bar, diagram, 126
Chappelle, Howard I., 57
Checking for fairness of radiused chine, 47
Chip brush, 17
Circular fabric cutter, 137
Cladding the exterior hull, 90
Clamp pads; need to use, 127
Clamping the outer rails
    Always done together, 52
    Proper procedure, 33
Clamps, low cost alternative, 128
Clean Up, 88
Closing up the chines, 30
Closing up the stem, 29
    Lower stem, 30
    Stranded copper wire, 29
    Upper stems, 29
Colloidal silica, 90
Colloidal silica; epoxy thickener, 111
Comments on the Building Sequence, 25
Conjuring a wood canoe, 12
Connett, Eugene, 95
Conover, Garrett, 94
Conrad, Joseph, 102

Contamination; surface of wood, 110
Copper pipe coupling, 16, 65
    Used as bushing, 63
Correct length for single bladed paddle, 149
Costs
    Materials, 14
    Paint and varnish, 14
Culler, R. D., 52
Curved hull parts, 95
    Backrest pad, 101
        Diagram, 102
    Carved, 95
    Laminated, 99
    Steam bent, 97
    Structural members, 95
Custom sanding tools, 70
Cutting out the hull shape, 26
Cutting the scarph, 119
Cutting the sheer, 41
Cutting the side halves to length, 34
Cutting the thwarts to length, 34
    Procedure to do accurately first time, 56
    Serendipitous omission, 58
    Simplifying assumptions, 56, 58

Decision Guide, Hull Length, 20
Deck screws compared to drywall screws, 113
Deglosser for paint, 74, 79
Detailing the hull, 68
Determining and marking a waterline, 90
Determining the Sheer, 137
Differing ply thicknesses, effect on scarph, 122
Double bladed paddle, aka kayak paddle, 147
Double paddle backrest, 122
    Arrangement, diagram, 143
    Parts, dimensions, 62, 144
    Stretcher support block shapes, 145
Dragon's teeth, 52, 130
    Diagram, 131
Drill guide, 59
Drilling holes for electrical ties, 27

Dryer, paint and varnish additive, 76
Drying time, paint and varnish, 78
Drywall screws with pressure pads, 51, 128
    Compared to deck screws, 113
    Take out before epoxy fully cures, 54
Dust mask, 17
    Use when sanding, 73
    Paint and varnish, 82, 83
Dylan, Bob, 140
"Dynamite" Payson butt joint, 118

Eight coats of varnish recommended, 74
Eight siding the thwarts, 60, 17
Electric drill as rotating sander, 142
Electric sanders, 73
    Respiratory protection, 73
Electrical ties, 17
Epoxy, 109
    Always wear plastic gloves, 109
    Amine blush, 111
    Can cause allergic reaction, 109
    Clamping pressure, 110
    Curing or hardening, 111
    Curing by polymerization, 111
    Glue line, 110
    Graphite filled, 90
    Measures defined, 111
    Mixing containers, 111
    Non-slumping mix, 111
    Safety glasses, 109
    Sanding before using, 110
    Source of supply, 18
    Thickeners, 111
    Uncured, removing with vinegar, 112
    West System®, 17, 110
Exothermic reaction; epoxy, 111
Exterior alkyd enamel paint, 74
Exterior latex paint, 74

Fatula, George, 67
Feeler gage, 56, 62, 64
Felt tip marker, do not use, 92
Fiberglass tape, 17, 39
  Butt joint, 36, 118
    Diagram, 118
  Joining the bottom pad halves, 36
  Joining the side halves, 34
  Tapering the edges, 142
Fillet at edge of bottom pad, 38
Filleting and taping
  Breasthooks, 44
  Inner chines, 38
  Inner stems, 39
Filleting blend; epoxy thickener, 111
Filleting tools, 39, 130
  Diagram, 131
  Plastic, 132
  Wood, 131
Finishing the Hull, 67
Finishing; a different activity than building, 68
Fishform, asymmetry, 108
Flat finish for paint and varnish, 74
Flattening agent for paint, 74
FLOAT PLAN, 153
Floatation for the hull, 151
Forefoot; drawn as segment of circle, 27
Form for steam bending and laminating, 97
Fowler, Edwin, 119
Frost, Robert, 8, 9
  "The Road Not Taken", 8
Fulgum, Robert, 158
Further Canoeing Adventures, books to read, 154

Gadgets and geegaws, 26
Garrett Wade; source for gouges, 144
Girl Scouts, 151
Gouge; used to trim fiberglass tape edges, 144
Graphite filled epoxy, 90

Great Dismal Swamp, 14
Green, Phil, 19, 160
Gutter of paint can, keeping clean, 82

Hand sanding, 14, 60, 144
Hardwood dowel, 17
  Backrest stretcher, 63, 117
Herreshoff, L. Francis, 19, 109, 145
Hile, James R.
Hill, Tom, 1114, 45
How Many Clamps?, 127
Hull alignment, 34, 37
  Forefoot, 30
  Stem bevels, 128
Hull capacity, limits, 19
Hull interior finished bright, 73
Hull Layout Plan
  Sweet Dream 12, 22
  Sweet Dream 13, 23
  Sweet Dream 14, 24
Hull Length Decision Guide, 20
Hull length, picking a, 19
Hull number plate, 150
Hull numbers, 150
Hull views, 16

Industrial Revolution, 69
Inner rail, 116
  Attaching, 54,
  Built up, 117
  Diagram, 117
  Milled, 117
  Solid, 116
Installing
  Bottom pad, 36
  Breasthooks, 42
  Inner rails, 54
  Outer rails, 51

Seat, 61
Thwarts, 56
Interlux® paints and varnishes, 75
Invisible butt joint, 118

Jacobson, Cliff, 12
Japan dryer, paint additive, 78
Jerome, Jerome Klapka, 80
Johnson, Beth, 92
Joining plywood sheets, 118
    Butt joint, 118
    Fiberglass tape butt joint, 118
    Scarph joint, 118, 125-127
Joining the side halves, 35
Joyce, James, 111

Kesselheim, Alan S., 72
Kinney, Francis S., 139

Lake Drummond, Great Dismal Swamp, 14
Laminated plywood breasthook, 141
    Diagram, 140
Laminating
    Backrest stretcher support blocks, 64
    Breasthook blanks, 42
    Curved backrest pads, 101
    Curved thwarts, 95
    Double paddling backrest pads, 92
    Single paddle seat, 61
Lap joint
    Diagram, 33
    Temporary, at rail ends, 33, 41
Leibnitz, Baron Gottfried Wilhem von, 11
Lists
    Materials, 17
    Recommended tools and equipment, 18

Longfellow, Henry W., 159
Lord Jim, 102
Lower stem, filleting, 40

Maine
    Brooklin, 11
    Hartford, 11
Maine State Fastener; the drywall screw, 113
Making a single paddle, 149
Making filleted and taped joints, 135
Marine grade alkyd enamel paint, 74
Marking a waterline, 90
Marking the sheer, 33
Marryat, Fredrick, 155
Masking tape, 78
    Removing, 89
    Using, 78, 89
Mason, Bill, 37
Material costs, 14
Material list, 17
Material Safety Data Sheet (MSDS), 10
Maybe (Maybe Not), 158
Microlight™, epoxy thickener, 111
Mid-Atlantic Small Craft Festival, 150
Milling the parts for the hull, 26, 116
    Batten, 116
    Inner Rails, 116
    Outer rails, 116
    Seat beams, 117
    Thwarts, 117
Mixing containers
    Epoxy, 41
    Paint, 81, 86
Most important building activities, 34

Naming Your Canoe, 156
Natural sheer, 138
Native American boat names, 158
Navigation Rules, 152

Near yacht finish, 75
Neutral color solids, 79
Nessmuk, 141
Newton, Sir Isaac, 11
Notched epoxy spreader. 17. 38

O'Reilly, John Boyle, 70
Oil/alkyd varnish, 75
Okume Panel Layout Diagram, 21
Okume plywood, 17, 18
	Easily scarphed, 119
	Sources of supply, 19
On the River, 67 109
One part marine polyurethane paint, 74
Optical Illusion, figure, 138
Optional Accessories, 95
	Curved backrest pad, 101
	Curved Structural Members, 95
	Tuffet and Tuffet II, 102
Organic vapor mask, 18, 109
Outer rails, 32, 36, 46, 116, 140
	Cross section, diagram, 116
	Permanently installed, 51
	Square vs. beveled, 116
	Trial fitting, 52
Overtightening electrical ties, 30

Paddle
	Double bladed, 148
	Single bladed, 148
Paddle Styles, Shapes, and Lengths, 147
Paddle Your Own Canoe, 155
Paint
	Automotive acrylic enamel, 75
	Exterior alkyd enamel, 74
	Exterior latex, 74
	Marine grade alkyd enamel, 74
	Neutral color solids, 79

One part marine polyurethane, 74
	Two part polyurethane, 75
Paint and Varnish, 73
	Adding agitator to can, 82
	Bugs, 83
	Clean up, 88
	Dealing with dust, 83
	Drying time, 78
	Need to be thinned, 78
	Painting sequences, 84
	Required equipment, 79
	Roller and brush technique, 79
	Shrinks as it dries, 77
	Tipping, 87
	Wet edge, 80, 87
Paint costs, 14
Paint, deglosser or flattening agent for, 74, 79
Painting technique, 76
Path of the Paddle, 37
Payson, Harold "Dynamite", 18
Permanently attaching the outer rails, 51
Personal floatation device (PFD), 151
Phil Green Designs, address, 19, 160
Picking a hull length, 19
Pinning the outer rails, 33, 46, 140
Plastic filleting tools, diagram, 131
Polymerization, epoxy, 111
Possible Boat Names from
	Native American sources, 158
Post Script, 160
Powdered graphite, 111
Primer for paint, 76
Press, laminating, diagram, 101
Pressure pads for drywall screws, 51
Pump; epoxy measure defined, 111

Radiator hose, used in steam bending, 98
Radius the Chine Joints, diagram, 47
Radiusing the outer rails, 55
Rail tapering fixture, 132
	Diagram, 132

Ransome, Arthur

Recommended tools and equipment, 18

Regular fiberglass tape, 50

Regular vs. bias cut fiberglass tapes, 136

 Circular fabric cutter, 137

 Diagram, 136

 Making bias cut tape, 137

Resilient spacer, 65

Respiratory protection; use when sanding, 73

Rewards of canoe building, 12

Rocker, setting, 31

Roethke, Theodore, 77

Roller and brush, 67, 75

 Painting technique, 79

Router guide, 129

 Diagram, 130

Router, used to make milled inner rail, 117

𝒮

Safety glasses

 Use when mixing epoxy, 109

 Use when sanding, 73

 Use when steam bending, 97

Safety in the shop, 109

Safety on the Water, 151

FLOAT PLAN, 153

Safety tips for canoeists, 152

Sand paper

 Abrasive material, 70

 Backing, 70

 Fastening methods, 70

 Glue, adhesive, or binder, 70

 Release agent, 70

 Using properly, 71-72

Sanders; electric, 73

Sanding alternative; the gouge, 144

Sanding and sandpaper, 69

Sanding block

 Resilient backing for, 72

 Stiff foam rubber, 72

Sanding the scarph joint, 127

Sanding

Major component of painting, 69

 Between coats of paint and varnish, 89

 Primer and undercoater, 90

Saving weight, cautions, 18

Sawhorses, 114

 Cutting the legs level, 115

 Plan, 115

Scarph, 118

Scarph in progress, diagram, 122

Scarph joint, 36, 118-127

 Cutting the scarph, 119-125

  Aluminum straight edge, 119

  Differing ply thicknesses, 122

  Glue lines as planing guides, 124

  Scarph in progress, diagram, 122

  Set back line, 120

  Setting up to scarph, diagram, 121

  Work surface, 120

 Joining the sheets, 125

  Aligning the sheets, 125

  Center pressure bar, diagram, 126

  Epoxying the joint, 126

  Sanding the scarph joint, 127

  Scarphing fixture. diagram, 126

  Space required, 125

Scarph joint, diagram, 118

Scarphing bottom pad for 14' hull, 134

 Diagram, 134

Scarphing fixture, diagram, 126

Schoolcraft, Henry Rowe, 159

Scoop; epoxy filler measure defined, 111

Scoring the bottom pad, 37

Screw clamp pressure pads

Sears, George Washington, "Nessmuk", 141

Seat beams, 61, 117

Seating Options, 144-146

Sensible Cruising Designs, 19, 148

Set back line; scarph, 119

Setting up to scarph, diagram, 121

Settlers in Canada, 155

Shakespeare, Wiliam, 82

Shaping the external chines, 46

Shaping the external stems, 48

Sheer Determining, 138

 Optical illusion, 138

Sheer adjustment lines, 42, 139

Side half ends, trimming chine edge, 37

        Cutting to length, 34

Silicon carbide, abrasive material, 70

Simmons, Walter J., 34

Single bladed paddle

        Correct length, 149

        Making, 149

Single paddle seat, 61, 146

        Diagram, 61, 146

Skene's Elements of Yacht Design, 139

Skiffs and Schooners, 52

Snaith, Skip, 29

Special bottom coatings, 90

Spirit of Adventure, 95

Stability; factors in, 144

Station lines, 27

Steam bending curved hull parts, 97

Steam box, 98

Steam generator, 98

Stelmok, Jerry, 75

Stem Bevel, 128

Stem bevels, 28

        Aligning, 128

                Thin putty knife as tool, 128

        Diagram, 128

Stems

        Drawn as straight lines, 27

        Taping external, 48

Stevens, W. P., 154, 157

Straight edge, aluminum

        Used in scarphing, 119

        Used in shaping lower stems, 49

        Used to make bias cut tape, 137

Structural fillets, 111

Surfacing compound, 76, 90

Support blocks

        Backrest stretcher, 63

        Alternate shapes, 146

Sweet Dream, design features, 10

Swedeform, asymmetry, 108

T

Tack cloth

        Storing, 77

        Using, 77

Tales from the Skipper, 95, 108

Taping the external chines, 48

Taping the external stems, 50

Tapering the Edges of Fiberglass Tape, 60, 142

Tapering the outer rails, 51, 132

        Curved taper, 132

        Straight taper, 132

Teller, Walter Magnes, 67, 109

Temporarily attaching the outer rails, 32

The Basic Essentials of Solo Canoeing, 12

The Chesapeake Bay of Yore, 158

The River Home, 11

The Road Not Taken, 8

The Sea and the Wind that Blows, 108

The Shape of the Fire, 77

The Song of Hiawatha, 159

*The **Sweet Dream** Register,* 150

The Thousand Dollar Yacht, 106, 156

The Wood and Canvas Canoe, 75

Three Men in a Boat, 80

Thickened epoxy, 39

Thickeners; epoxy, 111

Thin putty knife, used to align stems, 30

Thurlow, Rollin, 75

Thwart

        Installing, 56

        Procedure to cut accurately first time, 56

Thwarts, milling, 117

Tilp, Fredrick, 158

Time to

        Build, 14

        Paint and varnish, 14

        Sand seams, 14

Tipping, paint and varnish, 87

Tools and fixtures; builder made, 129

Tools, recommended, 18

Toothed epoxy spreader, 17, 38

Torn out holes in the hull, 30

Torque driver, 114, 125
Tortured plywood. 13
Traditional breast hooks, 140
Trial fitting the bottom pad, 37
Trial fitting the outer rails, 52
Trimming
      Breasthook sides, 46
      Hull at the rails, 55
      Outer rail ends, 55
      Side half ends, 31
Troilus and Cressida, 82
Tuffet and Tuffet II, 102
Twisted stem, corrections, 34
Two part epoxy based varnish, 75
Two part polyurethane paint, 75

Ultralight Boatbuilding, 114
Undercoater for paint, 76
Upper stem, filleting, 39
Using steam to soften wood, 97
UV block needed in varnish, 74

Vaneigem, Raoul, 142
Varnish (see also Paint and Varnish)
      Building film thickness, 77
      Detailing trick, 69
      Oil/alkyd, 75
      Required equipment, 79
      Storing unused, 82
      Two part epoxy, 75
      UV block, 74
      Water based, 75
      Wet sanding, 77
Varnishing the rails before painting, 77
Views of the Hull, 16
Vinegar; to remove uncured epoxy, 112
Virginia, 146
Volatile Organic Compounds (VOCs), 74, 77

Water and Sky, Reflections of a Northern Year, 72
Water based varnish, 75
Waterline
      Determining and marking, 90
      Marking with awl punches, 92
West System® epoxy, 17
Wet edge, 80, 87
Wet sanding varnish, 77
Wharram, James, 135
What's in a Name?, 156
While Readying the Fleet, 94
White, E.B., 108
Womack, Winslow, 150
Wood; Surface contamination, 110
Woodcraft; source for gouges, 144
WoodenBoat Magazine, 135
WoodenBoat School, 11, 67
Work surface, 112
      Cutting diagram, 112
      Exploded view, 113

Young, Terrence D., 15
Yukon Wild, 92

Do You Liveaboard?
Do You **Want** To?...

Ever found yourself out on the water, just wishing you could keep on cruising? What feeling do you have when you leave your boat behind after a pleasant weekend cruise? Have you been thinking that here is **Something More** to life?

The Benford Design Group is committed to the advancement of the Liveaboard Yacht. We find this lifestyle to be both challenging and fulfilling, wholly satisfying those wishes for a simpler life.

We can help you in your search. SMALL SHIPS covers the spectrum of Liveaboard power designs. And these designs are enchanting - having a rare blend of grace and purpose. But we're not done yet! Our current projects continue our thirty-four year history of bringing dreams to life.

Take the 35' Packet (above right) for example. This Small Ship has just what you need for living in comfort, for a long time - like air conditioning, a washer and dryer, and porches. There's room to walk about and room to cook great meals. Room to store your clothes and room to fly a kite. Room for you **and** your friends. On this boat the rooms **are rooms** - more generous than anything now in production - so it's easy to sprawl out and get comfortable. But even with this

unparalleled space and comfort, she's every bit a **boat**, having been conceived as a strong and practical vessel, born to the water.

As is her cousin, our delightful 100' Fantail Motoryacht (below). Equipped for extended cruising and with luxurious accommodations, this ship could be your **castle**. She has the spirit of an elegant old Trumpy in a new and easily maintainable form. Our modern design and engineering once again give life to these beautiful ships.

So if **your** dream combines "man-

sized" comfort with solid naval architecture, come and see what we have. Look at the boats we've done. Imagine yourself on board. Think what life on board would be like. We know **you'll feel right at home!**

> *Home is where*
> *the chart is....™*

For more information on these and scores of other liveaboard designs from the Benford Design group, read our SMALL SHIPS book.

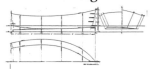

7-3" Dinghy
7-3" x 6'-9" x 3'-9¼" x 0'-4"

7½' Dinghy
7'-6" x 7 x 3'-9" x 0'-5"

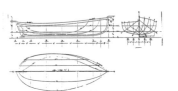

8' Double-Ended Dinghy
8' x 7'-3¾" x 3' x 0'-4"

8' Portland Yawlboat
8' x 7'-6" x 4' x 0'-5"/2'-6"

8½' Dinghy
8'-6" x 8'-2½" x 4' x 0'-9"/2'-6"

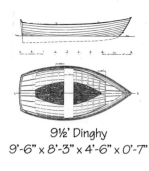

9½' Dinghy
9'-6" x 8'-3" x 4'-6" x 0'-7"

11'-4" Dinghy
11'-4" x 10'-1" x 4'-6" x 0'-3"

9' Pacific Peapod
9' x 8'-6" x 4'-6" x 0'-7"/2'-9"

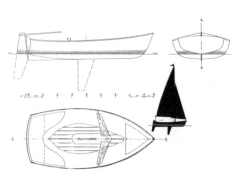

11' Dinghy
11' x 10' x 5' x 0'-6"/3'

11' Oregon Peapod
11' x 10' x 4'-6" x 0'-6"/3'

11' Dinghy Night
11' x 9'-6" x 4' 0'-6"/2'-11"

SMALL CRAFT PLANS

"Let's get it straight up front: This book is more than a catalog of designs. The 96 pages between its covers contain plans for 15 small craft. Designer Jay Benford knows that readers will build directly from the book — bypassing the formality of ordering plans from his office. In fact he encourages the process by including full working drawings and tables of offsets for all of the designs." **WoodenBoat**

The 15 sets of complete plans for skiffs & tenders from the Boards of the Benford Design Group (as shown on these two pages) will help you build your own dinghy, small craft, or tender. Plans for 7'-3" to 18-footers in cold-molded, carvel, lapstrake, plywood, and fiberglass construction are included, along with photos of some completed boats. 96 pages, softcover.

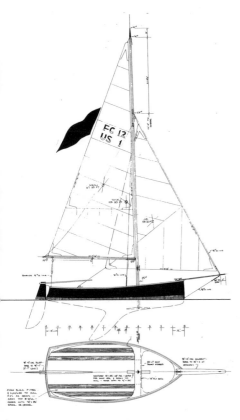

12' Keelboat
12' x 12' x 5' x 3'-4½"

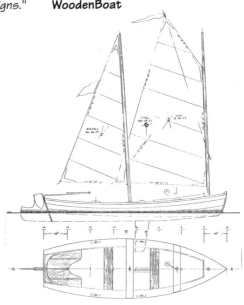

16' *Conch Ad Libitum*
16' x 15' x 5' x 0'-9"/3'-3"

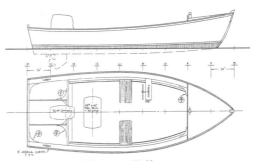

18' Texas Skiff
18' x 16' x 6'-8½" x 0'-5"

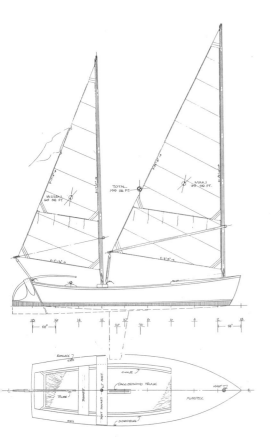

18' Cat Ketch
18' x 16' x 6' x 0'-8"/4'-6"

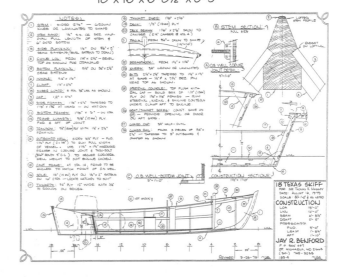

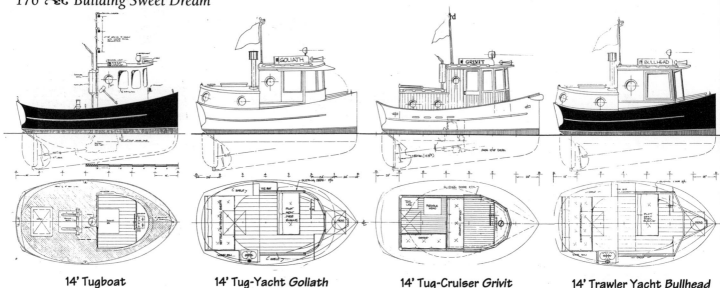

14' Tugboat
14' x 13' x 7 x 3'

14' Tug-Yacht *Goliath*
14' x 13' x 7 x 3'

14' Tug-Cruiser *Grivit*
14' x 13' x 7 x 3'

14' Trawler Yacht *Bullhead*
14' x 13' x 7 x 3'

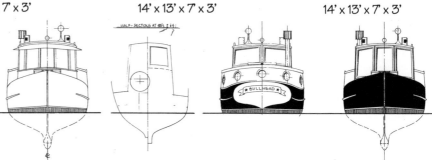

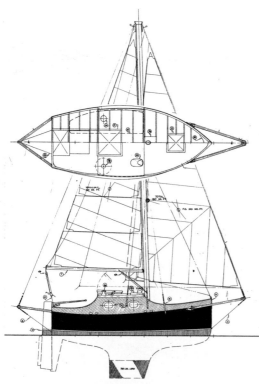

14' Cruiser *Happy*
13'-10" x 18'-8" x 6'-3" x 3'-7"

POCKET CRUISERS & TABLOID YACHTS
— VOLUME 1 —

Complete building plans for the small cruising boats shown on these two pages are in our book, **POCKET CRUISERS & TABLOID YACHTS, VOLUME 1**. These boats are some of the most popular plans from the boards of the Benford Design Group. They're shown in full detail in this 96 page, 8½" x 11" softcover book.

"All of the plans exhibit the professional presentation and well-conceived accommodations typical of the author's work."

WoodenBoat

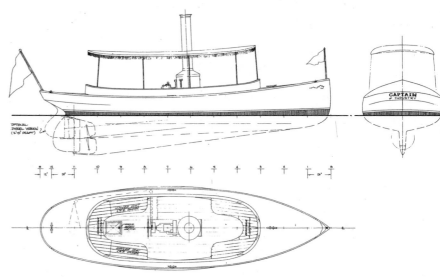

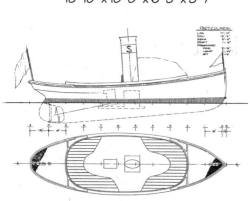

17' Fantail Steam Launch *Myf*
17 x 15'-6" x 5'-3" x 1'-8"

25' Fantail Steam Launch *Beverley*
25' x 22'-6" x 7 x 3'-3"